Starter Kit

This Book Includes 4 Manuscripts:

Wicca For Beginners

A Simple Guide to Understanding the Basics of Wicca and the Magical Properties of Herbs, Crystals and Essential Oils. Start Practicing Wicca and Follow the Modern Witchcraft.

Wicca Herbal Spells

A Practical Guide About the Healing Power of Plants in Harmony with Wicca. Improve your Everyday Life by Connecting with Nature Thanks to Herbal Spells and Modern Witchcraft

Wicca Moon Magic

How does the Moon Affect Nature, Animals and People? Find out How to Understand Moon's Magical Properties According to the Philosophy of Wicca, With Rituals and Spells

Wicca Crystal Magic

A Practical Guide on How to Improve your Life with the Magical Power of Crystals Used by Witches. Attract and Maintain Healthy Relationships, Reduce Anger, Stress and Anxiety

Justine J. Scott

© Copyright 2020 - Justine J. Scott
All rights reserved

The content contained within this book may not be reproduced, duplicated or transmitted without direct written permission from the author or the publisher.

Under no circumstances will any blame or legal responsibility be held against the publisher, or author, for any damages, reparation, or monetary loss due to the information contained within this book. Either directly or indirectly.

Legal Notice:

This book is copyright protected. This book is only for personal use. You cannot amend, distribute, sell, use, quote or paraphrase any part, or the content within this book, without the consent of the author or publisher.

Disclaimer Notice:

Please note the information contained within this document is for educational and entertainment purposes only. All effort has been executed to present accurate, up to date, and reliable, complete information. No warranties of any kind are declared or implied. Readers acknowledge that the author is not engaging in the rendering of legal, financial, medical or professional advice. The content within this book has been derived from various sources. Please consult a licensed professional before attempting any techniques outlined in this book.

By reading this document, the reader agrees that under no circumstances is the author responsible for any losses, direct or indirect, which are incurred as a result of the use of information contained within this document, including, but not limited to, — errors, omissions, or inaccuracies.

Stop! Take Your Gift!

To thank you for showing interest in this book I have the pleasure of giving you an e-book on Wicca. More specifically, it is the relationship between **Wicca and Sex** and how the Wiccan live the relationship of a couple.

Go to thewiccaworld.com/wicca-sex/ **and download it for free!**

Avalaible in Audible!

Wicca for Beginners is available in Audio format to listen to it even while you're doing something else during the day. Find out on Audible!

Table of Contents

Wicca For Beginners 7

Introduction 9

Chapter 1: So, What is Wicca? 11

Chapter 2: A history of Wicca 18

Chapter 3: Wiccan Philosophy 26

Chapter 4: Altars and Rituals: What they are, and How to Set them Up 35

Chapter 5: The Wiccan Relationships 49

Chapter 6: Understanding Seasonal Cycles 59

Chapter 7: Wiccan herbs, candles, and Crystals 67

Chapter 8: The Essential oils of Wicca and what they are 87

Chapter 9: How to Use Modern-Day Witchcraft 97

Chapter 10: Basic Wiccan Spells to Try 109

Chapter 11: You Wiccan relationships with the World and Others 121

Conclusion 131

Wicca Herbal Spells 133

Introduction 135

Chapter 1: What is Wicca 139

Chapter 2: Introduction to Herbalism 169

Chapter 3: Herbalism relationship with Wicca 172

Chapter 4: Types of Plants used in Wicca 177

Chapter 5: Spells used for Wicca 201

Chapter 6: Application of wicca spells in everyday life 283

Conclusion 287

Wicca Moon Magic 289

Introduction 291

Chapter 1: Wicca and the Moon 293

Chapter 2: Lunar Cycles and Events 307

Chapter 3: Ritual and Spell Basics 325

Chapter 4: The Lunar Grimoire – The Full Moon 345

Chapter 5: The Lunar Grimoire – The New Moon 367

Chapter 6: The Lunar Grimoire – Eclipse Magic 395

Chapter 7: The Lunar Grimoire – Moon Magic Spells 401

Conclusion 419

Wicca Crystal Magic 421

Introduction 423

Chapter 1: What is Wicca 429

Chapter 2: Introduction to Crystals 459

Chapter 3: List of specific Crystal that have a direct relationship with Wicca 475

Chapter 4: List of several spells and magical workings 483

Chapter 5: How to apply spells in everyday life 551

Conclusion 557

Wicca For Beginners

A Simple Guide to Understanding the Basics of Wicca and the Magical Properties of Herbs, Crystals and Essential Oils. Start Practicing Wicca and Follow the Modern Witchcraft.

Justine J. Scott

Introduction

Do you feel like you could benefit from Wicca?

Wicca is oftentimes considered "modern witchcraft." When we hear that, we probably think of Harry Potter or other popular witchcraft series. But it is a legitimate means of living, and it's a very popular way to improve your life.

Wicca isn't just casting spells, and it actually is used for good only, and not for bad. While some people look at the modern "witch" with rolled eyes, it's actually a legitimate religion, and it can help you.

But, how do you get into it? And how can this practice of witchcraft help you? Well, you're about to find out. Wicca is a little different from what you may think it is, and if you have an interest in it, this book will help you understand it more.

In this book, I'll give you the lowdown on a beginner's level what wicca is, including the history behind it, the original beliefs behind it, what exactly Wicca is in our society today, the philosophy that they have in terms of God, and also how to get started on your journey into Wicca.

I'll provide the basics that you should know about this, and also some basic practices. You'll also learn the basics of essential oils, healing crystals, herbs, and other items used in the Wiccan rituals.

I'll also tell you a little bit about what it means to practice modern Wicca, and the relationship you should have with this. You'll have a practical understanding of Wicca by the end of this and be able to utilize it in your life. I want you to use it, and I want you to understand the beauty that is Wicca, which is why I encourage you to continue on in your journey to reading and learning about Wicca on a beginner's level.

But first, I want to thank you for choosing this book and I'd be really happy if you left me a quick review on Amazon. Enjoy the reading!

Chapter 1: So, What is Wicca?

Before we continue with anything else, I want to educate you on what Wicca is on a basic level, and also dispel a few myths about Wicca that are prevalent in our society. The reason why these myths are here is due to not understanding, whether by choice, or involuntarily. But I want you to learn about Wicca, and here, we'll tackle the basic principles of it, and why they matter.

THE BASICS OF WICCA

Many people believe Wicca is actually just witchcraft, but it's not that. It's actually a modern understanding of pre-Christian traditions and beliefs. However, some do believe there is a connection to the practices of the ancient Druids. It is oftentimes practiced individually, or in groups called covens.

While Wicca does involve witchcraft, it's actually more of a religion than anything else. However, while many religions encourage you to worship a god, Wicca has more of an Earth-focused aspect to it.

The practice does date all the way back to the old shamans, hence why there is such similarities to people such as the Druids. However, it's a little different than that.

Wiccans actually honor the powers of nature, and host rituals and commit to providing earthen balances. Wicca is considered paganism, but not every Wiccan is a Pagan, and oftentimes there are many Pagans who don't consider themselves Wiccans.

Wicca is a very evolving religion, so it is changing immensely. However, most of them do have nature at the focus, and their beliefs and practices encompass nature, celebrations of the seasons, and the like.

We'll go more into the beliefs in the following chapters and sections, but that's at the core of what it is. It's a religion yes, but it isn't monotheism, nor is it centralized like Catholicism or Judaism.

Of course, when people hear religion, they oftentimes cringe due to the doctrines that are usually a part of modernized religion. People don't want to be a part of organized religion in many cases, which is why they turn to Wicca. Wicca has their own set of gods, and there isn't an official "holy book" with rules they need to follow. There isn't one particular way to interpret Wicca, which is pretty cool. It's incredibly fluid, and it encourages you to follow a spiritual path that works best for you.

So, in essence, you're the creator of your own life, and you're the one who takes the journey. There is no pastor who you need to see every week, nor is there one set of rules written by men thousands of years ago that you have to follow. It's your own code, your own understanding, and it allows you to practice the way you want to.

Of course, you can follow ancient rituals that can be practiced honoring a particular deity, and also to help benefit your life. But of course, this is all based on what you want to do, rather than what one particular scripture or code tells you to do.

But What About the Magic?

When we think of Wicca, we think of magic. However, not every Wiccan practices magic. But magic is essentially the intimate connection you have with the Nature energies around you, and the utilization of this people use to help improve their own lives, and the work they do to help others. The practice is called magic of course, but it's not the magic that you know from various media.

It actually is mostly done with rituals, and various tools, and it involves different tools, ingredients, and the like, such as herbs, crystals, candles, and affirmations. These are the "spells" of Wicca, but oftentimes it's calling upon one of the deities to help with the outcome that is desired.

The Myths of wicca, Debunked!

Here are a few of the myths of Wicca that we hear oftentimes, and the truth behind them all.

Wiccans Can hurt others with Spells!

That is incredibly untrue. Wiccans have one rule with their magic, and it's one of the very few actual "codes" they have. Their magic can only be used for positive actions, and never done to others in harmful ways, whether it be on purpose or not.

Witches are Evil!

Again, another myth that involves the concept that Wiccans harm others. They can't use their magic negatively, and they encourage people to use it positively. There is a Threefold law that says if you use your magic for evil, you'll get that back three times the power. So, Wiccans know better than to harm others, and instead, they use their magic for the good of other people.

WICCAN ISN'T A REAL RELIGION

It is in fact. It was actually recognized by the American government as a religion, and there are actually Wiccan holidays observed by people. There are eight different holidays Wiccans believe in, and while some of the Christian-dominated regions in the country may think otherwise, Wicca is a legitimate religion.

THEY ONLY WORSHIP THE DEVIL!

The common misconception that Wiccans are Satanists is prevalent. Wiccans don't believe in the devil, and the concept of Heaven and Hell isn't a part of their doctrine. They've never existed in common Wiccan practice. They also don't have one particular almighty god, but instead have many different deities, including gods and goddesses they may acknowledge. It's more similar to Buddhism and Hinduism when it comes to the types of deities they acknowledge.

THEY SACRIFICE ANIMALS!

Wiccans actually respect all living creatures, since the religion is based on nature. They do make offerings and sacrifices yes, but it's usually inanimate objects such as fruit, flowers, and bread, and oftentimes they wish only good for animals. They aren't allowed to make blood sacrifices, and its nonsense if stated otherwise.

THEY HAVE AN EVIL BIBLE

They don't even have a bible. Some Wiccans might make a "Book of Shadows" which is used as a generalized spell book or compilation of spells, but that's literally it. It's a reference book, just like any old textbook.

Some Wiccans call it a grimoire, magical diary, or a book of spells, and really, it's just an informational text, and it does have some myths, spells, various rituals and ceremonies, prayers and affirmations, as well as the herbs and lore behind them, or even personal records they find.

It's not an evil bible. It's a reference book. It's not made to hurt others, it's just there so they don't have to write down twenty times to use a certain crystal when working on a practice.

IT'S JUST A WEIRD CULT!

Nope. There are obviously "weird" Wiccans just like every other religion, but for the most part, it's incredibly individualized and personal to yourself. Again, some people can practice in covens if they want, but oftentimes it's easier to practice alone, which is totally fine.

Wicca is a legitimate religion and an interesting practice, and you learned here a little bit about it, along with the truth of Wicca, and what it really entails.

Chapter 2: A History of Wicca

Wicca actually has a rich history that's worth learning about. Here, I'll take you through the historical aspects of Wicca, and why they matter. Wiccan history isn't as old as you may think it is, although it does have ties to ancient practices, and we'll highlight as well some of those beliefs, and the importance of them.

THE ORIGINATION OF WICCA

As we've said, it's not an old religion. It's actually very new. Like less than a century old.

The origins of it were dated all the way back to 1954, which was when it was originally developed. It came forth in England during then, and Gerald Gardner was the first to bring it forth, talking about the diversity of it, and how it has many different ritualized practices.

There were a couple of other prevent Wiccans at the time, such as Gardner and Doreen Valiente, who both published works on these teachings and arts of the practice. However, the core structured was varied immensely, and it grew over time, and there are many different denominations and sects of it.

The type of Wicca that was practiced initially was called British Traditional Wicca, which followed the initiation elements of Gardner, and it is usually just the application of the older traditions.

So, there is an old-form of Wiccan tradition, which was the type of beliefs that were purported originally.

However, old Wiccans didn't call it Wicca at all, but it had similar practices. It was later during the 1960s that the name originally came about.

Some do believe it was the hidden lore that was passed during the Dark Ages when the pagans were persecuted, only to come about during modern times, which may be a theory, but it only takes from that in a very generalized sense.

The influences of Wicca are older however, so there is the argument there that Wicca was one of the old religions.

But Who was Gerald Gardner?

He was a man who was originally a civil servant who became interested in folklore, anthropology, the occult, and spiritualism. He was a part of the Rosicrucians who were around in the 1930s. He met some friends at that point, and it was revealed that they were a group of witches. And from there, he was initiated in 1939 to them.

He did travel a lot, and while ancient paganism was stamped out due to Christianity, it was still practiced in secret groups, and they were called a "witch cult," which asserted that those who were surviving were actually part of these covens. Gardner met with these people, and he was convinced they were part of a pre-Christian religion, and he wanted to make sure this survived well into the 20th century, hence how this was born.

Gardner founded his own little coven called Bricket Wood, and he drew inspiration from the previous covens he had heard about. He teamed up with Allister Crowley and Cecil Williamson, and from there, the core values of Wiccan were born, such as the worship of a god and goddess in your own way. But of course, they didn't really adopt the name Wicca until almost a decade later, when it spread.

There were other important figures who came about with this, including other occultists. Some do believe Gardner revived it, but there were others who played a key role in the revival of it, such as Margaret Murray, who wrote many books on it, and was a first-wave feminist who wrote about this religion all the way back in 1921.

But, with the rise of feminism in the 1970s, Wicca grew in power, and we'll dive into how this plays a part in modern society today.

WICCA AND FEMINISM

Feminism did play a part in Wicca becoming popular, especially during the 1970s, and this was due to women who were attracted to this, because of the female deity, but oftentimes were limited because of restrictions women had in other patriarchal religions. Wicca also became more magic-based, especially since it was a spiritual movement. Wicca still has heavy environmentalism tones to it, along with feminism, and it's why it became one of the major religions that came about in England.

There was even matriarchal lunar worship practiced in Wicca, and it was in Dianic Wicca, and a Wiccan activist even wrote a feminist Book of Shadows, and there are still popular feminist covens that grew out from it.

THE ORIGINAL BELIEFS

While the original beliefs weren't wrong, it was a little bit different. The idea was for two different gods to be in place, and there was a self-designation that had more of a "witchcraft" term to it. The original Wicca was of course referred to as witchcraft, and it was less religious in terms of connotation.

However, the original covens did collectively call themselves "the Wica" with only one C in it, and this was the British term that was in place.

Early Wiccans followed the duo theistic Horned God of Fertility, and the Mother Goddess. With the practitioners typically thinking these were the ancient deities who were worshipped by the old hunter-gatherers you hear about in the Stone Age, and the veneration of these gods was passed down in secret all the way to present times. This was derived from Margaret Murray's claims that she put in place about the witch-cult that was the early form of Wicca.

There were only two core venerated gods at this point, the horned God, and the Mother Goddess, both of which were also a part of Gardner's teachings, but he said that the roots were from the Stone Age, so Gardnerian Wiccan did have this at the beginning of it. However, the names were secret initially, but were later called Cernuous and Aradia, but those were later changed as well.

One of the deities was considered the "prime mover" who was an entity who was too complex for humans to understand, but there was also the terms called Cosmic Logos, Supreme Cosmic

Power, or the Godhead, and this deity was the one who created the undergods as well.

Gardnerism Wiccan did focus a bit more on witchcraft, and while it did dismiss the sacrificing, cannibalism, orgies, and Satanism that's oftentimes considered to be a part of "witchcraft," there is actually a series of rituals that are there, in order to provide a framework the person can use for themselves, and this was brought into modern context as well.

Today's Wicca: No, it isn't Harry Potter

Wicca wasn't an officially recognized religion until 1986, and that came about due to a court case called Dettmer V. Landon, and the case was based off a Wiccan who was incarcerated who was refused the objects they needed for rituals, and the ruling made Wiccans entitled to the same First Amendment protection that every other religion has.

In 1998, there was a Wiccan student who also got help from the ACLU after the board tried to prevent this person from wearing black jewelry and clothes, and of course since it was recognized as a religion, the view was reversed.

The Indiana Civil Liberties Union back in 2004 also tried to help purport the rulings that were in place, and they fought to reverse the idea that Wiccans who were divorced couldn't teach this religion to their children.

There are Wiccans in prominent positions. Sgt. Patrick D. Stewart was the first Wiccan to serve in the military who died in combat. The family wasn't allowed to put a pentacle on the gravestone, but there was a court case that was pushed in 2005 that was initiated to help push for the symbols to be put on Veteran's markers. Today, it is now acceptable to do that.

While there isn't an exact number of Wiccans in practice, there's an estimated number between a few hundred thousand to 3 million different people practicing at this time.

THE BELIEFS TODAY'S WICCANS HAVE

Today's Wiccans do have similar beliefs to the original, such as the idea that they aren't evil witches who hurt people, but instead they use spellcasting and magic in order to link themselves with this. They also don't execute or hurt people in the Wiccan religion.

However, their idea of the gods and deities has changed. The truth about modern-day Wiccans is they actually don't have to follow one specific god, or the Horned God and Goddess idea that Gardenerism originally had. Instead, they're allowed to have a monotheistic, or a polytheistic look to their understanding of their own spiritual journey.

It's a more impersonal religion. While some people like to follow a more monotheistic type of Wicca, such as the Dianic

Wicca groups that followed one specific goddess, it usually is multiple gods that are there.

Some don't even believe that the gods and goddesses really exist, but have an archetype that's Jungian in origin.

Some of them have the idea that all the gods are one god, or all the goddesses are one goddess, so some even believe that Kali in Hindu, as well as the Virgin Mary, and others are essentially the manifestation of one specific goddess. This is also seen in Dionysus, Yahweh, and others. However, most of them have a more polytheistic approach to all of these deities, but of course, it's all up to interpretation, and what you believe.

The history of Wicca is important to understand, since it's a little different than the other religions that are out there, and here, you learned a little bit about the different aspects of this as well.

Chapter 3: Wiccan Philosophy

Understanding the Philosophy of Wicca is important to really getting ahold of the different rituals and rites in Wicca. Beginners often think it's just casting spells and wearing crystals, but it's a little different than that. Here, we'll give you insight on Wiccan philosophy, and their beliefs on different parts of it.

THE PHILOSOPHY ON NATURE, AND GOD ITSELF

There are a few different philosophical aspects on Wicca we'll touch on here, and I'll give you an idea of each of these different philosophies and what they mean.

ON NATURE

Nature is one of the core aspects of Wicca, and it should be respected. They want to have a balanced life with nature, and it promotes the idea of oneness with nature and the Earth. It encourages appreciation of the sunset, sunrise, the moon, the world around you, and even the small little aspects of life. These are all part of a presence of Mother Earth, and should be revered. It encourages people to have a more humbled view of nature, where you aren't trying to hurt the environment, and you walk in nature with the integrity and light that you should have.

Wiccans believe nature is sacred, hence why they discourage hurting the world around them. While Wiccans do use modern technology, they're encouraged to care for the environment, and the others in it, which is why many Wiccans oftentimes like to help the Earth by cleaning it up, such as through recycling and other means.

THE TWO MAIN GODS

While it is polytheistic, and there are many gods, there are two supreme deities in this, who were responsible for creating everything. They're both altered at every ritual, and oftentimes, when magical work happens, they are as well. Some call them a Sky Father, or Earth Mother, but there are other deities you can worship as well through their existence. But their union is what creates and sustains life.

The feminine half is both the Earth itself, and the Moon too, and this is what controls the night, sea tides, the reproductive cycles females go through, and their psyche. The Goddess can also take different forms, sch as the Maiden, Rone, and Mother, based on the cycles of the moon. This Goddess oftentimes is associated with emotion, wisdom and intuition that happens when it engages with the shadow side, such as that of the moon.

The Mother Earth does encourage life to flourish, and she takes care of the world, and is a mother, but also is a partner to the God, and they work together to keep everything going, clearing away the old and bringing forth new elements.

The masculine side is the God, who is responsible for the sun, and the male energy, along with the growth of different creatures. He's also responsible for the forest, animals in it, hunting, and also the changing of the seasons, and they're often associated with the Holly and the Oak King. The Oak King is the lighter half and is part of the lighter seasons such as the spring and the summer, and the Holly King is associated with the Autumn and winter months.

However, some Wiccans like to work with ancient deities, which is why this religion is so incredibly versatile, some of which have existed since the beginning. Venus and Osiris, for example, are ones some Wiccans count upon, and they feel connected. They are usually part of the lesser aspects, but some polytheistic Wiccans may worship not only the divine pair that we discussed above, but also these ancient gods.

On Magic

Magic is a huge part of Wicca, but it's often misunderstood. Spells are used, and they are a big part of Wicca, and here, we'll dive into what they are, and why they matter.

Magi was used in early practices, and even Aleister Crowley did believe magic would cause changes in the world that conforms to the will. Many people do believe Magic is a type of law that's part of nature, but because of the way modern science treats it, it oftentimes it is viewed as supernatural. However, some Wiccans think magic is using the five senses in order to create results that are surprising. However, some Wiccans don't even use magic, or don't know how to use it, and just think that because they believe it happens, it just does.

Some Wiccans do use some sacred circles, and oftentimes, the spells they are using will change the physical world, such as through healing, fertility, protection, and also getting rid of negative influences. There is mostly white magic practiced with this, since black magic harms people.

They don't need to believe that it's there, but essentially, they use techniques to work with the universe, and the right magic can be experienced. But of course, not every Wiccan will practice magic. However, all spells that are cast are those that won't harm others, and if you do harm someone, you'll get it back three times as bad.

But the threefold law doesn't just impact black magic, but white magic, or the good magic, can also be affected by it. It's similar to karma in the Eastern religions where what you put out will come back to you. But, it's three times very specific. It's good for those who may have an inclination to do something bad.

Whether or not it's true is really based on interpretation, but the idea is that whatever you send out will come back to you threefold, so if you do send out a good affirmation to protect your home from any evildoing, or a shield to protect your space from negative vibes, that protection will come back to you threefold. If you want to heal from an illness or injury, the right spell will protect you threefold.

In contrast, any harmful spells will come back to you threefold. So, if you are harmful in your intents, that harm will come back to you threefold. It's there to help you resist the temptation to use the harmful spells, but also so you won't be tempted to use the manipulative magic that's out there.

The idea of magic is to use it in a way that benefits others. Some witches may have good intentions though, and sometimes may mess up the spell, so it has manipulative or not so positive intents. Of course, the witch will learn from their mistakes and will not do that again.

Wiccan spells for the most part though, are written in a way where you can't really do any harm. Basic witches won't have to worry about their spells going out of control, nor do they have to worry about any ill intent. The spells we'll mention later on will help protect you and benefit your life, not do any harm to you or others.

THE AFTERLIFE

Most religions in our world have an afterlife, a place where you go after you die. However, the belief in this is varied between Wiccans, so it's not a real focal part of this religion. They instinctually believe, however, that if one person does the most in their current life, and they are good in their current life, they will benefit from it later on. So, basically don't be a bad person in your current life and things will be good later on.

But some Wiccans don't believe in it either, and that's because some believe that once you physically die, you don't have a spirit or soul, and some people don't believe you have one initially, since it isn't something that can tangibly be seen, so once you die, that's it.

But some Wiccans actually have the idea you have multiple souls too, and where they go when you're done is based on a reincarnation sort of way. But of course, this is all a personalized aspect of it.

Some Wiccans also believe in reincarnation, and that's a more dominant practice since Gardner himself believed in it. The idea of how the cycle of reincarnation happens however, does differ between each person, since some of them insist the human souls would only go to human bodies, but some Wiccans believe a human soul can become virtually anything at all.

Another common Wiccan belief is that witches who practiced it in their current life will be reincarnated as witches later on, and this is also an idea that was espoused by Gardner as well. He also believed the human soul would rest for a period of time between when the body dies, and reincarnation, and this is called "the Summerland," which is kind of an in-between place.

Some Wiccans also believe they can contact the sprits of the deceased, and are mediums as well, but that's more of a spiritualism concept than a Wiccan one.

So, the concept of where you go when you pass on varies between everyone, and that's okay. The idea of Wiccan is that it's your journey, your beliefs, and you should take your own pathway.

MORALITY

Morality again, follows that threefold law. The idea, however, can also be extended. Their idea is to be nice to everyone as much as you can. If you're not harming people, do whatever you want. The general concept is you're free to practice how you want to, so long as you're not harming anyone, and if you do end up harming someone or something inadvertently, you've got to take the right precautions to prevent it from happening again.

This is a bit different from other religions, which have almost a cherry-picked, vague idea of what's good and what's bad. But Wiccans believe if you can do something that helps others and doesn't harm then, than that's fine. As long as you're not doing any harm, then there's nothing bad about it.

FIVE ELEMENTS

There are five elements in this, hence why you see the pentagram when you look at Wiccan materials. These represent the four elements along with aether, which is another name for the spirit. This is usually seen when Wiccans construct the magic circle. Oftentimes, it's also seen through the different actions on Earth. Such as Earth being the material itself, water being the water in the air or what's on the plants, the fire being the plant energy through photosynthesis, air being the oxygen and carbon dioxide that's in the atmosphere, and all of that is put together through the aether, the spirit itself.

In traditional Gardnerian Wiccan, the idea behind the five elements actually represents a cardinal point that's on the compass, but some argue that it only applies to the birthplace of Wiccan, which was southern England, and the directions should be based on your own personal region itself. But this is mostly important to know about, since you see these on the Wiccan symbol, and oftentimes, when you're asked to draw a magic circle, you should do so with this in mind.

Wicca is an interesting practice, and there is a lot you can learn about this. Lots of people who are into Wicca oftentimes like to know about the gods and goddesses behind their actions. These are the core beliefs that are worth mentioning, and if you've ever been curious about what goes into Wicca, this is definitely the way to do it, and it's what will help you better understand the practices too.

Chapter 4: Altars and Rituals: What they are, and How to Set them Up

All Wicca practices and rituals oftentimes require an altar, and a precise ritual. The rituals are based on events, and the altars that are crafted also have their own specifications. We'll go into detail on what these are, and why they matter here.

ABOUT THE ALTAR AND IMPORTANCE

The Wiccan altar is very similar to altars in other religions, but it has its own importance and relationships.

The generalized purpose of the Wiccan altar is to honor different spirits, deities, and the ancestors as well. It's where the offerings are done, and also where sacred objects are kept.

The altar is the main focal point of rituals and celebrations, such as the thirteen Esbats, and the eight Sabbats, both of which are very important ceremonies. The Wheel of the Year is also celebrated here, but you also can use this for meditation, prayer, or even spell work too.

Some people even have Wiccan altars outdoors, since it allows for a connection with nature. But, the altar itself is often nestled into a corner of your space and are pulled out and placed in the center during rituals.

There are various tools used as well, but the purpose of the altar is to create a space for Wiccans to practice, and oftentimes, you place different statues, candles, a wand, chalice, or even a ritual knife and various herbs onto this altar.

Typically, these altars are either permanent, or they are furniture that sets itself up as both a desk and a table. You only need for it to be a flat surface.

Some people like to have a rounded altar, because it makes it easier to put circles on it. But you should choose your altar that best fits you.

Basically, the altar is the media in which you practice your rituals and it is necessary for you to work on.

THINGS TO KEEP IN MIND ABOUT YOUR ALTAR

When you're setting it up there are a few things for you to consider when you're putting this together, and we'll list them below.

If you're struggling with setting up a Wiccan altar, you should focus on making sure it has the following properties:

- Reminds you of the ideals
- Allows you to echo your wishes and beliefs
- Is a focal point for your magical energies
- A home for your divine, whether it be a god or goddess
- Can help you do spells easily

If your altar doesn't have that, then chances are it won't be effective when you're using it.

Wiccan altars are a manifestation of your true self, and your soul's true potential. It's also the place where devotions happen, and it's a spiritual area for this, so you'll want to make sure that, when you're choosing a Wiccan altar, you focus on that point, so you're creating a space you want to work with.

Remember as well that in Wicca, you don't need to follow certain guidelines. Remember, that your altar is the manifestation of the relationship you possess with the god and goddess, so it's a confidential and personal matter. You shouldn't let people watch, and you shouldn't judge your altar on anything else other than what you want out of it, and what will communicate to the deities effectively.

Some Wiccans do like an altar made of natural materials, such as stone or wood. Metal is an option, but it's typically not the one that you go for. Wood is the most traditional of them all, since it's the easiest to obtain, and you typically can get an oak or willow altar pretty easily.

Of course, if you don't want to purchase a whole new table, you don't need to do so. A coffee table or household desk is fine, and you typically can get a Wiccan altar kit for a decent price. Of course, though, you must remember that the object will be charged with energy, no matter what you get. That's why, it's encouraged for you to get one that is natural, since it'll be closer to nature itself, which means it'll have more power.

This also means that you should avoid anything with synthetics or plastic as much as possible. If you do hold your rituals outside, you can literally use a tree stump, a big rock, or something else that's perfect for the altar. Some witches say that's the ideal situation in many cases.

But again, remember, this is something that you need to keep in mind yourself, and you should figure out the best course of action for your Wiccan practices.

Tools of Altars

There are certain tools you should also consider when putting your altar together, and we'll go over each of them, what they are, and their general purpose here.

- Athame: This is a ceremonial knife that has a black handle, and it is used to direct the energies that you have, especially in casting ritual circles.
- Bell: This brings attention to the divine that you're looking at, and you should get one that has a good tone, and has healing energy, since you can use this as well to clear your energies.
- Chalice: This is one of the most important items to have. You can get a fancy cup of your choice, or any type of wine glass is good. Silver is usually the ideal material it should be made out of, and you should make sure you offer liberations with this, or if needed, have it hold a saltwater solution.
- Libation Dish: This is a small bowl, typically near the center itself, that's used to give offerings to the gods and goddesses that are there. Some use a caldron for this purpose too, and you typically will get the offerings from the divine in this fashion as well, so you can offer it to nature at the end of the ritual.

- Pentacle: This is a five-point star that's within a circle, and it's put at the center of your altar, ad it offers you immense protection during magical work.

- Wand: You essentially need one of these, and they're made of a natural material, and they help with spell work. You should choose the wand that best fits your energies, but typically, they're used for channeling your energy, casting and recalling circles, and it can be used in place of your athame, and typically, it allows for you to absorb the energies of the world.

These tools are the basics of what you need, and it's very important that you have these, since they are valuable in putting together the right altar that helps you and can help with putting forth the effort necessary for good spell work.

TIPS TO SETTING IT UP

Remember that Wiccan altars are your own personal contribution, and you can decorate it as needed with fabric such as scarves and the like, which allows for you to transform various items into that of a magical nature. Many Wiccans do like to decorate their altars based on the season. For example, during Yule, putting some holly berries and bright leaves around it, or adding flower petals during the spring is good.

Crystals, stones, images of your deities that you're offering to, and the like can be there on the altar as well.

As for where the tools should go, it's based on different directions and traditions.

One puts all the tools associated with the Goddess and the elements such as earth and water on the left, and the God and his elements, which are air and fire, on the right. Another layout places the God and Goddess representations near the altar center, with the rest of the tools themselves arranged according to the directions and elements. This means the tools that are associated with the Earth for instance, will be the ones that are near the northern side, and then the fires will be to the south.

This is also based on the established patterns utilized for altar setups, and oftentimes, some people will be more intuitive with their patterns, and the way that their personal experiences resonated with this. Oftentimes, some people like to have more elaborate setups, but others prefer a more watered-down approach, with only a couple of objects at your altar.

Some people like to decorate their entire altar with all of their objects. The most important thing to remember, is to figure out the space, and if you are limited in space for your altar, you should design it based on a singular guiding principle and keep that vibe for the rest of the altar.

Some people do get down a little bit about their lack of items on the altar, or how extra their altar is. Oftentimes, people feel like their altar is boring, or maybe you feel like the altar is a mistake. But you should keep in mind that the God and Goddess don't care about the quality and the size of the Wiccan altar that you have, or the number of candles you put on it. You should work on making do with what you have, and if you need to, you should use something as small as the kitchen table for your space.

The general idea is to work with what you have, and don't worry all that much about how large, or how small, the area is.

When it comes to setting up your altar, you should figure out what works for you, and the right setup that benefits your life. Remember, this is your own choice, so you should figure it out for yourself on a personal level.

RITUALS

As we've said before, Wicca typically has rituals that allow for you to come together to encourage a closeness and union with the divine.

Sabbat and Esbat are two of the most important ones, but handfasting which are weddings, initiations, or even end-of-life ceremonies are also done. The purpose of these is to come together, either separately or in a coven or circle, to honor a God or Goddess, and the typically purpose is to celebrate the wonders of life. While most of these rituals are private, some will hold them in a public setting, so if you want to observe and learn about the craft itself, you can with it.

Solo rituals are also incredibly significant, and many Wiccans know that as they worship during each point of the wheel of the year, they're adding personal power and light to the magical energy that's there.

The basics of them are typically in many forms, and oftentimes, no two events are totally alike, and some may be more elaborate and structured, and others are very impersonal. Those that are practiced in solitude tend to be more on the spot.

It really does depend on occasion too, oftentimes some of them being more typical of a ritual than others.

The rituals begin with a purification, at the place that it's held, whether it be a bath, smudging to remove energies, or burning of sacred herbs.

After that, the altar is set up, and while some may set them up permanently, sometimes they may change the different foliage or items on there, such as fall foliage for the Mabon ceremony, or whatever. The altar also has various tools, offerings, and symbols, each laid out based on tradition.

From there, the circle is cast, which creates a boundary. The altar is at the center, with others to work in so that there isn't any stepping outside of the boundary or circle. There are also several candles, stones, or herbs, and oftentimes, circle casting is done at this point.

From here, invocations begin based on the ritual, elements, and the raw materials that are necessary, and the items are based on the cardinal direction.

The intent of the ritual is stated, and from there, there's a petition to the Goddess and God on behalf of someone who needs the help, and if there is magical spell work that needs to be done, they will do this as well during the ritual.

From there, various activities such as recreating scenes from poems or myths, liturgical materials, or even reading from ancient texts, poetry, chanting, singing, or decorating may happen during this time, and it is done with the purpose of informality reflecting on the event and ritual. Prayers may happen, and oftentimes they're personal.

There is also the cakes and ale, which is food and drink that's shared with the god or goddess at this time, and typically, it's near the end of the ritual. From there, the ceremony will connect on a spiritual level with the Earth, and most participants will then share with the God or Goddess before the closing proceedings happen.

This is more of a basic Wiccan ritual, and we'll talk about a basic one you can try later on in this chapter.

THE IMPORTANT WICCAN RITUALS

So, what are the most important Wiccan rituals to know about? Well, let's talk about some of the key wiccan rituals practiced in this religion:

- Mabon, which is done during the Fall Equinox, and it's used to thank the Goddess and God for the bountiful harvest, and to welcome the dark as you prepare for winter.
- The Sabbats, which are solar holidays that fall onto the different equinoxes that happen, and oftentimes are the cross-quarter days of the Sabbats
- Esbats are essentially the times when the moon is full. This is a ritual that's done with the purpose of honoring the Goddess, and are essentially the counterparts of the eight Sabbats, which showcase the journey of the sun and the God himself
- Samhain, which is done on Halloween and it has the themes of honoring ancestors, introspection, rebirth, divination, and revelry, and oftentimes also has the same themes as the fall equinox does, but with more mischief attached to it.
- Yule or the winter solstice, is held on the shortest day of the year, and it celebrates the beginning of the end of the year
- Brigid: This is the preparation for spring, where the Wiccans will also prepare for the growth of spring

All of these rituals are typically practiced, but they can also be done on a solitary level. You don't have to practice on an actual Wiccan holiday, but oftentimes, it's when the powers are strongest, so it isn't that a bad thing to consider, especially when you're thinking about partaking in Wicca.

A BASIC WICCAN RITUAL TO TRY

The best basic ritual to try is of course the solitary ritual. This is something you can do right now, on your own, without anyone else around.

First and foremost, figure out what ritual you want to hold, and if you want to do it in your own space, that's fine, or in a group of other witches, that's fine too. Figure out what you want to practice and write it down. Look up information on the rituals as well.

Plan what you need, including your altar, and any tools that are needed, and what quarters to use as well.

From here, prepare the space by either sweeping or smudging, and also clear up any debris in the space. If you're outside, you should do it barefoot, and prepare the practicalities that are used.

From here, take a bath and cleanse your body before you begin, using bath oils that you only use during rituals. From here, ground yourself by closing your eyes, and becoming relaxed.

Clear out all of the mundane aspects of life that are distracting you.

From here, you cast your circle by drawing it on your altar. Call the elements to your space, starting with air, then fire, then water, then earth, and finally, spirit. At this point, you should focus on the deity or deities you have at the focus and honor them. Symbolic pictures or sculptures are there for focusing the mind and should be used, especially in ritual groups where you need to be focused. However, closing your eyes and thinking of the deity when you're on your own works too.

Next, visualize and meditate. Take the spells you're using for the ritual, and from there, say them out loud. Use your wand or your athame to help focus the energy on them

At this point, offer to the God or Goddess the offerings that are there, thanking them in the process too.

Thank the elements in reverse order, going backwards from spirits all the way to air. At this point, open up the circle too, and do it as you say the elements. This in turn will get rid of the residual energies hanging around there and keep everything nice and fresh.

From here, ground yourself once more, whether it be by eating and drinking something, patting your body, or even visualizing some roots as they grow and hold you steady.

Solitary workings usually have the personal grounding, but if you work with people, they may have a wine and cake, where wine, along with bread and cake are passed clockwise, where you bless the next person. When everyone is settled, they may talk and express various emotions at this point.

From here, you may clean up, and you should make sure that you record your own personal experiences in your Book of Shadows. However, that step is optional.

Now what you use in your ceremony is really based on the deity who you're trying to get help from, but also the tools that you feel are needed. Some people may also use herbs, but the best thing to do in this case is to follow the guides that are there and the spells that are necessary. It's important that you take time to learn about it, and if there are specific instructions for certain rituals, do consider using them.

Sometimes the ritual may be based on a holiday, which is fine, because from there, you can thank the God or Goddess during that time, and also celebrate the holiday too.

Wiccan rituals, and the Wiccan altar are both interesting to learn about, and if you are curious about partaking in the activities of Wiccans, you should know about both of these.

Chapter 5: The Wiccan Relationships

Wicca offers different relationships between different concepts, and here, we'll discuss a little bit about each of these Wiccan relationships, and why they matter in the grand scheme of things.

THE RELATIONSHIP BETWEEN MALE AND FEMALE

There is one element that some people who are just getting started with Wicca are curious about: is gender important? What's the relationship between males and females?

Now according to Wiccan philosophy, the universe is created with a balance between both the feminine, and the masculine concepts and principles. So, union and individualizing, light and dark, activity and reception, and also matter and energy are both dualities that move the world. The world is basically a duality that's balanced, and when they're both balanced out, it creates peace.

This is manifested in gender, not just in Wiccan gods and goddesses, but in other elements of Wicca. The reality of it is, the God and Goddess are often perceived as what they are, where the God is the male and the Goddess is a female, but that's done more out of convenience than anything.

But of course, some Wiccan traditions are incredibly gender-focused, where some of the concepts are fueled by gender. Gardnerian Wiccan and the offshoots of that are more gender-based and rules. But that has changed a lot over the last century or so, where the concept of gender in it of itself is less and less aligned with the reality, or the spirituality and in essence, it changes the constructs of it.

Oftentimes, the God is the male and the Goddess is the female, but the reality of it is, they're both aspects in each person. It may be new to you, it may not be, but the truth is, anyone can invoke either of these energies, regardless of gender. So, anyone can hold the energies of the goddess regardless of their gender, so anyone can hold that god energy. So, if you're LGBT, you can actually take the opportunities to know both of these, and in essence, both male and female are of equal importance in this, and it creates a balance.

The concept of the deities themselves in many cases are also considered bi-sexual. This means it incorporates both genders at the end of it all, and in essence, it will allow for you to work with the traditions around the world. Krishna, Buddha, and other gods are oftentimes ambiguous within gender, and not overly feminine. It's important to understand the divine in Wicca is a duality, and it shouldn't be limited to just that, but instead recognize that it's beyond the entire gender identity, where the divine light, the forces of creativity, and the mysteries of life all have a similar oneness. When we look into each of these gods and goddesses, in a sense, they're kind of one and the same.

WICCA AND THE GENDER REVOLUTION

Did you know however, that Wicca actually played a major role in the cultural evolution of our society? In a sense, it makes complete sense, since in our society, the gender assumptions are breaking down more and more, with gender roles and rules slowly coming apart. That's because, in our world, there isn't such a thing as duality, that means that gender roles are more of a convenience that we use, and it isn't a part of the reality.

With that being said, you need one and the other, one in the same, but if you are worried about whether or not gender roles are a huge part of your life, the answer to that is no, they're not that important, and they oftentimes are not as big and expansive as you think they might be. Gender roles are often not the reality of life, and instead, with Wicca, there is an understanding of the fluidity of gender itself, along with the divine as well, allowing you to reach beyond the generalized beliefs and rules that you're programmed with, and from there, you accept the diversity of it with gratitude. For many people, it is a wonderful understanding, since you don't have to worry as much about whether you're doing something "feminine" or "masculine."

The God and Goddess are both incredibly important in the Wiccan religion. That's because, without one, the other can't be. This is quite a contrast from the patriarchal religions that are in our world. Oftentimes, women are not seen on the same level as men, and that creates a problem for many.

But, Wicca takes all of that away, destroying the gender and social constructs in order to create a better understanding of life itself.

WICCAN RELATIONSHIP WITH NATURE AND HOW TO PRACTICE IT

Nature is one of the most important parts of Wicca. It's essentially a big part of Wicca itself. Nature plays a major role in Wicca, and it's very important to respect nature in its own way.

Wicca aims to respect nature, as a spiritual teacher, and many Wiccans devote themselves to the integration of the Earth's cycles, and the inherent wisdom within it in order to create a spiritual tradition. They hold nature as a sacred part, since it's what keeps everything in place, and it's very important for many Wiccans to hold nature in place, and it is something Wiccans enjoy practicing.

Most Wiccan rituals are done by living in a harmonious means with the Earth. It has a spiritual worldview that many Native American and indigenous religions have. The practices of spirituality within Wicca are used to help coincide yourself and humanity with the natural rhythms of the Earth, and the cycles. The rituals as well will coincide with the moon and sun phases, and this is a big thing for women especially.

The goal of Wicca is to have a balance with nature, and that's really the ultimate result that Wiccans want from this. They want to practice spirituality in both sacred rituals, but also in the way that they live. Which is why, Wiccans will spend a lot of time outside in prayer, mediation, and they oftentimes will focus on shamanic work too.

Gardening and spending time outside is a big part of Wicca too. It allows for those to be connected with nature to have that purpose, and oftentimes, the focus of the divine presence is a part of this.

Divine presence is said to be everywhere. That includes the air that we're breathing, the water we drink, and the food that we eat. Wiccans do respect nature, which is why they try to have a natural life, opting more towards foods that nourish us, that don't harm the earth, and textiles that won't harm the Earth as well.

They revere the Earth, which oftentimes encompasses the divine, and they have a deep concern that's more pragmatic than anything. The Earth is not treated as something that you just use or exploit, pollute, or destroy in the short-term, but instead, they respect the Earth as sacred, and will make sure it is treated as such, and oftentimes, they'll keep everything in place, and keep a wonderful bond with nature whenever possible.

NATURE AND NOT HARMING IT

Remember the whole "if it doesn't harm anyone, do what you will? That's the principle Wiccans use when they're working with nature.

Whenever they're doing anything involving nature, as long as it doesn't harm someone, and it honors the divine in some way, you can live your own life. However, you need to be responsible in your actions, and you should make sure that you have that same concept when looking at what you eat, and how you live.

So, if you're curious about doing something, the Wiccan principles basically say as long as you're not harming someone, then you're fine.

That's why when you cast spells, you make sure that they're done in ways that don't harm people, and it's more of a ritual that you meditate on rather than actual practice. Oftentimes the divine energy and the power of the Earth is manifested into the world itself through that interaction. The idea of having domination over nature isn't the end-goal of wiccan practices. Wiccans won't work with supernatural forces, or work to hurt others, but instead, they'll call upon the help of the God and the Goddess, and together, it will work to showcase respect and the tuning of these natural energies so that everything is sacred.

In simple terms, it's actually unethical to do any spiritual work that will control, manipulate, or force you to have power over another. While work may be done on behalf of another, such as in the case of healing that's important in Wicca, you do it with the consent of the person, and you always do it with respect to nature.

Nature is a natural form of healing, where, when faced with situations that will crush your spirit, making you feel bad, and lost, you can focus on nature to help you, providing you with the strength to live once more. Once you do utilize the power of naturel, you'll be able to carry out different activities that will help you.

So, how can live in harmony with both nature and the duality of both female and male? Read below.

How to apply This

The best way to apply both of these principles, is first and foremost, realize that gender roles are a patriarchal construct you don't have to follow when you're learning all about this.

Second of all, you should work to do more activities that improve your environment. This can be something as simple as gardening or putting together an herb garden, planting some trees, or trimming hedges. You'll be able to divert your focus from your issues to the activities that are there, and from there, accomplish that feeling of happiness, and you'll feel great too.

This also applies to where you go when you're outside. Going on trips, such as camping or little adventures can help you get into contact with nature. Even little trips to the park will help you prevent burnout, and you can learn from nature in this case too. If you feel like you're missing out on some connection with nature, or you feel burnt out and not refreshed, this is how you do it.

Finally, focus on keeping your environment nice and serene, attempting to find calmness and peace in it. If you're tired and feel like you're never catching a break, take a few minutes and spend it outside in the sun, enjoying and basking in the heat, or breathing in the cold air as you sit outside and relax.

You can also participate in different ceremonies and festivals in Wicca as well in order to sacrifice or offer to gods, in order to prepare for the season. You can also do these to help commemorate the journey of the Earth going around the Sun. this in turn will help you stay in harmony with the natural gods and nature. Learning about the different Wiccan festivals, and potentially considering actually partaking in them might be a wonderful choice for those who are curious.

Most of all, be respectful to nature. Nature is hurting due to the way humans are treating it. The best way to exercise caution and understanding of this Wiccan principle is to be respectful to the nature at hand and understand that it's a big part of the way your life is. If you're worried about whether you're doing something that's helping the Earth or harming it, the best thing to do, is think about whether the divine would appreciate what you're doing.

If the answer is no, then chances are you're harming the Earth.

The principles of nature and gender in Wicca are important for understanding Wicca, and it's imperative that, if you do have considerations on whether or not you can fit into Wicca based on your gender or sexual orientation, or how you respect nature, know that it's quite easy to do, and the religion is very fluid on these concepts, especially compared to other religions in our world today.

Chapter 6: Understanding Seasonal Cycles

Seasonal cycles, or seasons, are very important for Wiccans. They are in fact, the days when rituals are held. Here, we'll highlight the seasonal cycles that are important in wicca, the rituals and how they play into this, along with some of the seasonal activities that they do.

WHAT ARE WICCAN SEASONAL CYCLES

The seasonal cycles are based on the wheel of the year, which is basically the seasonal festivals that wiccans, along with many other pagans, do observe. These usually are held on the different solstices and equinoxes, along with the midpoints between. The names are varied, but typically, they are usually called either quarter days or cross-quarter days. Usually, Wicca does observe those names. Wicca also celebrates different holidays based on the phases of the moon, but for the most part, the seasons are the major festivals.

The festivals in Wicca are called sabbats, which is based on the term that was originally used in the middle ages, and it also does refer to the Jewish term called Shabbat, which commingled with the celebrations too. Typically, the events are marked on our own calendars as well, which are represented by the beginning of each new season.

Typically, this time is often known as the growth and the retreat of people through the different seasons. In Wicca, these events have generally been based on a lot of the symbolism and solar mythology. The esbats as well, are typically tied to the lunar cycles, and the phases of the moon.

There are a few important seasonal cycles that are recognized in Wicca, and they are listed below:

- Yule: Celebrated on the first day of winter, and it's one of the significant points in this, and it is oftentimes associated with the solstice sunset and sunrise, and the reversal of the sun at this point is supposed to represent the presence of the solar god and the return of the fertile seasons

- Spring Equinox: The first day of spring and is often times called Ostaa in Wicca. It is the holiday of the spring celebrations, in which there is a balance of light and dark, with the light rising
- May Eve: This is the first day of summer in Ireland, but this is supposed to be the festival of flora, who is the Roman goddess of flowers, and it recognizes the power of life in its full nature
- Summer Solstice: This is called Litha, which is a name that holds Anglo-Saxon history in it. This is showing the light of summer, which is when it's greatest, and it's when the strength is the highest, is the turning point, and it also is when the sun starts to decline, and it's one of the most important seasons and one of the most important rituals
- Autumnal Equinox: This is a time of harvest, and it is a time when there is thanks given for the fruits that have come from the Earth, and they're used to secure the blessings of the Goddess and God during the winter months. It's often called Mabon, which was coined by Aidan Kelly in the year 1970, which was from a character in Welsh Mythology

So, all of these seasons are important, since they signify important spiritual rituals, and oftentimes, are some of the observed holidays.

How Rituals Play Into This

Rituals are a huge part of Wiccan season changes. For many of them, they are a time when you offer thanks or ask for the God and Goddess to offer a fruitful or bountiful harvest.

For example, during Yule, there is oftentimes sacrifices that are done, offerings that are there, feasting, and gift giving during this time. They often encourage wiccans to bring every greenery such as holly, mistletoe, ivy, pine, and yew, and this is a time when you decorate your home.

In contrast, during Beltane, which is May Eve and the first official day of summer in Ireland, it oftentimes is a time of festive dancing, used to help recognize the power of the fullness of the Earth, and the opening of the flourishing and youthfulness. During this time, a lot of rituals are held, because this is a time when people are thanking the goddess for this type of growth and asking the Goddess to help bring forth a fruitful summer.

Remember that, with Wicca, there is oftentimes a desire for people to ask the God or Goddess for help with the nature-related activities. That's because, wicca has an inherent connection to the earth, so a lot of the purpose of Wicca is of course, to thank the God or Goddess for the help in nature-related activities. Obviously, the turning of the seasons, and the different seasonal changes are incredibly important within

Wicca, which is why during rituals, seasonal activities are done in order to thank the deities for the help they've offered.

When it comes to the time it is celebrated, the dates are flexible, and oftentimes, you want to do it either on cross-quarter days, during the nearest full moon or new moon, or the nearest weekend at the very minimum. Typically, if you can, you should even wear seasonal clothing in order to celebrate it.

The different Wiccan seasonal activities

The first of the seasonal activities is of course, offerings. Now, Wiccans don't sacrifice animals and such, contrary to what others might think. Instead, they offer food, drink in a chalice, or different objects that are used as veneration for the God and Goddess.

Some Wiccans may not eat different animals at this time, and instead eat a more plant-based diet and the like. Sometimes though, there will be Wiccans that will eat meat as a celebration, where a little bit is offered, and the rest is consumed.

Most of the sacrifices to the deities are done via burning. Burying and leaving he is offering, however, are the most common of occurrences, where the purpose of his is to show veneration, gratitude, giving back to the world, and also strengthening the bonds between both humans, and the divine within the community.

Within Wicca, the Wheel of the Year is of course, the marriage between the God and the Goddess, and it's when the god is born during Yule, grows during the vernal equinox along with the Goddess, from there, court and impregnate the Goddess during Beltane, and from there, it will wane in power during Lammas, and will pass into the underworld during Samhain, which is Halloween, and from that point, the God and Goddess are both taken. This is core aspects and from here, they're born once again during Yule. The goddess will always rage and rejuvenate during the seasons, and each year, they're courted by the Horned God.

Many Wiccans oftentimes also incorporate the Oak King, and the Holly King into this narrative as well, where these two figures will battle completely during the season turnings. During summer solstice, the Holly King will defeat the Oak King, and will commence their own reign. During the Autumn equinox, the Oak King will then regain their power as the sun starts to wane. During the winter solstice, the Oak King will in turn vanquish the Holly King.

After this point, the spring equinox will then wax again, and the Holly King will regain his strength to once again beat the Oak King during summer solstice.

These two battles are essentially the two parts of the whole, and the light and darkness that make God, and you should realize that one without the other won't exist. The Holly King is often seen as a woodsy person, and Oak King is more of a fertility god itself. But this is also celebrated through rituals thanking both of the gods for their hard work.

Some of the seasonal activities that Wiccans do during this time include dancing, singing, and also reading poetry, to thank and acknowledge the work the God and Goddess do. For many Wiccans, this can be done alone, and sometimes Wiccans will pray in order to thank the God and Goddess. Some Wiccans, however, will just celebrate in joy.

When it comes to the harvest time, oftentimes the harvest for the year, such as your own personal garden, will be offered to the God and Goddess as thanks for the effort. Of course, this is all a personal thing and at the end of the day, is ultimately your choice in how you want to celebrate it.

Most Wiccans love to celebrate the seasons because it offers a connection to nature they may not have before. With the different seasons and activities, it's no wonder that you'd want to celebrate as well, and you can, with each new year, celebrate the activities, the different ways to acknowledge the seasons, and to have a wonderful time commemorating each of these different parts of the journey of the year.

Chapter 7: Wiccan herbs, candles, and Crystals

One part of Wicca a lot of witches are curious about, is of course herbs, candles, and crystals. Along with a picture of the deity that you're celebrating, or the one you're making an offering to, herbs, crystals, and candles are all used in order to help accomplish spells, and to ask the deity for assistance. We'll go over the main herbs that witches should know about, the candles, candle colors and their purpose, along with the purpose of healing crystals for witches.

All about the herbs used

The purpose of herbs is based on the different magical properties that you're trying to possess. Whether love, romance, or even just to cleanse your space, some of the herbs that are used in Wicca are very powerful, and they are incredibly potent.

The list of herbs is very long, but here, we'll highlight some of the best beginner herbs to start with, and some of the different factors utilized in each of these herbs.

Herbs should be ground up, and you should take care of them in the way that the spell requests you to. Otherwise, it could adversely affect the potency of this. When choosing herbs, always choose those that are fresh, and not filled with any pollutants.

Herbs can sometimes be carried around too and having them physically on your body can help with improving the magical properties of such.

Some of the top herbs that are used include the following:

- Caraway: Used to add charms to attract a lover, oftentimes used as well to help improve passion, and to protect you.
- Catnip: Is oftentimes used in cat magic, but can also be used to treat colds, insomnia, and also can help to consecrate your tools
- Chamomile: Used with protection because it's incredible calming, and it can also induce sleep. It's wonderful for

insect repellent too, and you'll have success if you plant this

- Cinnamon: This is a wonderful one for spiritual quests, improving power, your success, psychic work, and is used in healing, telling the future, and it is also a male aphrodisiac. It also has wonderful properties for skin issues, and it aids in digestion
- Clover: Associated with the Triple Goddess, and is used to help maintain beauty, youth, heal any injuries, and also cures madness, and if you find a four leafed clover, that's a proven good luck charm
- Clove: Used to help dispel negativity and those that will speak ill of you, if you wear it on a red thread, it's a protective charm, that helps with clearing out any gunk involving money, visions, and purification and cleansing
- Coriander: Another good one for keeping peace within your home, and overall serenity, it's used to help improve both longevity, and the love spells too. You can create a love potion with wo people who are consenting, simply by grinding 7 grains of this into a container, mixing it together with wine, and then drinking it. This is also the love potion herb, which is used in charms and sachets
- Lavender: Used to help with love, healing, protection, purification, sleep, and peace, also used to promote healing. Can be used to preserve chastity when it's mixed

with rosemary. Lots of flowers are burned to help induce sleep, and it generally helps cleanse the home in order to bring peace and harmony.

- Juniper: Will banish anything that's injurious to your health, attracts energies that are healthy, and it can increase the potency of males. You can string these over in order to improve your love, and it can be burned in order to safeguard your home and allow for magical protection. You can use the berries, or the wood itself
- Jezebel Root: Oftentimes popular in casting spells related to money and achievement
- Jasmine: Used in order to charge your healing crystals and is used in divination. Oftentimes used in sachets in order to draw love and attract soulmates. Carry or burn these around in order to create money and wealth. Oftentimes used in dream pillows to induce sleep within the body
- Hyssop: This is one of the most common herbs in purification magic, and will lighten the vibrations around, and also used widely in purifying herbs that are used in magic. This is also used to protect properties as well against people, and it's used to consecrate the magical tools, and is oftentimes used for general cleansing, and is used to help ward off evil
- Hyacinth: Used in order to help promote peaceful minds and a more restful sleep, allowing you to attract luck, love,

and often, and this is good for guarding against nightmares.

- Lemon: Is commonly used to help clean and protect the spiritual openings, and is used for purification, and also removing blockages. Oftentimes, lemon peels are used in sachets and mixtures. You can soak these and wash magical objects in order to get rid of the negativity that's there, and they're great for secondhand objects
- Licorice: This isn't the candy, this is the herb, and it's used to attract lust, love, and fidelity, and is used in many cases to attract lovers too
- Lotus Root: Used in many cases to help with maintaining clean and pure thoughts. You can mark one side yes, and then no, and then toss the root of this into the air, and from there, it will help figure out if wishes will come true.
- Marjoram: Used in order to cleanse, dispel and purify a space. It oftentimes is used in reading dreams, and you can put it in different areas to help protect it and is oftentimes used in food in order to strengthen this, hence why you see it in ingredients.
- Marshmallow root: Used to protect against psychic powers, in order to help stimulate the psyche. You can put this on an altar in order to improv your spirits, and encourage a good ones

- Mint: Used in order to promote vitality, communication, and energy, drawing customers to your business as needed. You can use this within a green paper in order to use it for healing. You can put it in a purse of wallet to draw money to you. Use it on your altar to help promote the spirit and the magic that's here. You can also put it into your home for protection
- Mistletoe: Oftentimes used to help improve your fertility, creativity, and prevent the misfortune and illness, protecting you against negative spells and such. You can also carry it around for good luck with hunting, drawing in customers, and improving healing in rituals. You should, however, know that it's used with caution, since it is poisonous. Don't use this in the presence of animals, and don't use it internally.

These different herbs are used in order to promote wellness and happiness in life. Wiccans should use this in your spell making as needed, in order to help with improving the effectiveness of spells and magical works. Lots of Wiccans have these on hand, and you should use these as needed in order to ensure proper happiness.

THE PURPOSE OF CANDLES AND HOW TO USE THEM

The next Wiccan tool we'll be going over is candles. Candles are often used during rituals and rites for different reasons, and they are oftentimes used for worshipping the deities, and you use them as well honoring these as well. Worshipping deities is often done with torches, flaming wheels, and balefires. It is the only source of natural illumination short of the sun, which makes it obvious why Wiccans would use something so natural. It's got sacred power, and it has been used throughout history.

While we do use electricity in our world today, there are still candles utilized in almost every religious service there, I order to create specific intentions, and you even use these in the secular world.

The custom is oftentimes done because it creates an atmosphere that's pleasant and peaceful, which means that when we look at this light, it calms us.

Some also say candles are used in spell work too, since it helps you practice better and incorporates concentration. These also help strengthen your muscles magically, and the ability to focus the energy in each direction. Plus, this is both the simplest, and most complex form of magic.

Candle magic is very interesting, because the concept is incredibly simple, where you simply send out an intent on the physical plane, a message of sorts, with the request being made in order to help signify an intention. You send it through, and from there, it transforms into a physical plane, and it carries the message and then some.

Candles are oftentimes used with color at the beginning of this, and it's done in a way that's focused ad d tangible. It allows for you to create the intent in a way that is possible, and it can help with this. Different factors such as luck, love, and the like, and even death can be associated with candle magic, and it's said that it's supposed to help make the intent of this much stronger, and it can help with improving the overall strength of the intent as well.

For example, red candles are associated with love and passion, such as the color of the heart. Green is associated with abundance and is often used in spells involving money cause it's a green color, just like money is. The growing season is identified by this.

You can use each of these candles in order to help you reinforce the intent of the spell. That's literally the purpose of this, and these spell candles are found in almost every single color that's there.

The process of candle magic and using candles in wicca is simple. Once you light the candle, you can sit there and watch the size, shape, flame, and just let it burn, with the intent of this in mind at this point to help you focus the energy in this.

If you send the intent out quickly, you'll have a quick manifestation. If you notice that the candle is flickering brightly and quickly, that means that this will manifest itself super quickly, whereas a low, weaker flame will indicate that there isn't much spiritual energy in it. It also is said that if the wick is black, or thickly smoking, there's an opposition in the intent, whether it be from a person, item, or unknown circumstances, and not even the unconscious mind may know that it's happening. But you just have to hope for the intent to push through.

Now, you continue to push that intent, and once it's all the way downwards, you can look at the wax that's left behind. Some witches will do that with the candles that are left, and it's called ceromancy, and it's suited for people to visualize, and if you get visions easily, this is a great way to do it. If you look at the wax, you look for shapes and the patterns that are there before you suggest the forces that are taking shape in terms of the wax. From here, you can look at where the wax is pushed when it melted, where the air went, and you can look at the mood of the wax, and what it seems to be.

Of course, if you are confused by this, you shouldn't worry too much about it. Some people get so hung up on the different aspects of this. You'll probably not understand this at first, but once you have a sense of where the flames and wax are communicating, you can do what you need to do with this.

Some of the different candle colors include the following:

- White: The goddess, purity, peace, virginity
- Black: Binding, shapeshifting, protection, and repels negativity
- Brown: Influences friendships
- Silver: The Goddess, female energy, astral energy, clairvoyance, and dreams
- Purple: Third eye, psychic ability, spiritual power, and influencing people in higher locations
- Blue: Water element, protection, wisdom, calmness, good fortune, and opening up blocked communication
- Green: The earth element, healing, success financially, and growth of the natural world
- Pink: Affection, romance, and care
- Red: The fire element, passion, strength, career goals, lust, survival, and the blood moon
- Orange: Generalized success

These candles can be used as you see fit, and if you want to try basic candle magic, you're welcome to do so.

Now, you should always practice safe candle magic when doing this. Most candle spells call for you to let the candle burn on its own, which is fine, but understand this may take a while. It's never a good suggestion to leave burning candles unattended, and you should make sure that you stay near it at all times. If you really, really must leave a candle burning for a long period of time, put it in a sink or tub, and away from where it might fall down and burn. You should also make sure that you are careful if you're adding oils to this too. Those things are incredibly flammable, and they can burn your fingers.

It is a great way to improve your focus and direction, and you can explore the magical arts with this type of magic, that's for sure.

WICCAN CRYSTALS AND HOW THEY'RE USED

Finally, we've got Wiccan healing crystals. Oftentimes, people will wear these crystals on their body physically in order to ward off energies, or they're used with different rites and intent in mind.

When you look at crystals though, you're going to see that there are 70 different ones that are used in Wicca. But, here's the thing, the average witch doesn't need to have that many. You can use over 100 crystals, ten, or just one. The reality of it is, don't take it as a set element to just have a certain amount of crystals.

With crystal, you need to ground, charge, cleanse, and recharge them, and that is a very in-depth process. Others might just like the fact that they're pretty. At the end of the day, crystals are what you make of them, and they're what you want them to be.

So, what are crystals used for? Well, here's the thing, crystals are used for your rituals, in order to appease a goddess or other deity, or they're used for grounding, which is used to help keep you focused on the Earth so you're not feeling the effects of negative energies.

There is also the fact that crystals are wonderful for power. Power is something that you'll want to work on, and something worth mentioning over time. But the right crystal will make all the difference. Crystals can be used as well to help make intents that you have come true.

For example, if you're thinking about trying to fall in love with someone, or you want to work on passion, you can take a crystal, and hold onto it.

Each crystal has a certain amount of power to it though. Think of it like a stamina bar in a video game. Each crystal needs a certain amount of charging in order to use it, and then needs to be recharged in order to maintain the effects of that, which is something most beginner witches don't worry about.

So, how do you do each of these? Read below to find out.

CLEANING THE CRYSTALS

You should clean these after another has touched them, if you have had guests within your space, if you've taken them with you, or a few days before the full moon.

You can typically clean them using a saltwater bath. Put them in there to help get rid of that energy. Everyone is different though, but 24 hours should be ample.

You can also bury them within the dirt. This is what many Wiccans do in order to help keep them nice and cleaned up. Plus, they're connected with the Mother Earth better, so they'll have more power.

Beaches are another good place, and this is great for blue and green-colored crystals. This is fast, and natural too. This is incredibly quick, and personally, if you live near a beach, this is a good way to do it.

Now, if you don't want to put that much work into cleaning, salt is the best way to purify these items. Salt will naturally purify things, so put them on top, or bury each of them for about 24 hours on average to help clean them up.

You can also use sage too. Burn some sage, and literally keep the smoke around each of the sides of the crystal, in order to clear away your energies. You can also do this with a selenite stick, which is used as a wand, and from there, it will help eliminate any negative energy.

Cleaning them is incredibly important, especially if you want to keep them free from negative elements.

RECHARGING THEM

Crystals are powerful, but if they aren't charged or recharged fully, you won't get the results that you want to from them.

You need to make sure you do this after you clean them, because otherwise, your intention will get mixed up with the intent of the others, and that's not what you want to do.

What you do, is you take each crystal, speaking the intent into each one that you have. For example, if you're sing rose quartz and say that you want to fill your heart with love. Black tourmaline can be used to help keep away negative energy. Essentially, speak what you want the crystal to be used for.

Next, put them by a window so they can charge in the sun. That's how they get energy.

Another time you can recharge these is during the full moon, where you leave them in a container or by the window outside.

At this point, you can use these in rituals, or even just on your own. Many Wiccans prefer to use jewelry than to have them just for rituals, and let's face it, they're incredibly pretty too.

GOOD BEGINNER HEALING CRYSTALS

There are a few good healing crystals for beginner witches to try out. It ultimately depends on what you want to use them for. Lots of people like something that's easily accessible, so something you can get from a natural shop is the best answer to this.

Clear Quartz is one of the most versatile out there, and it's the second most common mineral in the earth, and it's found on every continent but Antarctica, and it's the least expensive crystal to buy. It's wonderful for healing, clarity, and protection. It's kind of like the most universal stones out there, and if you don't have a particular stone for the job, then you should consider this. It's an impressive chemical, and it's wonderful for amplification, and healing spells too. It also is wonderful for clearing up any issues you have, and to help with focus. It's the most essential crystal you need, and it can be used for pretty much anything under the sun.

Amethyst is another one that's super popular for Wiccans, since it has the meaning of sobriety, self-discipline, inner strength, awareness, and peace. It can calm down fears, induce hopes and dreams that are peaceful. It's wonderful for cleansing energy, and to enhance spiritual growth. It can be used during meditation in order to heighten your own psychic abilities, along with improving intuition. This is also a beautiful gemstone that can be used to prevent overindulgence and also curb destructive habits you'd like to change.

Rose Quartz is on our list as the second most useful crystal in spell work. It's got the name from the pink hue this obviously has. It does have small traces of titanium within the crystal, but it's got a pale shade of pink, to rose pink. It oftentimes is used and associated with love, unconditional love to be exact. Oftentimes, these are carved into the shape of hearts to help push this idea.

They are good for promoting love, friendship binds, and deep healing on an inner level, and are wonderful comforts for those times of grief. It also can help promote the feelings of anxiety and heartbreak. It also is used to help dispel emotional pollution, creating a vibe that's loving and nice, and pushes acceptance and forgiveness, both of which are important aspects of building a happier, more reliable friendship not just with others, but with yourself as well.

You should consider getting some rose quartz if you feel stressed, depressed, or need to recover. While it isn't a replacement for medication and therapy, it's a wonderful way to cope with the various issues at hand.

Selenite is another very potent mineral. It's the crystal form of gypsum, and when put into water, it an revert all the way back to gypsum, and it's generally transparent and colorless. These are usually used in the form of sticks and points when used in wicca and are important because they help to purify the world around you.

This is actually named after the Greek goddess that's associated with the moon, Selene, and it helps clear the mind, expanding your own self-awareness and your surroundings, and it helps open up your chakras and get guidance from the spirits. Selenite also does instill peace and comfort, and if you use meditation in your Wiccan practices, this can help push judgement aside, and make seeing the deeper picture even more possible.

Finally, you have hematite, and that's a mineral with iron oxide in it. It's the oldest iron oxide out there and it's widespread in the soils and rocks. Typically, it's black to steel or silver-gray in color, or even reddish brown or red. These are wonderful for protection and grounding, used to strengthen the connection that's there with the Earth, making you feel secure and safe. It will allow for you to have the strength, courage, endurance, and the vitality that's possible.

It's essentially a "stone for the mind" which stimulates both focus and concentration and improves your memory and organic thinking. It also is potentially a good luck crystal, which the ancient Romans used to smear this onto their bodies, which they believed would make them invisible when used in battle. It is oftentimes used to bring you good luck during situations that are troublesome, especially legal ones.

It also helps to balance out the ethereal nervous system, along with the physical nervous system, helping with energy focus for the emotions between the spirit, mind, and body. It also helps to dissolve negativity within other people and is a valuable crystal to be used in practice.

USING CRYSTALS IN WICCAN PRACTICE

Crystals are oftentimes used in Wicca to mark out the sacred circle before you start, and it's often also used for honoring deities, and these specific stones are used to help honor the different goddesses and gods. Sometimes, pentacles and wands have crystals in them, and those Wiccans who wear magic jewelry can benefit from this.

In the Wiccan magic itself, it is used for everything from divination to healing, to even just manifesting wealth, along with love. It also is used in amulets, different talismans, and other "good luck" charms, along with scrying and protection too. They're a powerful part of spell work, whether it be ingredients that are added, or the main parts of a spell. Some Wiccan spells have these as the focus of the spell work, which is fine, and they're still quite powerful.

For example, you can use amethyst as a "power booster" for almost every spell. Rose quartz is used for sharpening your focus, especially if you're using spells that are more complex. You can also charge different crystals for different purposes, and you can even just charge and carry it for the proper results. For example, carrying red jasper for courage, or even citrine for attracting some money as well.

Crystal magic is also unique because you can take advantage of color correspondence in a natural way. You don't have to dye them like different cloth or candles, and the colors that are on the stone self are already available, and they resonate with all of the different parts of our existence, according to those vibrations. Pink for example is harmonizing, loving, and it is a powerful part of drawing love within your life. Green has a vibrational resonance with growth and abundance, making green stones, including bloodstone and jade, good for different spell work aspects, especially money and prosperity.

You can pretty much buy all of these stones at wiccan, or even New Age shops, and you can get ones that specifically focus on the phenomena at hand. However, lots of times crystal magic believes that the stones choose you, not you choose the stone. You might be given a stone that is a gift from a friend, or you just find it during a walk. You should find one that has an intention and comes to you.

Here's the thing about buying from shops. It might seem like a wonderful idea, but the thing is, you might be drawn to that stone without thinking much on it, and there will be a gravitational pull to certain crystals, but then, you may not even notice that there are energies associated with this. For example, if you do find one, scan your body, and if it makes you feel good, chances are, it's a good one. If you have a negative feeling, it might not be for you. Stones aren't harmful themselves, but if they aren't a good fit, they will just be ineffective.

That's really all there is to it. Wiccan crystals and herbs are very important, and the candles and candle magic change the game as well. As a Wiccan, you should always consider using these and from there, you can build a much happier, more worthwhile experience for yourself.

Chapter 8:
The Essential oils of Wicca and what they are

Essential oils are another part of Wicca, and while they are a tool used in spell work, they also have healing and other properties that are wonderful for you to use. Here is a list of some of the essential oils that are important for Wiccans to try, and also how to use these essential oils.

Essential oils are a component of ritual practice, and it's something that isn't totally new, since a lot of ancient healers used these to help with their creations. The oils in the past were of course made by heating up plant matter, and then the carrier oils are then put together with these in order to be used. Some of the earliest oils that were used were frankincense, cinnamon, and myrrh, and of course, cinnamon is still used today.

The oils today are extracted a little more differently, and there are other technologies that are discovered, letting the oils be extracted from different plants, especially citrus plants and flowers. These days, essential oils are used more in aromatherapy than anything else, but for Wiccans looking to get their hands on some good essential oils immediately, this is the way to do it.

How are they Used?

If you're familiar with Wiccan spell work, you probably think these oils are part of the main course, but they're not. The oils are used for anointing crystals, tools, amulets, talismans, and their own bodies. These oils are oftentimes sued to create incense, and this is great for making candles and charms. Pretty much anything that you' like to do on a magical level is enhanced by the utilization of oils, whether it's a single scent, or a blend of multiple scents that are used to help build a better foundation.

These are used for two reasons: they are from the earth, so naturally they have plant energies in them. Plants are living forms, and of course, they work with the harmony or nature to help others. Of course, plants also have the magical properties that are concentrated within essential oils.

The best thing to remember is that synthetic oils are nowhere near as good, simply because they don't contain the ingredients in botanicals. While witches have used synthetic oils with great success, most of them will say that botanicals are your best option, and they can't be rivaled.

THE POWER OF SCENTS

Scents have incredible power. Many of us are very in-tune with the scents and how we feel. Different scents will put us in great moods, letting us feel happier, and of course more relaxed. Myrrh and cedarwood, or even blends are really good since they awaken within something that's beyond ordinary scents of smell and such, putting us in different frames of mind. This is also a good way to get in touch with the invisible powers within the universe, letting us achieve the aims that are there. These oils provide a good and direct line between both the physical, and the spiritual world.

You can't summon the mind state you want if you're not in line with the universe. You should be in good harmony with both, which is why many essential oils and incense is used in Wicca. The richly-scented smoke that's there will help you keep a good frame of mind, and you won't be so focused on the worrisome details that might be happening outside of spell work. It helps create focus, and if you want the spell to be effective, then this is how you do it.

This focus will of course, help you connect with the higher deities, self, or whatever you're looking to use. They also promote inner focus, and they can even be charged as well by giving it a little bit of solar or lunar energy, and from there make them a powerhouse in your life.

The Best Essential Oils for Wiccans

So which oils work for you? The answer to this of course, is all relative. You may love the smell of something people normally don't like, or if you smell something that you can't utterly stand, don't use it. It's that simple.

Of course, with the commercialization of essential oils, you run into the problem of people selling cheap knockoffs that aren't that good. If you notice that the oil is a bit putrid, or just doesn't make you feel good, you shouldn't use this.

With that in mind, let's talk the best essential oils for Wiccans out there.

Basil

First let's talk about basil. This is one that stimulates the mind of the conscious, and it can be used for reducing fatigue in the body, and allowing for the mind to reveal itself, and it's good for understanding yourself on a different plane. Some also use it with spellcasting and different rituals that invoke joy and money.

It also has the power of creating sympathy between those who wear it, to avoid clashes that are there, and sometimes can be used in clashes that might be happening. It creates a harmony within others too, which is why people use it in order to help calm down negative energies between two people.

Anise

Anise is used within clairvoyance especially is you are trying to tell the future, and through divination. It's added to bath rituals that have divination as the focus, and it can be worn during rituals of divination.

It is also used to help scent a sacred space in order to help get rid of negative energies and also invoke the gods themselves so they can utilize their magical protection in order to help the caster.

Cinnamon

Cinnamon is used in many ways to access the realm of the psychics, and with visualization in order to strengthen the body itself. Many times, it's also a big part of spells that promote wealth. The leaf especially is used for this.

The oil is very vibrant, and it is great for protection, and for females, it's a sexual stimulant. If you add this to any other incense or essential oil, it will increase the powers. Some mix it with sandalwood to create a good incense for magic, meditation, good, and for illumination.

Cumin Seed

Cumin seed promotes harmony and peace within the home itself. Some witches will use this to anoint the doorways of a sacred space once a week before the sun is up, and when the house is asleep and quiet, and that in turn will help to bring a balance of all of these factors to the home itself.

Cypress

Cypress is one that's used for smoothing the transitions that the caster is going through, especially those who are suffering from the loss of those that they love, the separation of friends, or the end of a relationship. Cypress also bestows comfort and solace within a space, so it can help calm you down after all the negative energies have started to fall away.

Cypress in spell work is an oil that's used for blessing, protection and concentration. It is actually a symbol of the element of earth, and of course death, which is why it's used when there is a situation of those leaving for some reason.

Some wiccans will wear this at funerals, so that the oil is uplifted by the meaning of the death at the doorway, but another life at this point, and it will screen out those negative feelings that mourners have. Many will wear it on Samhain itself in order to become aware and help remember the people who have passed from here on out.

Eucalyptus

This is a healing oil, which is wonderful or those who are healing after an illness. It also can cure throat issues and colds when applied to the threat, wrists, and forehead, or used in healing baths. It also can be used for purification rituals with wonderful results.

Lotus

Lotus is a sacred oil that ancient Egyptians used, and it's got a very high level of spiritual vibration, and it's great for anointing, blessing, meditating on, and also as a dedicatory oil to the gods themselves. Many Wiccans will also use this in healing rituals. The idea of lotus is that if you wear this, you'll have good fortune, along with happiness too, hence why many Wiccans add it to their lucky and prosperity rituals.

Myrrh

Myrrh is a very old oil, used during ancient times, but it is incredibly powerful. Myrrh is used to protect, and purify the user, and it also is protection from hex breaking as well. It's got a very high level of vibrancy in it, which makes it excellent for most magic rituals itself. The house should be anointed every morning and evening with this in order to create a space that's protected in every shape and form.

However, it also will help with the awareness of the spiritual reality in our existence every day. It will calm the fears and stop the questions that are there in relation to the future. It also is used in meditation, and healing of the body itself in order to improve the connection that's there.

Orange blossom

Orange blossom, or orange sweet is used for people who want to get married. Many women who use it in baths do use it to help with their attractiveness. It's a good way to boost your own personal, and sexual prowess as well.

It also can purify the self as well, and if you feel sad, it will transform that depression into joy. I also increase the bioelectrical energy in most magical activities and is pretty strong in terms of an essential oil.

Patchouli

Patchouli is great for those who want to boost sexual desire and prowess, and also to help with improving the physical energy of a person's interest. Patchouli is also used as a way to manifest the money that you desire, so if you want money, or using a money spell, patchouli will be your best friend.

It is a very powerful occult oil too, and it's called a magnetic oil, which means it attracts the opposite. Oftentimes, men wear it to attract women. It also will ward off evil and negativity, giving peace and mind to the one who is wearing it, making is possible for the person to have a happier state. The oil is also very sensual in nature, heightening the senses as well.

Rosemary

Finally, we have rosemary, which is incredibly vitalizing in oil form. It's used in almost all healing rituals in order to make sure that prudence is followed, along with common sense, and general assurance as well. It aids the power of the mental plane when it's rubbed into the temples. It's used with rose in many cases, such as in terms of blessing homes and apartments, protecting the space, and warding off negative energy. It can also be used to help infuse peace and tranquility in the home as well, and when burned once a week along with rose oil, this will help with the domestic tranquility sense.

Essential oils are so good for wiccans to use, and many of them love to use all of these different ones to great results. Check them out and find the oils that work best for you.

Chapter 9: How to Use Modern-Day Witchcraft

Most people reading this wonder how they can use this. After all, maybe you're not ready nor do you want to use complex rituals or celebrate wiccan holidays. But wiccan spells and activities are incredibly popular in the modern world, and there are a lot of ways you can utilize wicca in modern society. It's a little different from what you think, and just like with Wicca principles, you don't need to use dark arts or anything in order to achieve the results that you want.

How to Use Wiccan Spells in Modern-Day World

Now most of us may be ready to take the plunge and start using Wicca, but some of us may not be ready to invest what you need to invest into Wicca. That's totally fine, because many people don't want to spend that money.

However, in the modern-day world, there are basic spells you can use.

Spells for money, for love, and for happiness are what many modern-day witches strive to use. These spells usually involve a few herbs, maybe a crystal or two, and a few incantations. You just have to work with what you've got, and from there, try out some spells.

We'll go over a few key Wiccan spells for beginners to use, but the best way to go about getting results with Wiccans in the modern-day world may be through just learning on your own.

Oftentimes, these beginner practices will help as a supplemental reason for you to get into wicca. There are many spells out there, and a lot that date back to ancient times, and you just have to, with this as well, create the best and most worthwhile experience that you can with what you have, and try it from there.

Ways to Learn About Wicca

How can you learn more about Wicca though, especially in modern society? While you may not be ready to join a coven yet, you can learn a lot about Wicca through different media, and through different activities.

Listen, watch, and read different pagan and Wiccan publications. There are tons of websites, videos, and podcasts, even social media pages that will help you figure out how you want to practice Wicca. For many Wiccans who are first starting out, it can be hard to figure out what your focus may be, and if you're ready to move to the next step. But learning is powerful, and Wiccan and pagan books will help you understand Wicca a little better, and help you get a feel for how you want to practice it. You can choose to be a more devout practitioner, or someone who is a little more casual with this. At the end of the day, it's your choice.

There are also Wiccan and pagan festivals you can check out. Festivals and Wiccan holidays might be a wonderful way for you to get to know those who are also interested in the practice and who may want you to join their coven. You also can find out about the traditions of pagans as well as Wiccans at these festivals.

There is usually holidays during summer and winter solstice that you can learn about, and these usually are found through websites, or even on social media. Social media is one of the best ways to connect with fellow Wiccans too.

Speaking of social media, this is how you contact other Wiccans in life. You can find people through both social media and email, and when you feel it's right, you can meet each other directly. You should definitely do this only when you're an adult, but if you are a child interested in Wicca, you should have a guardian that's with you if you do meet people. Most of the time, the groups, festivals, and teachers aren't even open to those under 18 unless they get parental permission, but for the most part adults are who are interested in Wicca, so it makes sense that the festivals are more geared towards adults.

There are Wiccan and pagan centers and sacred sites. You can visit these during their sabbat festivals, the classes, full moons, or other visiting days. You might have to put a little effort into finding these, but once you do, you'll have a lot of good opportunities to meet other Wiccans, and if there are places where this is being practiced, then you're in luck as this can help.

There are seminars, classes, and retreats that offer valuable learning experiences. You should consider potentially looking into these. Circle Sanctuary is one of the best resources, and they offer a wide variety of different classes, and you can work on trying to get with other Wiccans within this.

Sometimes, it takes a bit of time to find those who are interested in working with you, but it's possible to find fellow Wiccans ready to work together, and this is something that lots of Wiccans can benefit from.

How to Practice Your Connection with Nature in the Current World

In our current world, tis hard to connect with nature. With all the tumult that's happening with a lot of the issues in our world, it can be hard for a wiccan to toss that to the side for a second, and spend time connecting with nature. But Wiccans have a deep connection with nature, and you should as well.

It is hard to just do away with all modern conveniences especially since we often rely on those. But it does involve taking care of the planet, even just a little bit, and many Wiccans will practice this connection to help better their experience in the common world, and here, we'll talk a little bit about building that connection in modern times.

The Power of Nature Rituals

Nature rituals are one of the best ways to connect with nature, especially in our modern world. Oftentimes, you don't spend enough time in nature, and we are typically stuck in the rut of our spaces and rooms, instead of just getting out and exploring.

But journeying into nature, and divine interconnectedness will help you.

The way to do this is simple. You should find a place within nature that's special in your eyes, such as the woods, a meadow, a lakeshore, or even a small brook, or the ocean, a mountain, or even just a pile of rocks or a small hill. You should find a space where you can be connected with animals, plants, and elements, but also away from other humans and ideally away from modern conveniences.

As you journey there, you should commune with nature of course, but you should shift your focus from a human-centric mindset to a nature-aware mindset. The journey there should remind you that you're a part of nature, that you as a human are a part of this.

This journey will help nurture the spirits that you have, and also strengthen the relationships that you have with lifeforms that aren't humans, a part of the biosphere.

You should, once you get to the chosen place, sit down. You should be seated and relax. Take deep and slow breaths that will help you relax. You should become aware of yourself resting at where you are. You should experience the planet as mother earth is holding you to her. You should feel the sky lightly caressing you, along with the Earth and the sky energizing one another.

You should express appreciation at the core for the planet, along with the cosmos for nurturing you, and the other lifeforms. You should drink the life energy that nature has, and is surrounding you, and from there, become aware of the energy as you feel it hits you. This nature connection is oftentimes known as the divine communion.

From here, you should become aware of the plants that are here, and their own aliveness, such as a tree or something that's near you. But, don't just look over it in a glossed over manner, but instead, merge and become one with it. Imagine you're literally that plant, experiencing the world at the level these plants do. You should then focus on yourself as a human once again, and mentally thank the plant that you have as a friend, relative, and teacher, and from there sit and reflect on the experience.

From here, shift to another plant and do the same thing, and you can continue to do this until you start to feel one with nature and the plants themselves.

From here, you want to pay attention to the sounds, the birds, the wind, and the other nature sounds. You should also pay attention to your sights, and from here, you can see the nature and beauty in different shapes, patterns, and colors that are around you.

From here, focus on the rhythms of nature, such as touch, taste, and smell of nature, and as you expand the awareness of the sense on a physical level, you should allow yourself to experience the place with your sixth sense, intuition, and where there is neither space nor time, only the sense of being.

You can from there open up your mouth and let the sacred vibrations of sounds flow within you. Let the sound be pushed from deep within your being, but also from your diaphragm, heart, and your entire body. You should fill this with sound, creating a oneness with it. From there, you can rise and celebrate by dancing and celebrating nature, living, and celebrating the spiraling circle of change and rebirth.

From here, be quiet once again. Take the time that's necessary to reflect on this, and then give thanks with the divine and all of nature once you're done. You can connect with wisdom through this, which is around you, and is a part of nature, and you essentially connect with the spirit that possesses a deeper part of meaning.

As you go back, reflect on what you've done, and from there, you can picture the level of thanks and happiness that thinking about and connecting with nature has bestowed to you.

MEDITATION

Meditating within nature is the next thing you can do. Lots of us don't have that good of a connection with nature. You can do this in a similar way to the nature journey, but you can do this with walking. As you walk, notice the sounds, the sights, and the feeling of nature. Become aware and mindful of it. From here, reflect upon yourself: how could you do that better? You can figure out how you can have a better oneness with nature as well. There are a lot of different ways, but as you meditate on this, you'll be very happy with the results of this, and in turn, create a better, more worthwhile experience for yourself.

As you meditate, if you notice intrusive thoughts start to come in, you can always banish them as you continue. These intrusive thoughts will happen regardless, so you should definitely make sure not to dwell on them.

If you feel like there is nothing you can do to help nature, then as you meditate on this, meditate on what you can do in order to help you with this. For many people, meditating and being one with nature is hard, but it's completely possible, and worthwhile.

At the end of it, thank nature, and point out three things about nature you're thankful for. Send out your vibes, and let nature know how important it is to you, and how much it matters.

Understanding the importance of nature, and what you can do with it is important, and you'll be able to understand what you're doing with this too.

Give Back to the Community

In many instances, being in contact with nature is good, but if you feel like you can't do anything about the way life is going, modern Wiccans try to give back to nature.

Some of the different ways they do it is ultimately dependent on what they're working with.

For example, many Wiccans actually love working in gardens, tending their own garden, but they might get that urge to work with a community garden to help others.

Many Wiccans will volunteer at forest preserves and at different animal shelters, or work to help bring nature to others, along with the benefits of it. Many Wiccans do love volunteering in nature, such as by helping to plant a tree and the like. They want to give back to nature, since nature is so important to them.

Lots of Wiccans try to reduce their own personal carbon footprint and energy output. Many of them will try to recycle or save energy as much as they can. They're conscious of it, and while you might not think that what you're doing is much, remember a little bit goes a long way. Caring about the planet is important too, since we are on the precipice where we need to start being mindful. Some Wiccans may choose to eat less meat, but of course, this is ultimately up to them.

With that in mind, Wiccans may consider practicing more within nature than in their home. The connection with nature will help them improve their own understanding of this, and it's quite helpful especially if they want to build the connection with nature and want to know more about it. Wiccans oftentimes will struggle with that connection, but going out in nature and casting spells in regard to nature is a good way to do it.

Even just being mindful of Wiccan traditions and beliefs is a good way to practice modern Wicca. Many Wiccans do become more mindful of this as time does go on, and it's important that you understand the importance of Wicca, and its own characteristics. Wicca is possible to practice in modern times, just consider these different nuances of practice before you begin.

Chapter 10:
Basic Wiccan Spells to Try

For those who are beginning on their Wicca journey, they may wonder what the best spells to try are. There are a few that are wonderful for beginner witches, and here, we'll give you a few to choose from, and those that let you ask the deities for extra help. These spells are basic, but they are wonderful, and should be used.

PETITION MAGIC

This type of spellcasting is used when you need something, and you want to ask the gods for help. In our world, we have most of the resources, and they should be used both responsibly and ethically, but they are meant to be used. You don't have to as the gods for things all the time, but if you do have something that you can't get yourself, it is a good action to take. If you're asking for stuff that's feasible from the gods, then future spellcasting might be affected by this. Petition magic is basically used whenever you have a warranted excuse, and it's essentially a magical prayer.

Now of course, you must remember that not all prayers may be what you want. Sometimes, you might not get what you want when you ask, and that's okay.

To do this, you first and foremost need to write the petition. You also can choose a candle for this so that you're able to get extra help from the gods as well. You should make sure that you do this in a way that will be meaningful, and if you need something else, add it to this. For example, a bag of sugar to "sweeten" the situation is a wonderful addition. If you want guidance on what job to take, you might print out the housing listings. You can also use this with various photographs as well. Basically, the goal is to be very heartfelt and meaningful, no matter how you do it.

From this point, once the petition is written, you can cast your magic. First, you need all the supplies, and go to a well-ventilated room. From here, you can do your spell as a full circle ritual and start with that by creating the casting circle. Ground and prepare for this, and make sure if you need to dress the candle, you do that, but also do it with the goal as the focus.

From here, light the candle, and from there invoke the deity that's there.

You then meditate on the goal, actually focusing on this. Take the writing implement and the paper, and from there write or draw out the petition that you have, with all the focus being on what you want from this. You might need to add things to the paper as well, and fold it in. You can actually use herbs, nail clippings, hair, or even blood if you want to do blood magic, and from there, make the statement and tell the deities that you want something, and from there, you light the paper towards the candle. Hold it without getting burned, and when finished, put it in a pot that holds heat well.

Finally, thank the deity for their cooperation with this, and once that's done, you can from here finish the ritual. You can at this point finish up, ground yourself once again, and finish all the ritual activities.

This type of magic should be used only if you really want something, and if you feel like you're unable to get it otherwise.

FREEZER SPELL

Chill out! Well, maybe you want someone to keep their mouth shut, or you want people to stop being gossipmongers. If that's the case, then you should definitely learn this one. Ice, freezers and the like are oftentimes used in various Wiccan spells, since they are effective for freezing or keeping one quiet.

Freezer, or icebox spells are great for beginners, and this is good to help cast spells that stop you from getting harassed. To use this, you'll need to get a freezer bag with a seal that zippers it, or some container that you can fill up with water, and from there seal. If you do have a glass jar for casting, make sure you can keep it in the freezer.

You'll need a piece of paper as well with the person's name on it, and from there, you should also get some water that is consecrated, or even vinegar and urine. From here, you write the name of the person on the zippered bag, from there fill it up with some consecrated water, or whatever liquid you'd like to use, and from there, you put the bag directly into the freezer. As the person's name freezes up within the ice, they should "chill out" from this point forward.

Some Wiccans have used this with beef or even animal tongue on a lemon, which represents sour words being said, the paper is then put into the slit of the tongue, and then the whole thing is wound up with some twine, and from there it's placed in the freezer to freeze up. You can also use this to keep someone in check, especially someone who is having sexual exploits that are harming others. A veggie that looks like genitalia can be used, such as a peach, or even a zucchini can be used with this type of spell.

This spell is oftentimes done with the intent of your own benefit in place. This means that you're not cursing or hurting another person, but instead, you're actually using this to stop those harmful words from hitting you, which is a good thing for most people to utilize.

Protection Magic

Another common type of magic hat wiccan will use is of course, protection magic. Protection magic I wonderful, since it helps keep you safe during those trying times. If you're worried about whether or not you'll have someone intruding in your space a lot or if you are someone that is going through a situation that's rough, then you should consider some kind of protection magic.

Protection magic comes in a number of different forms. It is actually the oldest spell work documented, all the way back from ancient Egyptian times, where they had simple protection spells that were used both in the home, but also with the dead to protect them and provide for a journey.

One of the simplest spells comes in the form of making an onion braid to protect your home. You essentially braid an onion, and you can do this as well when preparing them for winter storage. You need lots of onions with the top of the greens attached, and a few feet of heavy rope or twine.

Fold the twine in a halved manner, and from there, tie a knot at the end, making a loop, and from there you put the twine onto a surface, and put the onion in an upside down fashion so the greens create a third string, along with the two extra ends of twine. You then braid this until it's all in place, and do it with all of the onions, braiding them and also doing it between the stems too.

When you braid these, have an intent in place, and continue to focus on making sure that you're protecting something. You can put together a magical incantation and link them to the protection that you need.

You can ask for protection of your home, or even just protecting yourself, asking for you to keep the negative energies away from you.

Another thing you can use during ceremonies is protection oil. Protection oil is something you can use to protect yourself from magical, along with psychic attacks. You can also use this within your home, car, or even anoint people during rituals to help keep them protected. You need about an eight of a cup of the base oil you want to use, and then 3 drops lavender, 4 drops patchouli, a drop of hyssop, and a drop of mugwart.

Combine and blend the oils that are here, and from there, you want to visualize the intent, and from there, smell the aroma that's there. You should know the oil itself is sacred, and magical too. You can then keep this labelled and dated, and then stored whenever you need it. You should use this for protection of yourself, and the protection of others too.

Finally, you have the wolf protection spell, which summons the spirit of a wolf that's ferocious, and it's used to protect against people and evil forces that you feel you need. To make this, you need a picture of a wolf, specifically one that's an artists' rendition, two candles that are green, a white candle, holy water, and the protection oil from before. As well for offerings, you need a drink that's lunar focused, such as wine or even ale, and it doesn't have to be alcohol either. You should also have some sort of small cake.

Put these on your ritual space in the way you want to and do this during the full moon and from there chant the incantation of, "Three candles, both green and white, give me protection tonight. The sky is cleared, the moon full, and make the evil around me disappear. The wolf that runs over and gives me protection from harm come hither, please come hither!"

From there, you continue chanting that as the candles go out, and from there, lightly put the oil on your hands, and rub it in. Offer to the deities the food that you brought, and end the ritual with food and drink.

Wiccan protection spells will keep you safe, and you'll be much happier with the result if you have this in place as well.

TEA SPELL FOR ANXIETY

For some who practice Wicca, they may use it to help them get through a hard time, and to help quell the anxiety in their body. This spell can relieve it, and you just need tea that's been brewed, a little place for sitting, and a few minutes. You probably will notice it's a pretty similar spell to what you've read before, but what you can do with this spell, is to write one up that's meaningful for you. Do that in a way that lets you put together a wonderful spell that will help you get through the issues in life.

The first thing that you do, is you make the tea. A nice, lavender blend will do just fine with this. From here, you then sit down, and you think of the incantation and chant, and then you sip the tea. You also can say it while you mix the tea. It definitely is a good one to try if you have recent issues. It can be used to help calm you down after a rough day.

You shouldn't, when you're canting, say anything about others or wish ill upon them. Make sure that you don't say anything about the person within the spell and keep the intentions mostly private when you're using this. Don't do this in a public setting either, especially one that would frown upon Wiccan spells.

Tea magic is mostly enchantment, and you can actually do this beforehand as well if you know your week is really going to be rough. The magic happens when you take honey, or something else that's sweet, and from there, stir the tea in order to activate its powers.

When you do this, first simmer and steep the tea in a container for about 20 minutes, and from there, you can strain and put it into a teacup. You can then add honey and stir it in a way that's clockwise, and this will make the intent sweeter, helping you have a sweeter situation. From here, say the spell, encouraging that no harm is happening to either you or the other person. When everything is complete, you finally drink the tea, savoring the taste of it.

This is a wonderful way for you to get the most that you can out of your work, and you'll be able to, with this as well, create a better, easier week for yourself.

Full moon Compassion and Self-Love Spell

Do you feel like you're too hard on yourself, and you like to second guess yourself all the time? Well, if you notice you don't take your own advice enough, then perhaps a spell is in order. Oftentimes, if you're the type who struggles with mistakes, beating yourself up over the simplest things, and generally feeling terrible, then you need to start working on yourself, and here, we'll tell you how.

The full moon is a wonderful time to do spells, for the sole reason of you'll be able to cultivate compassion and have better compassion for yourself. First, you must release what's blocking your self-compassion, and from there inviting that which is needed for this to grow. You can from there do this on the full moon, but it also may be done at any point in time that you need to use it. It also includes meditation, and various items around the house that you can use.

To do this, you need to do this on either full moon days, or on Mondays when the moon is waxing. It will take about thirty minutes to do. You'll need a pink candle, a cauldron or a container that's fireproof, two bay leaves for each person that's doing this, a book or Book of Shadows you can use for recording, a writing utensil, crystals and incense that helps with self-love, anything with pink, green, or blue, rose quartz or selenite for the healing stones, and lavender or sandalwood or anything that relaxes you.

To begin, you want to create a sacred space, and you can cleanse it by casting the circle or using a sacred space ritual. From there, sit yourself down in the working space or altar. Take some breaths, and from there, bring the body and mind to the moment, reminding yourself of the intention needed.

From here, create the intention by lighting the candle, looking at the flame. You should remind yourself of the intention of this.

At this point, close your eyes and start to visualize yourself within a room, whether the one you're in now or another. From here notice that there's a mirror here, either full-length or a mounted or small one. From here, visualize yourself going to the mirror, picking this up, and then holding it in your hands, and then gaze at it to see your face. You can from here face your own reflection, understanding the person looking back at you currently. Start to visualize this reflection smiling and looking at you, feeling the love from all of this.

From here, receive any messages, such as those that you need for self-love, and what you need to take in your self-compassion and growth, and from here, stay like this for some time. After you feel this, you then can start to ground yourself, writing the experience down within your journal. You should note what you need to release, and what needs to be taken in to cultivate your self-compassion.

You can then consecrate the bay leaves by taking one of these, using them to represent what you must release. Hold this into the palm of your hand, and send the intent to the leaf, imagining that it will embody what you need in order to let go, and bring more self-compassion.

Finally, you should then say out loud "I release ____ to allow for more self-compassion within me." From here, light the bay leaf on fire, putting it into the cauldron or fireproof receptacle. And that is your intention that you're releasing into the world.

From here, grab the second half of the bay leaves, which represent that which you're going to need to take in so that you can grow your self-compassion within your life. You can from there have it take that in by saying so, and then light that same bay leaf on fire, doing the same thing as before, and then dropping it into the cauldron.

At this point, you close the circle by taking in what's been done, and when you are finished, put out the candle, closing the space as well. Bury the leaves that are there into the earth, since you want the connection of nature and the Goddess, and from there, you can let it break down the intention as you go along.

So, if you want to reinforce this, you do this by reinforcing the spell every single waning moon, and you should light your candles each time you use this, since it will help with growth and building the compassion and self-care that's necessary.

These spells can all be used in a ritualistic sense, but also used for many who want to utilize this type of magic for themselves to benefit them. If you're curious about it, try one of these, and work on trying this each time, so you can build the best and most rewarding experience possible.

Chapter 11:
You Wiccan relationships with the World and Others

For you as a Wiccan, you may wonder what your relationships with the world currently are. You may wonder how you fit into the grand scheme of things, and how to really go about bringing your own personal spiritual growth and wellness into this.

When you start on your journey into Wicca, one of the best things to do to better understand your relationship with the world, is to read. Before you even think about finalizing decisions, you should study this. Some will say that studying this can be hard, but the thing is, wicca doesn't have a dogma to it, so unlike religions such as Christianity or others, there isn't one set of steps for you to take. So, it's important for you to understand that, when learning about Wicca and practicing it, it isn't just one set of beliefs, but instead, it's what you feel is right.

Also, one book shouldn't be where you start. You should consider multiple books and study, and study it for a bit before you make the decisions necessary to be a Wiccan.

A THINKING PRACTICE

With Wicca, it isn't just you following one doctrine. When you talk with other Wiccans, chances are you're going to notice that you might have different beliefs from others, whether it be in the realm of love, of the deities, or even rituals. It is not a dogmatic type of religion, unlike others, so anyone who comes into this looking for one set of directions will start to realize it's a little different.

The goal here, when you study Wicca, is to figure out how your personal beliefs fit into wicca. Is there a certain deity that you feel is a part of your life? Do you feel a connection to the moon? Do you want a religion that's focused more on a spiritual pathway, or one that's focused on one delineated book? Wicca is a religion that has many different parts, and there are some parts that don't even fit underneath the definition.

If you don't believe in gods, and you just want to practice magic, then Wiccan rituals may not be for you, since those rituals are centered around gods and goddesses. Witchcraft is something you can practice without being a wiccan. If you are someone who believes in Jesus, chances are Wicca may not be ideal for you, since there are two deities, both of which fit on the same plane.

If you wat to practice Wicca, the beauty of it is there's no certain practice that you have to follow no matter what, but you also need to accept responsibility for reasoning and logic, which are really two of the core beliefs of Wicca. This may be one of the few things that may attract you to Wicca, but if you don't think you can at least practice the rituals, you may just want to consider the spellcasting elements.

If you have a connection with nature, then Wicca is perfect for you, since it does involve a deeper, more pronounced understanding of this, and if you feel you can appreciate nature more and more, then you're in the right business.

Conversing with Other Wiccans

When you do converse with other Wiccans, the first thing you might notice is that your beliefs are a little different. Remember that that's fine, everyone has their own set of beliefs, and their own ideas of how they want to practice.

You should be respectful, and if one Wiccan likes a certain aspect of their religion that you're not interested in, respect it.

You should always talk to others as if they have their own beliefs.

You can partake in rituals together, or even pray and meditate together, but you don't have to. Some Wiccans like the conveyance that happens within covens, and if you feel strength in numbers and actions, this is the way to do it. But, if you feel like it's not your thing, and you're not sure whether you should do that or not, then you may want to consider your own personal spiritual growth and wellness first.

The idea of being a Wiccan isn't that you have to practice it one way or another, but instead, you do what works for you, what's best for you, and you respect the beliefs and religious ideas of others.

Praying as a Communication

One aspect of being a Wiccan which might be a bit odd for some, is of course praying. If you know that you want to worship as a Wiccan, you should start praying, whether it be to the gods, or whatever. You should introduce yourself and tell them who you are. You can ask for understanding, clarification, or even guidance. Rituals accomplish this too, but it's a little different, since it involves actual steps that you may not be used to.

However, praying is very similar to meditation. If you're someone who believes Wicca might be the answer you're looking for, but you're not sure about the prayer parts, then consider meditation. Meditation is where you sit quietly, and you begin to close your eyes and focus on one thing for a period of time. Remember that meditation is wonderful both physically and mentally, and it works for both spiritual development, and your personal health as well.

Praying is something that anyone can do, and you can actually do it on your own. Some people like to spend lots of time praying, others may just do it every so often, checking in and saying what's happening. It doesn't have to be something you should force yourself to do, but instead be realistic in the way you handle your own personal needs and actions.

WICCANS AND OTHER RELIGIONS

One of the common misconceptions is that Wiccans are so different from other religions, such as Christianity and otherwise. Many times, lots of Wiccans feel like they are ostracized or different from the Christians that are out there.

But it doesn't have to be this way. The truth of it is, you're more similar than you'd think. While Christianity does believe in one singular god, and Wiccans the two deity beliefs, oftentimes when you come together, you'll realize you're not as different as you'd think. Some Christians may believe that Wiccans worship various strange creatures, such as unicorns or the like. The biggest thing to learn, is that Wicca doesn't do that, and instead, understand that as a Wiccan, you harness divine magic, and you work through that with others.

You may run into those who don't understand. This is common, and lots of times, those who are meeting you with hostility only do so because they don't get it. But as a Wiccan, you don't have to have that mindset. Instead, you should learn to help branch the gaps, and learn to understand.

Some of the ways you can help branch into the conversations with others about Wicca include the following:

- Tell them about it
- Show them that it's not just witchcraft
- Talk to others about their beliefs, and work together in order to come to an understanding
- From here, both of you can work on the similarities, rather than the differences, between each of these.

Lots of times, some people will meet those in Wicca with that hostility because they believe that all they do is cast harmful spells that hurt others. Which isn't even the case. Some people don't realize that there is a big difference between witchcraft and Wicca. Oftentimes, people don't realize that Wicca can be a conglomeration of many different things.

WICCA BRANCHES

Of course, if you want to learn a bit more about Wicca, there are different branches. Oftentimes, people just think Wicca is rituals, but in reality, it's actually a bit more than that. Wicca has secular practices as well that you can utilize different types of branches of Wicca in order to improve your own wellness.

If the religious and worshipping aspect isn't for you, there are other ways to practice different Wiccan concepts, and they include the following:

- Faith healing
- Tarot reading
- Spell casting
- Connection with nature

All of these are different parts of it. It does have a small bit of doctrine of course, but it isn't just that. It involves many different other aspects of it too.

Practicing on your own is usually the way most people begin, since it's how you push forward, and how you can better yourself. If you find likeminded people who want to practice with you, then great. Otherwise, if you're fine with a singular type of practice, then so be it.

Some people like to practice it all the time, some during rituals. It's your practice, your own personal connection with the world. Do as you must to benefit from this.

Contributing to the Better of the World as a Wiccan

So how can you better yourself in this world as a Wiccan? You may wonder how this is possible, but the connection with nature is the one that you should focus on. Building a connection with nature that helps benefit you is one of the best things that you can do as a wiccan.

Some ways you can build your spiritual connection as a Wiccan include these:

- Going outside and appreciating nature
- Taking a meditative walk
- Cleaning up the planet
- Not littering
- Focus on recycling
- Start a compost pole

All of these things are a good way to begin with this. For many people, this can be a bit of a struggle though, since oftentimes their connection with nature is one that's deep, and one that is important.

With Wicca, you can practice this as you go along. Lots jump into it thinking they need all of the ritual objects, when in reality, all you need is a few small tools and the like, and then you're fine. Lots of Wiccans overprepare, but you can always invest in more as you go along to help with this. You just need to do a few things here and there, and you'll be well on your way to being the best Wiccan you can be.

You have to remember that as a Wiccan, you'll probably meet those who don't understand, and those who won't get it. But, with the right mindset, you'll be much happier, and by better understanding what being a Wiccan is, you'll be able to create a better, safer experience for yourself as well.

Conclusion

This beginners' guide taught you a little bit about Wiccan spells, concepts, and the like, so you'll be able to, quite easily really, take care of yourself. With the right mindset, and the right ideas, you'll be much happier with your life, and you'll be able to create a much more immersive experience for yourself too.

For many Wiccans, these different spells, incantations, and rituals may take a bit of time to master, but they are very important for those who are interested in learning about the concept of Wicca. Wicca has a lot of freedom to it, especially compared to other religions, so how you practice it is ultimately based on what you want to do.

So, the key takeaway here is, that you can practice Wicca as you see fit, in the way you feel is right. Lots of people like that about the religion and learning the different practices will prove to you that Wicca is a wonderful religion, and one that you can use to better your life.

Plus, the spellcasting, which is a big part of it, are quite wonderful to try. The reason why so many people like Wiccan spellcasting, is it's done in a positive manner, which means that you'll be able to, with the right concepts and ideas at hand, create a better life for yourself. You can use this for anything from creating spells to help improve your luck and health, to even spells to help eliminate the negative energy that you might have. Lots of Wiccans are definitely happy with this, and the freedom to do the type of spellcasting that you desire is a big part of it.

So yes, your next step is to figure out the way to use Wicca, and how to master it so that you can improve your life. This beginner book will help you get a better understanding of how to be a Wiccan, and it will start you on your spiritual journey.

As a Wiccan myself, I know it's a bit complex at first, and oftentimes, people don't realize the problems that come about when you start with this religion. You probably are going to be hit with so many apothecary ideas, and different mindsets as well. But, Wicca is easy to grasp at the end of the day, and it's quite wonderful to use. You'll be able to with the Wiccan practices in here, use it to improve your life on every level.

If you enjoyed this book, let me know what you think and leave me a quick review on Amazon, I'd be really happy, thanks!

Wicca Herbal Spells

A Practical Guide About the Healing Power of Plants in Harmony with Wicca. Improve your Everyday Life by Connecting with Nature Thanks to Herbal Spells and Modern Witchcraft

Justine J. Scott

Introduction

Herbal magick has been used for as long as Wicca has been around, as you are going to learn about within this very book. This particular type of magick is one of the most ancient traditional forms of Wicca magick practices. To begin embarking on your own Wicca journey, knowing how to use herbs in spellcasting is going to allow you to begin engaging with Wicca in an even deeper manner. Regardless of what type of witch you are, from a hedge witch to a white witch or anything in between, you are going to benefit from understanding herbal magick. Herbal magick has roots in virtually every type of Wicca, and it can be incorporated into every spellcasting ritual.

When it comes to working with herbs, it is natural to realize that certain herbs are made more easily available at certain times of the year, depending on when they are naturally available to harvest.

This is one big reason why magick follows the wheel of the year: typically, the herbs that are best used for certain rituals are harvestable at the same time that the energy for those particular rituals to be done is at its highest.

It is important for you as a practicing witch to understand the sheer value herbs have in rituals, spells, and the Wiccan faith in general. Through increasing your knowledge in this, it will be easier for you to see just how many ancients and energies you are invoking with each herb, as you tap into the energy and intention of something that has been used in magick for hundreds and thousands of generations before you.

Herbs are something that will always be available so long as the Earth is in existence because they are a natural part of the environment here and virtually nothing we can do can completely halt their growth, short of us throwing down cement on every inch of the planet and self-destructing. This makes them a powerful tool of longevity and magick that can be used in many different ways.

When you use an herb in a spell, you are not only tapping into the elemental magick of that plant, you are also tapping into hundreds of thousands of witches before you who have performed magick with that same plant. The energy associated with each plant is massive, making them not only the oldest tools to work with, but also the most powerful tools to work with, too.

When it comes to magical symbolism, plants interact with all four of the classical Wiccan elements so that they can sustain life. They grow in the dirt to interact with the element of earth, they require water to grow, they absorb sunlight or fire energy to produce photosynthesis, and they cleanse the air. They are connected in every way imaginable, so even though they typically represent the earth element, they are actually powerful representations of all four elements.

If you are looking to do elemental magick, working with herbs, even if they have been dried to be used in spellcasting, is a great way to invoke all of the elements through one simple medium. Although many people will go on to find more elements to incorporate, it is not necessary so long as you are working with any form of herb in your magical rituals. This means this particular type of magick is amongst one of the most versatile and easily accessible forms of magick available to mankind.

If new to the journey of Wicca, this path is a great one to start with. This herbal magick helps you to do almost all things you want in the journey of spellcasting from getting more money, love and beauty to you setting your intentions with the full and new moon.

You can also call in any number of different opportunities or experiences, as well as virtually anything else that you desire.

But first, I want to thank you for choosing this book and I'd really happy if you left me a quick review on Amazon. Enjoy reading!

Chapter 1: What is Wicca

Wicca is a way of life, often called a religion. It lays the groundwork for people to live and work harmoniously with the world around them. When you live life the Wiccan way, you are living in a way that encourages togetherness with the godly and with everything that has been brought into existence from the Divine.

When you choose to live life the Wiccan way, you agree to live in profound awe and appreciation of the world around you. You are expressing gratitude for the world that you experience from the sunrise and sunset to the growing and harvesting of plants and the natural lifecycles of the animals around you. Everything that is a part of your natural world becomes sacred to you as you see it as being a sacred gift afforded to you by the world surrounding you.

This particular belief system predates Christianity, and it originates in Ireland, Scotland and Wales. There, the ancient ancestors learned how to live together in unity with the world around them, honoring the Divine in everything and cherishing all that was. Much of the information that is used in modern Wicca stems from these ancient traditions, although there is plenty of modern information and twists that have been incorporated into the tradition since.

It is important to understand that Wicca has multiple "types" of belief systems to it. Plenty of off-shoots of the original traditions have developed, allowing for many different types of belief systems to be incorporated into their lifestyle. This way, regardless of what your beliefs are, you will likely find someone in the Wiccan faith who believes similarly to you, allowing you to connect with others who can help you advance your own practices and learn more about yourself and this intricate belief system.

We are but a part of the Earth, no greater and no less than any other creature that crawls, flies, or swims. Thus, it is our duty to care for, heal, and protect every being that exists. To be Wiccan is to give selflessly, to take on the role of a teacher, and to go on a continuous quest for improvement.

To be Wiccan is to recognize power in everything and every creature that you behold. As Wiccan, it is for you to see the divine power in whatever face it chooses to manifest itself. That face can be in the form of the naked tree branches shivering in the autumn wind or in the promise held by each petal of a budding flower in spring.

The medieval church made great efforts to demonize the image of the Wiccan faith. But if anything else, to be Wiccan means to become a promoter of peace and to lead by example by living a violence-free lifestyle. Our goal is to co-exist in harmony with all creatures in this Earth and with the divine powers that surround us.

As Wiccan, it is important for you to understand that we do not acknowledge the idea of an absolute evil such as Satan. Unlike believers of other religions, Wiccans are not driven by fear of "punishment in the afterlife" or "eternal damnation." Instead, Wiccans are encouraged to be kind to others and to "behave" in this life simply because it is the right thing to do.

Another misconception that is as old as time is the idea of Wicca as a cult. Increasing our numbers and manipulating people's heads to gain power has never been the Wiccan way. On the contrary, to be Wiccan is all about embracing diversity. As Wiccans, we always respect and uphold the individual's right to choose the way he wants to live his life.

Does this mean that there are no rules that govern the Wiccan faith?

As a religion, Wicca functions with a basic set of rules. The first among these set of principles is the Wiccan Rede which states that as long as you harm none, you are free to do as you choose.

It is because of this rule that Wiccans are discouraged to use magick to intentionally harm another living being.

To be Wiccan means to be in sync with the universe. Thus, you will be able to tap into the infinite pool of universal wisdom and gain access to the knowledge of magick. That privilege is accompanied by a great responsibility. As Wiccan, you are encouraged to use magick exclusively for doing good.

According to the Law of Threefold Return, whatever energy you send out into the world, whether it's negative or positive, will return to you and when it does, it shall be three times stronger. It is important to note that this rule is by no means a way to reassure obedience by striking fear. The universe does not seek to punish anyone. This is simply a natural reaction. Think of the universe as a vast ocean of energy which connects and encompasses the individual energies of all living beings, including you.

When you send out ripples of energy, be it in the form of an action or an intention, it will be released into that vast ocean and will touch everything and everyone. But just like ocean waves, that energy will eventually return to touch you as well.

In the '70's, there was a rise in horrible criminal activities done by members of Satanic cults. Sadly, the media wrongly associated these activities with Wiccans and these misconceptions were spread among the public. Feeling the threat, the Council of Witches formed the 13 Principles of Wiccan Belief to regulate Wiccan practice.

Up until today, a great number of covens use this model when creating mandates. The main idea behind these principles is that we are to care for nature just as we must allow nature to care for us. Within us lies an innate power which we must control and wield so that we are able to live in harmony with nature and with all beings.

Each of us consists of internal and external dimensions, inner and outer realities, and it is our duty to nurture both dimensions. As Wiccan, you must appreciate the universe's creative power which is revealed through the merging of the masculine and the feminine energies. To Wiccans, sex is symbolic of life and a source of energy which can be powerful when used in magick.

Additionally, it is necessary to note that different covens are run by different rules created by their committees. Such rules serve to guide you in the prudent use of magick. Each coven is ruled by the High Priestess or the High Priest. To become a member of a coven is to agree to live according to these rules.

You also have the option to become a solitary practitioner. Whichever path you choose, remember that the goodness in your heart, your conscience, and the purity of your intention is a far greater guide than any rule set in stone.

What is Magick?

Belief in magick is an essential part of the Wiccan religion. In the simplest sense, magick means harnessing the energy of the universe to make something happen. Everything in this universe is made up of energy. You are made up of energy. And all of our energies are interconnected by what is called the Universal Energy that flows freely and endlessly around us. Everyone was born with the ability to tap into and wield these energies to create a certain effect.

As Wiccan, you must believe that it is your birthright to access this illimitable supply of energy so that you may improve your life and those of others. Tapping into this energy and using it is done through magick and spellcasting. Each time you cast a spell; you are borrowing energy from the divine essence of the universe. You can understand now why spellcasting should be a sacred act and is not to be taken lightly. It is not for you to abuse the powers of the universe. Practicing Wiccans utilize magick for meaningful endeavors such as to help a friend recover from an illness or from grief, to attract love for others of for oneself, to heal the Earth, or to invite happiness into one's life.

History

Wicca is not a new thing, but the concept of this practice has only been available with a Western cultural openness since the early to mid-20th century. Believe it or not, Wicca was popularized in the 1950s in Europe by an Englishman named Gerald Gardner. Gardner was an advocate for the natural rituals and paganistic practices of early centuries which were only beginning to renew themselves at this time as a result of the overall popularity of Spiritualism and the Occult.

As early as the mid-1800s, people in America and spreading into Europe, were looking for "new religion" and looked toward the less commonplace and more controversial forms of religious pleasure and doctrines. Contrary to the religions of Christianity, Wicca is celebrated as one of the most original pagan practices that pre-dates a long line of civilizations and cultures. Many people have practiced the fundamental concepts of Paganism and later Wicca for centuries. But as it happens, the practice of such knowledge or craft was banished for its heresy to the church of God, or rather the business of religion as seen by Christian faiths.

To be plain, Wicca has been built from the foundation of Pagan religions and was not really called Wicca until more modern times. It is the practice of worshiping nature. The Gods/Goddesses and the energy of all life on Earth through rituals and casting spells, as well as a great knowledge of the herb and plant life used for healing purposes. Today, people who call themselves Wiccan, or who aspire to practice Wicca, are really practicing the ancient arts of Pagan and pre-pagan spirituality.

Let's take a look back at the origins of Wicca and why it was not popularized until later in the early part of the last century. Witchcraft had its place in all cultures and still does today. Throughout the world, different cultures and people celebrate various types of shamanism, herbal magick, and spirituality.

Many of these cultural ritual practices and beliefs have a common thread throughout all Pagan or Wiccan cultural beliefs, as well as demonstrating a link between all of these shamanistic and natural practices. They often used nature as a guide and benefactor to their practice; they worship a divinity or deity to assert their power and energy, and; they use specific rituals to realize intentions and promote energetic life flow through their spells and incantations.

All over Europe, the Americas, China, Russia, Africa, and beyond, there are cultures who perform magick rituals that bring about an energetic influence into the life of the practitioner and the people around them who they offer these practices to. Plenty of people have been persecuted for their beliefs and practices and the most notorious example of this is the great witch hunts of the 16th and 17th centuries.

Primarily taking place in Europe and North America, the Witch hunt, or trials, were an ongoing attempt made by the Christian faiths and religions to cut out the work of witchcraft, often seen as a worship of the Devil. The basic beliefs of Wicca have nothing to do with Devil worship nor did any of the Pagan rites and rituals performed in those days, which were carried over from a time pre-dating the orthodox churches of the time.

The terror of the Christian church was the practice of anything that worshipped a faith outside of their beliefs and so it was up to these clerics and inquisitors to smudge out the very essence of anything that was not in accordance with the laws and edicts of the God-fearing Christian faiths. Oddly enough, a majority of the Christian religion's celebrations, rituals, and practices are derived from Pagan rituals and practices and still, to this day, bare a resemblance to these ancient ways of connecting with the divine.

The hypocrisy of this era of persecution against Pagans has left a great wound in the reality of human history, and so it wasn't until later, in the early part of the 20th century, that practice of witchcraft was less likely to get you mutilated, tortured, or burned at the stake. With the evolution of faith and religion throughout our history, we have evolved a broader view of all peoples practicing what works for them despite regularly dissuading or discounting more esoteric leanings from the point of view of the church.

At the time of these witch hunts, the reality of witchcraft was much like it has operated today through the practice of Wicca. Those who were practicing witchcraft in those times were mainly just women, and as often men, who were supporting their lives through the daily rituals and practices of worshipping nature and goddess or god figures.

There was a great knowledge of healing and how to provide remedies for sicknesses, even curing the diseased. Women who were involved in covens or group rituals were seen as high Priestesses who were revered for their power and strength.

Worship of the divine feminine was not a product of the Christian faiths, which forced a more patriarchal view of religion and belief and so were determined to decrease the worship of the Goddess and bring about the worship of only one God and his son. The women who were considered to be witches at this time were a danger to the morals of the church of God and were therefore against him, consummating their own religions by practicing Devil worship, according to the Christian faiths.

Even if you weren't blatantly practicing witchcraft, or Pagan rituals at this time, if you had a knowledge of herbal magick and remedies and had a capacity to heal without the word of the Lord, then you would be considered a witch and sentenced to death for your crimes against God. The blame from the church on the practice of nature-worship and herbal plant knowledge left a huge gap in the religious realities of connecting with the divine energies of the Universe.

Thankfully, Wiccans, or Pagans as they were called in those times, were never truly gone and continued to practice in secret, away from the watchful eye of the God-fearing man who would seek to eliminate any and all traces of Paganism from the planet despite the church being heavily influenced by Pagan rituals.

Over time, the practice of such work seemed like a lost art and craft and was passed down secretly and quietly, from generation to generation, until the time came when it would know popularity and acceptance. These witch hunts were largely occurring in Western civilizations while many other cultures have respected, revered, and exalted those who know the magick and mystery of the elements and the energy of all things.

At the same time as women and some men were being burned alive for their witchcraft, people in China, Tibet, and India were being acknowledged and celebrated for their connections to pagan-like practices. Though they appeared differently and had different context for practice, the messages and intentions were a lot alike and were born of a desire to become closer to the divine through the magick of the self.

A majority of uncivilized cultures in our world have some kind of religious practice, often involving Shamans or those who can communicate with the spirit world. The belief in these abilities and these energies was usually considered important in these tribes and many Shamans and healers utilized herbs and a close connection with nature and the cycles and seasons of life in order to communicate the divine to the people who worshipped it.

Wicca is primarily focused on the Paganistic religions that were spread across Europe and North America after it became colonized. The reality of Pagan religious practices was born out of early human's connection to their spirituality while they were still hunting and gathering. Even before we knew what we were doing, we were inventing an understanding of the world around us through sacred rituals and rites and our learning of how to heal ourselves with the magick of the plants, herbs, flowers, trees, and shrubs that grew all around us.

People were finding out how to coexist with nature and began to identify it with something bigger than what they could see and comprehend and as these energies were also aligning with humans' ability to speak directly with spirit and the voices of the divine. They were becoming acquainted with the magick and the mysteries of the world and what lies beyond, slowly developing religious practices to accommodate that reality.

As people have grown more into a rational and logical mind imprint, as the Age of Reason and Science took a greater force in the world, humans are less and less connected to embracing the spirituality of nature and the source of all life. What once was common practice and an everyday part of life, communing with nature and the realm of spirit, became a blight of the church that needed to be extinguished, but also something that wasn't likely to be easily proven by scientific evidence.

Interestingly enough, early physicians in the Age of Reason, following the backlash against Paganism and occult rituals, were borrowing and absorbing the practices of witches who used herbal remedies to heal and cure the sick and ailing. Though they would never admit it themselves, these often male doctors were actually practicing the witchcraft that was the cause of many deaths and burnings by the church.

Fast forwarding to the early 1900s, the Victorian era saw the rise of popularity in occult and spiritual matters that were practiced outside of the Christian faith and so it wasn't considered taboo to involve yourself in such practices or experiences. In fact, it was Queen Victoria herself who popularized this practice when she began holding séances to speak to her deceased husband, Prince Albert.

The resurrection of the occult in popular Western culture allowed for more practices, including Paganism, to have more prominence in the world of religion as an acceptable form of spiritual practice. Gerald Gardner's promotion of Wicca through his books and religious circles was only the beginning of a widespread journey across many cultures, particularly Western culture, allowing people to regain their relationship to Mother nature and the divine goddesses/gods through the art of practicing these spells, rituals and practices.

Wicca is not an ancient religion, although its practices stem from them, as Gardener pulled a majority of his practices from the types of Pagan practices being practiced across time. Some of Gardner's ideas also came from Eastern mysticism, the Kabbalah and British lore, legend, and folktales. Originally, his practices and techniques involved oaths, initiations and secrecy. Today, practicing Wiccans follow a wide variety of rituals and spell work that stems from Gardner's original concepts and ideas but that may allow for more freedom and creativity overall.

Some people argue that Wicca isn't Pagan at all, however almost all of what Gardner promoted in his Wiccan ideals came from a general faith in the same energies, essences and divinities as the

Pagans had. Gardner's public introduction in England in 1954 of this Neo-Pagan religion included duo-theistic beliefs, meaning that there is worship of both God and Goddess and many practicing Wiccans today uphold and support these originally traditions while some others prefer worship of the Goddess only, or vice versa.

Since the 50s Wicca has transformed into a wide variety of practices and beliefs, mainly because of its tendency to be a creative religion. Most people, or covens, create their own rituals and divine rites to practice based on their own personality, or group beliefs, taking from the basic concepts outlined by Gardner.

It's hard to say how many people in the world today are currently practicing Wiccans, but a recent consensus shows that the number could be somewhere between 1-2 million. That is a pretty large number of people who celebrate the Wiccan beliefs, compared to how it was at the time of the earlier uses of herbal magick and leading up to the witch hunts of the 16th and 17th centuries.

It has been largely a hidden religion, mostly due to a fear of persecution; however, more and more today, people all over the world are eager to celebrate one of the most original religions in the history of the world. Wicca is an expression of the ancient practice of connection to the Earth and worshipping her divine energies through the use of regular ritual, spells, craft, and appreciation. To resurrect your inner Pagan God or Goddess, today's Wicca is the path that leads you back in time to the way we all used to live when there was no one to tell you not to worship the Earth and her bounty.

Principles

Wiccans practice rituals in order to live according to the rhythm of nature. These are observed as the Lunar phases, the equinoxes, the solstices, and the other sabbaths.

Wiccans realize that human intelligence comes with a responsibility towards one's environment, therefore, Wiccans try to live in harmony with nature, with practices that benefit the environment and the evolution of all life.

Wiccans acknowledge the fact that through the practice of magick, they possess a power that is greater than most average persons. Although it may be called a "supernatural" ability by some, Wiccans propose that is actually part of the natural world, merely overlooked by non-practitioners.

Wiccans recognize the duality of the Universe as possessing both masculine and feminine, similar to the concepts of Yin and Yang. Neither is greater than the other; they are supportive and necessary to one another, and also exist in all humans. Wiccans look at sex and sexuality as a gift from the Goddess, and not as something to be ashamed of, so long as mutual consent is given. Sex is also a divine act and a symbol of life itself.

Wiccans recognize different planes of existence, such as the material world and the spirit world.

Wiccans do not allow an absolute hierarchy within their ranks, but they honor the teachers, elders, priests and priestesses who give their time and devote their lives to teaching future generations the Old Ways.

Wiccans view their practice as combining magick, religion, and nature-based wisdom. Together these elements form the Wiccan life method. A witch is such because he or she practices witchcraft, not because of lineage or false claims. Degrees and initiations are the individual's choice, but they do not determine who is a witch and who is not. A witch strives to control forces within his or herself in order to live a better life, and in greater harmony with the natural world.

Wiccans believe in seeking fulfillment and affirmation in their lives by seeking to give greater meaning to the Universe and by examining their individual roles within that Universe.

Wiccans keep no animosity towards Christianity, save for the fact that Christianity insists it is the only "true" religion, and all others are false. Wiccans have no issue with other faiths, so long as those faiths do not strive to suppress the religious freedom of others.

Wiccans resist feeling threatened by other members of the Craft engaging in debate about the tenets or practices of Wicca. They welcome dialogue that seeks to further the cause of Wiccan and pave the way for the future.

Wiccans refute the idea of "absolute evil" and do not worship entities like "Satan" or "the Devil" as defined by Christian principles. Wiccans abhor the search for power via the suffering of others.

Wiccans believe that everything we need in life can be found in Nature and its mysteries.

Uses in Present time

Today, many people think that Wicca and Witchcraft are one and the same. However, it is important to understand that this is not necessarily the case. Although all Wiccans are typically witches, not all witches are Wiccan. Many witches prefer to identify by other terms or use other belief systems to hone their craft, meaning that the two are not one and the same.

Wicca people often engage in witchcraft, although not all Wiccans will identify as witches. For some, they see these natural rituals as simply being rituals no different than having Santa Claus appear at Christmas or using a Menorah at Hanukkah. These are simply traditional rituals that they use at certain times of the year or for certain purposes that allows them to harmoniously engage with life and the world around them in a way that feels positive and fulfilling to them.

Common Myths About Wicca and Modern Paganism

Of course, despite the great advances that Wicca has made in becoming a legitimate, accepted modern religion, there are still many misunderstandings and prejudices regarding this peaceful, nature-worshipping faith.

Wiccans do not believe in or acknowledge a "devil," or Satan character. The Wiccan Horned God is symbolic of the virility of nature and of the masculine, it has nothing to do with any Christian notion of evil or of the Devil. They believe in the ebb and flow of the natural world, and that sometimes there is growth, and sometimes decay, but darkness is not evil—it is simply the absence of light. As they worship the departure and return of the Sun God, so do they commit themselves to the faith that even in the darkest hour, so will Light return to the world.

Wiccans disregard moral absolutes. They strive to practice their magick and their faith with a portion of humility, never seeking power over another or practicing magick that aims to directly harm or disable someone else.

Wiccans and other pagans do not seek to recruit others, for Wiccan is not a cult. It is a calling to those who wish to pursue its path, and Wiccans take personal choice very seriously.

Wiccans do not sacrifice animals. That would directly contradict their law to "Harm None".

Wiccans do not take the energy from another person in order to make their magick powerful. Wiccans and other pagans believe that we are all imbued with divine energy, as well as the potential to utilize that energy in order to practice magick and witchcraft.

Witches aren't real. Of course they are; a witch is simply a person who practices magick. (Some Wiccans and witches prefer to spell magic with a "k", i.e. magick, in order to differentiate it from performative stage magic. Either spelling is acceptable). A witch is a self-aware scholar of ways both ancient and modern to utilize the power of the natural world and of themselves to make changes in their lives and in themselves.

You are not a "real" witch or Wiccan without years of commitment and training. This is a personal choice; you're a witch if you practice magick, and you're a Wiccan if you decide that you are, it's as simple as that. Some Wiccans prefer to pursue their path alone, and we call these individuals "solitary" witches. Others feel more comfortable surrounded by a formal community, and to be taught by ordained elders, priests, and priestesses. There is no wrong way to be a Wiccan, so long as you adhere to the Wiccan Rede and try to practice Wiccan tenets throughout your daily life.

You need the proper tools in order to practice witchcraft. Tools are wonderful, they're fun to use and enjoyable to buy, but at the end of the day, it's a Wiccan's mind that enables he or she to practice magick. You can easily cast a spell with nothing more than your imagination and a stick you found in the woods.

A male witch is called a warlock. Not all witches or Wiccans are female. A male witch is simply a witch.

If your family are not witches, then neither are you. There is no pedigree needed to be a witch or a Wiccan. Wiccans and other pagans highly prize the force of one's will: if you desire it to be so (for yourself), then it is. It's as simple as that.

Hexes do not work. Unfortunately, any magical intention set forth into the universe will have some effect. For Wiccans, casting magick with the intention of causing someone else harm goes against everything Wicca stands for. Additionally, Wiccans strive to work their magick in tandem with nature, not against it. Causing harm for no other reason than the ego demands it is unnatural and disrespectful to the universe.

"White magick" is completely ineffective, while "black magick" is evil. This is another misconception perpetuated by Hollywood. Magick is most effective when the spellcaster is specific in their intention and works with the natural laws of the time and place the spell is cast. Magick can be used for any purpose—a healing spell cast during the new moon can bring relief to someone who's needed to get more sleep or change their diet for better digestion, and a protection spell cast during the dark moon on a Saturday can suddenly distract the originator of hurtful gossip and redirect their attention elsewhere. Nothing here is either "black" or "white," it simply works with nature and the witch's intent to produce results.

Joining a coven is a necessary part of becoming a Wiccan or a witch. It's not; a coven is a small group of individuals who come together to celebrate the sabbaths, esbats, or perform magick together. A community is larger, and less formal. And then there are individuals who prefer to practice alone—these are referred to as "solitaries."

Wiccans have orgies. Again, more Hollywood, but one thing to note is that Wiccans do believe that sex and sexuality are sacred and blessed by the divine. Some solitary practitioners or covens may prefer to be "skyclad" (without clothing) during a circle, but it is not for any sexual purpose, merely to feel closer to the God and Goddess in a natural form. There are never any sexual, public rites performed at a sabbath or esbat.

The pentacle is the sign of the Devil. This could not be farther from the truth. The pentagram is a symbol of a five-pointed star; it can be right-side up or upside-down, and neither represent Satan, a figure created by the Christian Church. With the single point up top, the pentagram is a symbol of the elements: Earth, Air, Fire, Water, and Spirit. It is also a symbol of humankind (if you imagine the single point is the person's head, and the other four are their arms and legs). With two points up, the pentagram is a symbol of wild nature (think a goat, stag, or ram).

How do Wiccans and Pagans differ? A Wiccan is a type of Pagan, just as a Baptist is a type of Christian. There are many different pagan faiths in the world, such as Stregha, Heathens,

Feri, and Druids. The word "pagan" comes from the latin paganus, or "of the countryside."

Wiccan Tools for Spells and Rituals

Before casting any spells, you must first familiarize yourself with the basic tools used in spellcasting and in performing rituals. Each Wiccan tool is rich with meaning. Some Wiccan tools are living beings plucked from nature's womb, but it is important to understand that as Wiccan, you are entitled to only take what is willing. Remember, each time you harvest a plant or use a crystal for your spell, you are asking that living being to sacrifice its life for you. In the end, you must make sure that your intention is worthy of their lives.

Wiccans typically have altars that they use for rituals and ceremonies. The altar is actually an important focal point in their rituals. It does not really matter that much if it is elaborate or simple. So, you can tailor your altar according to your personal preference. You also do not have to spend too much money on it. You can simply use the materials that you already have in your home. Remember that it is not the appearance of your altar that counts, but rather the way you use it.

You can use a fixed altar if you have one. You can also use a folding table if you live in a small home and do not have a lot of space. Folding tables are great because you can easily fold and store them away after you use them. There is no single rule for decorating an altar. A variety of tools, clothing, and jewelry may be used. It is up to your discretion whether you will use these tools or not. You should go with whatever feels comfortable for you. Nevertheless, there are certain items that are recommended to be used for your altar.

The following are the most commonly used tools for the spells and rituals done in Wiccan traditions.

Wand

This tool is actually optional. You can choose to have a wand or not. You can buy it from a store or have it custom made. If you choose to have a wand, you can refer to various traditions. In general, a wand has to be the length of your elbows, fingers, and hand but it can also be twice or half its size. You can choose any material for your wand, but woods are more ideal because they are used by ancient Druids. They are also more connected to nature.

Athame and Sword

An athame is a small knife typically made with wood. It is basically a mini dagger. A sword, on the other hand, is much bigger. It generally comes in a variety of sizes and shapes and is bigger than an athame. You can choose whatever athame or sword best fits your personal preferences. Nonetheless, it is ideal for your athame to be double ended. It also has to have a dark wood on its handle. If you want to personalize it, you can carve symbols on its handle.

Boline

This one is also a knife. It has a white handle and a curved blade. It is mainly used to cut sacred items that have to be used for rituals and ceremonies. When you use a boline, see to it that you are careful so that you can avoid accidents. You can order this tool online or buy it from a store that sells garden supplies.

Besom

It is a broom that is used in the cleaning process during a ritual. However, you do not necessarily have to sweep the floor. You can use this tool for a symbolic purpose. When you choose a bosom, see to it that you go for something made with natural materials. If you cannot find a besom from a store, you can make your own. Depending on which Wiccan coven or group you belong to, you should follow certain specifications when making your own besom.

Chalice

It is a container used to contain wine, fruit juice, or any other liquid needed for a ritual. You can find chalices in numerous sizes and shapes. Generally, a chalice is simply a cup with a long stem, similar to that of a wine glass. You can get a chalice that is made from any material. Glass and brass are the most commonly used materials for chalices.

Bell

It is used to attract positive energies and invoke deities during rituals. Bells come in different sizes and shapes. They are also widely available, so you can easily purchase them from anywhere. It is up to you what kind of bell you use for your altar. You can use a small one or a big one. You may prefer a small bell since it is easier to hold and has a mild tone. This is especially ideal if you live in a condo or apartment unit and do not want to disturb your neighbors during rituals.

Cauldron

This tool is perhaps the one most associated with Wicca. It is used to stir and combine ingredients used in rituals. As with many of the tools placed on altars, you can find cauldrons in various sizes and shapes. However, you do not have to put your cauldron on your altar if it is too big and heavy. Cauldrons are basically iron pots that have large bottoms and three legs. If your altar is small, you may get a small cauldron that does not take up much space.

Crystal Ball

This tool is used to represent the Goddess. Wiccans gaze into their crystal ball to have a vision. You can find crystal balls in different sizes and types. However, once you acquire a crystal ball, make sure that you charge it magically as soon as you can. Crystal balls have long been used in witchcraft and other similar practices.

Sensor

This tool is used to hold the incense that you burn during your rituals. You can find sensors in different sizes, shapes, and materials. They are typically made of brass. Nonetheless, you may also use a hanging sensor or a glass tray if it is more convenient for you. A hanging sensor is actually ideal if you wish to disperse the smoke from your incense during your ritual sessions.

Altar Tile

This tool is used as the central area during the ritual process and may contain a pentagram. It is available in different materials. Your altar tile can be of any size, but it is better to have one that fits your altar perfectly. You can also choose to have symbols engraved on it if you want. If your altar tile has a pentagram, see to it that it points upward, not downward.

Clothing

You are allowed to wear whatever you want during a ritual, provided that it is approved of by the members of your coven. If already a solitary practitioner, you can wear whatever you want as long as you feel comfortable in it. You should be able to easily stand up, sit down, and move around. Most Wiccans wear robes that feature embroidery, hoods, and flared sleeves. If you are not comfortable wearing a robe, you can wear something casual such as a pair of jeans and a t-shirt. You can even be nude if you like.

Jewelry and Accessories

The use of jewelry and accessories is open to many different interpretations. Wiccans are not really required to wear jewelry during a ritual. However, if you wish to wear any celestial symbol or an amulet, you can wear it. You may also wear a bracelet or a ring that features a special gem or stone.

Wiccan Tools from Nature

Stones and Crystals are natural element Earth symbols. They denote the North when they are used in rituals and spells. They are usually used in healing spells.

Crystals can be used to clear oneself of bad energies that are the cause of illness and negative thoughts and feelings. As such, they are often used in spells to heal one's body, mind, and spirit. Furthermore, crystals can aid you in connecting with your divine self, that part within yourself that is constant and unaffected by external realities. Crystals are also used to trigger your innate clairvoyant powers.

Another natural tool that symbolizes the North is Herbs. Even though they come from the Earth, when used for spells, each herb may represent a different natural element.

Chapter 2: Introduction to Herbalism

It all begins with a tiny seed, hidden under the soil, invisible and silent. In due time, the first delicate green shoots emerge, growing taller and stronger as the hours and days go by.

Soon enough, leaves and stems are taking their shape and drinking in the light they need to survive. Under the soil, the roots are also expanding, with the help of the water that moistens their dark surroundings.

As the plant grows and flourishes, it produces buds, blossoms, fruits, and more seeds, in order to start the process all over again. Depending on its type and what it experiences, it may live only for a season, or for thousands of years. But no matter what form it eventually takes, it was once simply a seed.

You don't have to be a Witch to witness this kind of magick. Anyone who has ever done any kind of gardening has experienced it in one form or another—with the possible exception of those who didn't meet with success at first and decided they don't have "the green thumb."

Herbalists, botanists, master gardeners and farmers are of course intimately familiar with plant life. But it could be argued that Witches have an extra degree of appreciation for the processes that create and sustain plant life (and therefore all life), as they know that plants have even more power than non-Witches—even the experts—are able to comprehend.

There has been a resurgence of interest in herbal knowledge in many healing fields over the last several decades. But since the beginning of human history, we have been making use of these gifts of the Earth. In fact, there is anthropological evidence that herbs were being used for deliberate purposes as long as 50,000 years ago.

Around the globe, all ancient societies had their own working relationships with herbs. We see this, for example, in clay tablets from the Sumerians, which listed hundreds of plants with medicinal properties.

The oldest known book on herbal medicine was written by a Chinese emperor over 5,000 years ago, and is believed to be based on even older oral traditions.

The ancient Greeks and Romans also had extensive knowledge of herbs, which was spread throughout parts of Europe as the

Roman Empire expanded, and was still being used in medical texts 1500 years later. The ancient Druids—the healers and magical practitioners of the Celts—were also well-versed in the use of many herbs.

Chapter 3: Herbalism relationship with Wicca

When it comes to magical symbolism, plants house the power of the four elements. They start as seeds of the Earth, where they find the minerals to sustain life. They work with the Fire of the sunlight, which helps them to convert carbon dioxide into oxygen.

Air fosters plant life in the wind, which helps to stimulate the growth of leaves and stems and scatters seeds around for the cycle to continue. Plants also, of course, need Water to live. But it also plays an important part in the regulation of the Earth's water cycle by helping to purify the water, and helping to take it from the soil to the atmosphere. This is the best way to see the four elements work together.

But herbs are powerful in other ways as well. When used as medicines, they don't come with all the side effects that regular medicines have, and they support internal balance.

Every spice or herb comes from a plant. They are created from the roots, leaves, barks, seeds, fruits, or flowers of plants. They not only make food taste amazing, but they can help to preserve them. Spices and herbs have antiviral and antibacterial properties and they are full of trace minerals and B-vitamins. They also contain disease-fighting antioxidants than veggies and fruits.

Herbs can also help people improve their spirituality. Herbs have a consciousness. It is an extension of Earth consciousness, and they want to help to protect, heal, and support us.

The power of herbs weaves throughout the body and works on our cells. They can help us to rationally understand things so that we don't make decisions with our ego mind, and let intuition guide us.

Herbs give us the power to connect with the energies of the Earth. Herbs are also very versatile when it comes to magick. Herbs can be burned to purify the air and can be used to make incense and oils. Herbal magick is very practical, and you most likely have most of the stuff you need already in your kitchen.

Believe it or not, the medicinal herbal benefits and magical herbal benefits are often connected in a profound way. In most cases, they are actually entangled together and there is no way to really tell what came first: the traditional medicinal uses or the magical uses of each plant.

For many, the healing properties of plants in terms of their medicinal benefits are considered to be magical because they can offer so much relief from so many things. Of course, there is typically strong scientific reasoning behind this from a medical perspective, but from a magical perspective, the intention infused with each of these practices is just as powerful as the medicinal and scientific properties of each plant.

Honoring both backgrounds is a powerful way to ensure that you are harnessing the power of each plant, as it allows you to tap into the tangible and scientific-backed proof of plants' powers, as well as the ancients' and ancestor's proof of the magical properties.

Physical Herbal Healing Combined with Spiritual Rituals

When you are performing a ritual with herbs, you will find that the herbs magical properties often mirror their medicinal properties as well. For example, rosehips are traditionally used in magical practices as being a symbol for immunity and physical wellness, and they are used in medicinal practices for the same as they are known for being high in Vitamin C.

Alternatively, roses themselves on a magical level are known for beauty and love and when it comes to their medicinal values we know that they offer many benefits in the way of beauty as they can brighten skin, relieve blemishes and heal acne scars.

It is incredible to realize that long before modern medicine and science were a thing, people were properly using these plants for their medicinal properties and for the spiritual correspondences as well.

It is hard to deny that plants are magical and that we have such a strong ability to communicate with them when you realize how accurately people have been using plants in healing for hundreds of thousands of years.

Traditional Magical Healing Rituals

When it comes to traditional magical healing rituals, typically a witch would use an herb that is relevant to a certain style of healing in a practical way as well as in a way that combines the power of intention, chanting and perhaps the proper cycle of the wheel of the year to maximize the magical energy.

By combining the practical healing properties of various plants, which was not known in ancient history, with the magical healing properties, people were said to have experienced miraculous healing benefits from plants. In traditional tribes, the witches or healers of the tribe were the ones who hold all of the knowledge of how the plants and rituals worked, and it was believed that if the ritual was not performed correctly the plant may not have the healing benefits that it was meant to have.

This was often proven as rituals that were ill performed or that lacked certain elements were often noted for now being as powerful or effective as those that were done at the right time and in the right way.

This is why people often turned to witches, medicine women, and healers when they were ill. They knew that these individuals in the traditional tribe would have access to all of the knowledge and would be able to perform the ritual in the best way possible to maximize the person's ability to heal and recover from an injury or illness.

Although we do not typically see medicine in such a sacred way in this day and age, it continues to be just as powerful. Knowing how to effectively work with medicinal plants and the energies and spirits of plants is a powerful opportunity to achieve traditional healing in a way that keeps you connected and in touch with the healing that you are doing. This is an incredibly sacred and harmonious way of life that many still believe is essential in experiencing a complete recovery from various ailments.

Chapter 4: Types of Plants used in Wicca

Basil

This is a kitchen herb found in various Thai and Mediterranean dishes. Basil is known for its deep and wide green leaves. These leaves are useful in dried and fresh forms in cooking, but its magical uses have a tendency to include leaves that are dry only because the fresh ones, may wither soon after they are harvested.

Basil as a yearly plant is easily grown and makes an outstanding multi-purpose essential in a magical garden of herbs. Leaves of basil are also usually available in grocery stores in dried and fresh form.

Medically, basil's calming quality is also used for easing upset stomachs and helps in digestion. More so basil essential oil has anti-fungal and antibiotic properties.

In English traditional magick, basil was useful in guarding against harmful spells that others have cast and also keeping away pests. Am ancient tale has it that the witches used to drink basil juice before they fly on their broomsticks. This can advocate that is was useful in interacting with the world of spirits in an experience of out-of-body and astral projections. In Italy, Basil was used as a love symbol and for the women who were prepared to welcome suitors, they would put a pot of basil on their balconies.

Today, basil has various magical uses like exorcism, protection, courage, fertility, wealth, love, luck, harmony, and happiness, etc.

In its uses of protection, it is sprinkled on floors to remove negative energies and is taken to encourage bravery in dangerous situations. It can be worn in a charm bag for money attraction or scattered outside someone's business. Some people also carry fully dried leaves in their bags and wallets for this use. It can also be used to make the mind clear from feelings of inadequacy or fear, confusion and anxiety. And during love spells, it is usually useful in encouraging understanding between couples.

Bay Laurel

Most commonly known as the leaf you put in soups and sauces to flavor them while cooking (and then remove before eating!), the leaf of the bay laurel tree has a long history of magical importance.

Bay laurel is an evergreen shrub, generally 3 to 10 feet tall, with shiny oval leaves that are brighter green on top and lighter on the bottom. Once dried, the leaves begin to fade in color, so you can tell when bay leaves are old by whether they are still somewhat green or have faded to brown. Bay leaves are widely available in the spice section of grocery stores.

Some healers make a poultice of the leaves and berries of bay laurel for relieving head and chest colds. The essential oil can be included in massage oils for the relief of arthritis and sore muscles.

Bay laurel was associated with nobility, honor, and triumph in ancient times, and was used to crown heroes, poets, and other people of high regard in both Greece and Rome. Wreaths of laurel were worn to protect against any vengeful tendencies on the part of sky gods, and by doctors who considered laurel to have highly curative properties.

Bay leaves are useful during spell work for strength, good fortune, success, money, healing, purification, protection and clairvoyance, divination and psychic powers.

A common form of bay magick is to write your wish on a dried bay leaf and then burn it to seal the spell. Bay leaves are placed in one corner of each room in a house for protection, as well as under pillows—or in dream pillows—to encourage prophetic dreaming. In keeping with its ancient associations, bay leaf can be carried to promote luck in athletic games and competitions.

A sprig of bay laurel can be used to asperge a space, a person, and/or magical tools in preparation for ritual. Some healers wear laurel wreaths while treating their patients in order to increase positive energy and ward off any negative energy resulting from the illness. After recovery from illness, burning bay leaf in the room where the person was treated can purify the space.

In fact, bay leaf is a great smudging herb for banishing unwanted negative energy in the form of poltergeists or other disturbing spirits. On a more mundane level, bay leaves can keep bugs out of a sack of flour, and keep clothing and linens fresh and moth-free.

Be sure not to confuse bay laurel with other plants with similar names, such as mountain laurel, which is poisonous.

Chamomile

This plant name comes a Greek word for ground apple.

Chamomile is recognized by lots of people for its soothing effects as tea, but it also has many magical uses too. This attractive plant has flowers that smell sweet and fluffy leaves which look like small daisies.

Chamomile flowers can be dried and then crushed in order to make tea and the essential oil from chamomile can be used in aromatherapy and skincare products. If you can't access heavy herbs, you better not order it online, instead you can buy its tea, open each teabag and use chamomile in your spell work.

Chamomile was useful as an incense in early days of Rome and to heal fevers in Egypt. It was recognized as one of the nine revered herbs in Anglo-Saxon traditional witchcraft and is still known that way by current followers of this tradition.

Today, it is useful in calming stress, menstrual cramps, indigestion, colic and teething in babies. Though, most professionals in healing give a warning against consuming chamomile while pregnant. Always consult your doctor before you try any herbs.

Chamomile is a great herb to be with, especially for those who deal with so much anxiety and stress. Though its mostly known to be a herb that heals, the fresh leaves are awesome when mixed with butter or sour cream for flavoring potatoes.

The calming properties in chamomile are also useful in reducing stress, promoting peaceful sleep, and promoting healing. Other magical purposes include it works for money, love and purification. It can as well be added to bags for prosperity or burned in spells for money.

Cinnamon

One of the world's favorite spices for thousands of years, cinnamon comes from an Asian evergreen tree with leathery leaves and brown, paper-like bark. The tree also produces yellow flowers and purple berries. The bark, leaves, and buds are used for many purposes beyond adding flavor to hot cocoa and baked goods.

One of the more unusual uses for cinnamon in ancient Egypt was as a mummification agent. It was also beloved by Chinese healers and is referenced in the Bible. Once cinnamon found its way to Europe, it motivated explorers to locate its source, which led to the colonization of Ceylon (present-day Sri Lanka) and its reputation as "the spice that launched a thousand ships."

Cinnamon is still used medicinally, to relieve upset stomachs and other digestive problems. Pregnant women are advised to take it easy on cinnamon, but it can be effective for morning sickness. Cinnamon taken in combination with other herbs is also known to boost the action of the combination.

Magical goals for cinnamon include love, lust, luck, protection, prosperity, spirituality, power, and success.

It is used in sachets of corresponding colors for a number of these purposes, such as pink or red for drawing love. Cinnamon also makes a very pleasant incense, and is burned to increase connectedness to spiritual energy.

Interestingly, cinnamon works particularly well in money spells in combination with its culinary companions—cloves, nutmeg, cardamom, and ginger. Cinnamon-scented decorative brooms and pinecones, which you can find commercially available at gift shops, can be charged to bring love and happiness into the home.

Cinnamon, also known as sweet wood, is classified as a dermal toxin (or skin irritant), and so should not be applied topically. If using cinnamon essential oil to anoint candles or other magical objects, wear gloves or dilute heavily in a carrier oil.

Elecampane

Elecampane is probably the least known herbs of this set of 13, but it's well worth getting acquainted with.

Popular in Celtic-based Witchcraft and used for healing purposes since ancient Rome, this helpful plant grows to be between 4 and 5 feet tall and resembles the sunflower.

Since it's not really a culinary herb (though the root was candied and enjoyed as a treat in Europe prior to the 20th century), it's unlikely to be found in grocery stores. It's popular with herbalists, however, so it should be available in a local natural foods store or any number of online botanical dispensaries.

The second part of its Latin name, "Helenium," is a reference to Helen of Troy in Greek mythology, whose tears are said to have given rise to the plant. When it was introduced to the rest of Europe in Medieval times, elecampane gained a reputation for being useful for infections, which may be why chewing it was thought to "fasten the teeth"—that is, it likely took care of inflammation of the gums.

Elecampane root was also worn as a protection against snake bites and poisonous insects. In Celtic countries, it was known as "elfwort" due to its ability to attract faeries.

Modern healers love elecampane root for its help with relieving ailments of the lung. It's an ingredient in many medicinal teas and cough syrups, and can be made into a tea on its own, though its bitter taste definitely calls for plenty of honey to make it go down easier!

The leaves and flowers are also used by some herbalists for dealing with digestive issues, but the root is the most widely available part of the plant.

Magically, elecampane is used for protection against the energies of disease and to promote general good luck. Some wear it in a sachet or other charm to attract love, though it's not exactly known as an incredibly romantic herb.

The energy of elecampane is more geared toward soothing feelings of conflict or uprootedness, and it's quite effective at dispelling anger and/or violent impulses or vibrations. It can be sprinkled around doorways to keep such vibrations out of the home.

It is also used to promote a stronger mind-body connection, particularly for those whose lifestyles are largely sedentary and don't get much exercise.

As a "faery herb," elecampane is particularly effective in workings for communication with the spirit world, and intuition. Drinking the tea before divination activities can strengthen the connection between the Witch and the divine.

Hibiscus

Hibiscus is usually thought of only as a flower, but its petals are used medicinally as well as for culinary purposes, and the color of red hibiscus—whether it's used in a tea, a magical sachet, or some other Witchy creation—is a delightful addition to the usual greens and browns of an herbal magician's pantry.

You can find dried hibiscus in the herb section of any natural foods store, or online. If you live in a warm climate, you can also grow it in your garden and harvest and dry the petals yourself!

Hibiscus is found in a few different colors, but its red hibiscus that best serves both medicinal and magical purposes.

Hibiscus has been used in various parts of the world in teas and jams, and even for paper making. In some places, fibers from the stem of the hibiscus are used for making sackcloth and twine.

High in antioxidants, the tea is beneficial for regulating appetite, protecting the liver, and helping the body speed up healing from a cold or flu. It can lower blood pressure and cholesterol, and has even been used in some parts of the world for encouraging hair to grow more thickly and keep from turning grey prematurely.

The primary magical uses for hibiscus are love, lust, and divination.

The flowers can be brewed in a strong tea which is drunk for inducing lust and passion. It can also be carried in a sachet or burned as an incense to attract love.

Loose dried petals in a hot bath are a delightful way to raise one's vibration and induce a general sense of well-being, which is a precursor to attracting new love. (Test your bathtub's stain resistance before trying this—the color may rinse out more easily in older porcelain tubs than in newer acrylic ones)

For divination and clairvoyance, mix hibiscus into an incense. The flowers can also be used as a scrying tool when placed in a wooden bowl filled with water.

Lavender

Lavender is well known as a very fragrant, calming herb used in many bath oils as well as sachets and sleep pillows.

Although it isn't widely used in cooking these days, culinary lavender does make a nice addition to teas and many desserts.

A member of the mint family (though known for having more of a "tangy" than a "minty" taste), lavender is somewhat similar in appearance to rosemary, with narrow green leaves resembling short pine needles. Both the leaves and the purple, white, and/or blue flowers blooming at the tops of the plant hold a unique flavor and an unmistakable aroma.

During Cleopatra's day in Rome, lavender had a reputation for attracting love and passion. However, other cultures prized it for its apparent protective properties, and used it to keep away the "evil eye" and/or unwanted spirits. It was found to be useful against the plague in the Middle Ages, most likely because it repelled the fleas that carried and spread the disease. Bundles of lavender were traditionally given to women during childbirth to hold onto, in order to promote courage and strength.

Lavender is an incredibly versatile herb in magical workings as well. While it's very often used for love, peace, and restful sleep, other purposes include clairvoyance, consecration, happiness, healing, money, passion, protection (both physical and psychic), purification, relief of grieving, longevity, memory retention, meditation, divination, and wedding blessings.

Lavender is a classic staple ingredient in dream pillows, bath spells, sachets and love spells.

The flowers are particularly effective in love spells, especially those aimed at attracting a man into one's life. The ashes of dried lavender flowers can also be sprinkled around the home to promote peacefulness.

For those who have trouble falling asleep at night, burning lavender incense can be tremendously helpful. (If you can't find lavender incense, a few drops of essential oil sprinkled on your pillow can also help.) For purifying a space, lavender makes for a great asperging herb as well.

Because of its calming and centering energy, lavender can be of great benefit to use before working magick of any kind.

For example, if you're wanting to work a Full Moon spell but can't seem to get in the right frame of mind after a busy day of work, try taking a ritual purification bath with lavender flowers or essential oil. At the very least, you can inhale the fragrance of lavender as you breathe deeply for a few moments, readying yourself to begin your magical work.

Mugwort

Mugwort is a member of the daisy family, and though it's not quite as pretty to look at as some of its cousins, it is a favorite herb among Witches.

Growing between three and six feet tall, with a subtly purple stem and small, reddish or greenish yellow flowers, this versatile plant was used to flavor beer before the cultivation of hops became standard. Some say that this is where the herb gets its name—from the "mug" that the beer would be drunk from.

However, like lavender, mugwort is also a great repeller of moths, and some believe the name comes from an older word for "moth."

Aside from its early role in beer-making, mugwort is not considered a culinary herb, but it has many medicinal and magical uses that make it worth adding to any Witch's herb pantry.

Like chamomile, mugwort is among the nine sacred herbs in the Anglo-Saxon Witchcraft tradition.

Roman soldiers valued mugwort for its ability to combat fatigue, and put sprigs of it in their sandals to keep their feet from getting worn out on long marches. Later, as Christianity spread across Europe, mugwort was associated with John the Baptist in Germany and Holland. People would gather mugwort on St. John's Eve—a holiday coinciding with the Summer Solstice—and make crowns of it to wear for luck and prevention of illness. Other reputed reasons for carrying mugwort were the prevention of backaches and the curing of "madness."

Today, mugwort is used medicinally as a topical anesthetic, and for relief of burning and/or itching of the skin.

Some people chew fresh mugwort leaves to alleviate tiredness and clear their minds. An infusion of fresh leaves can calm chronic stomach issues and help increase appetite, and dried mugwort mixed with honey can be used to fade bruises.

However, mugwort is a very potent herb and should not be used internally on a regular basis, as it can cause a host of problems, especially for pregnant women. If you are just beginning your education in herbalism, stay away from ingesting mugwort until you have done thorough research and have developed a strong intuition about what will serve your body well.

For now, it's enough to stick to external, magical uses for this powerful herb. These magical uses include dream work, divination, safeguarding the home from unwanted energies, and protection during travel.

Mugwort added to dream pillows can encourage prophetic dreaming, while placing sprigs of the herb near divination tools, such as Tarot cards and runes, can increase their power and accuracy. Some Witches like to use an infusion of mugwort to clean their ritual tools, and especially their scrying tools, such as crystal balls and mirrors.

Burning mugwort during divination sessions can also enhance receptivity to the messages coming through. Hanging mugwort on or over a door protects the space inside from unwelcome spirits or other energies, and carrying a mugwort sachet while traveling can help prevent delays and mishaps.

Finally, the "St. John's Eve" tradition continues today in its pagan form, as Witches may wear a garland of mugwort while dancing around the fire at Midsummer's Eve. Throw the garland into the fire at the end of the night for protection throughout the coming year.

Nutmeg

A favorite winter spice for baked goods and hot drinks, what we know as nutmeg is actually the grated or powdered seed of an Indonesian evergreen tree.

The herb known as mace comes from the same tree, and is derived from the covering of the seed. The nutmeg tree also produces a fruit, the skin of which can be used to make jellies and jams, but this is a more rare use for this exotic plant.

The potent fragrance and taste of nutmeg are a testament to its overall power as a culinary, medicinal, and magical herb.

The whole seeds were worn in charms and amulets in the Middle Ages for protection against malicious deeds and danger of all kinds. Some also believed it could attract admirers, and men would wear it in combination with wood, silver, or ivory to promote strength and energy.

Medicinally, nutmeg can be used to aid digestion and appetite, as well as promoting restful sleep.

Like mugwort, nutmeg is very potent and should be taken only in small doses—no more than 1 teaspoon is generally recommended. Large amounts can be toxic and even induce hallucinations, so be careful with this beloved spice!

Nutmeg magical purposes include protection, good luck, prosperity, money attraction and dissolving negative energy from another person. Scatter nutmeg on a green candle in spells of money, or other magical tools and anointing candles with a mixture of other essential oils that draw money and nutmeg.

Like chamomile, nutmeg can help with games of chance, so gamblers will carry whole seeds for luck. You can also it in your pocket for luck during travel.

Wrapped in a purple cloth, whole nutmeg can be used for success in legal matters.

For enhanced meditation and/or divination, add powdered or grated nutmeg to a hot beverage to drink before the session, or rub a massage oil containing nutmeg into your temples.

If you like to bake, start experimenting with adding nutmeg to banana bread, muffins, and other sweet treats. Place an intention into the dry mix of flour(s) and spices as you stir them together, and take note of how your personal energy shifts into a positive state when eating your magical creations!

Rosemary

Another favorite of Witches and cooks alike, rosemary has long been used for a wide variety of culinary, medicinal, and magical purposes.

This fragrant herb tends to resemble lavender in appearance, but you can easily tell the difference between the two by rubbing the leaves with your hands, which will release the aromatic oils for easy identification. Another distinguishing characteristic is that rosemary leaves are whitish underneath and a deeper green on top, while lavender leaves tend to have a more blue-green hue.

You can find dried rosemary in the spice section of any grocery store, but it's also quite easy to grow in a garden or a kitchen window.

In the ancient world, rosemary was sacred in Greece, Rome, and Egypt, and had associations with both festive and somber occasions. While the wood of the rosemary bush was used to make musical instruments, and brides wore wreaths made from the branches, Egyptians used it in embalming the dead. It was also used in funeral rites in Wales, where mourners would throw sprigs into the gravesite while the coffin was being lowered into it.

In contemporary times, rosemary is used for improving circulation and warming cold arms and legs, as well as for improving the appearance of hair and skin. This herb has an all-around energetic quality of clarification, purification, and rejuvenation.

Magical workings for rosemary use its purifying properties, particularly for eliminating negative vibrations from a physical space or one's own person. For this reason, burning rosemary before spell work is highly recommended, as is using an infusion of rosemary in a ritual bath prior to magical work.

Alternatively, you can make a sacred water with rosemary to rinse your hands in before magick, or to purify and bless ritual tools.

Combined with juniper, rosemary makes a great smudge for healing, and for clearing out any residual energies of disease in a room where someone has been ill.

Other purposes of rosemary are strengthening mental focus and clarity, healing, love, lust, protection, jealousy and retaining youth.

In love spells, rosemary is stuffed into poppets or sachets to draw new suitors. This same method can be used in spells for focusing during an examination, so rosemary is a great herb for students to make regular use of. And a fresh sprig of rosemary placed by the pillow promotes a solid night's sleep, which is a key component in retaining one's youthful vitality.

Sage

Another member of the mint family, sage has been associated with healing for thousands of years. Its Latin name, "salvia," comes from the Latin word meaning "to heal," as in applying a salve to a wound.

Sage—sometimes called "common sage" or "garden sage"—is used as a culinary spice, particularly in its native region of the Mediterranean, and so is easily found in grocery stores.

It has long, pale, almost silvery-green leaves which are wonderful both fresh and dried, but the taste is very strong, so a little goes a long way.

Sage was both sacred and very practical for the Romans, who revered it at harvest time and also used it to clean their teeth, as well as to boost brain power and memory.

This particular power has been utilized consistently throughout history, including the 10th century, when Arab doctors boiled sage leaves and drank the tea with honey in order to increase their mental clarity. In the Middle Ages, sage tea was drunk to treat such diverse conditions as liver disease, epilepsy, and fevers.

The English drank it as a "healthful tonic," and made use of it in meat dishes as well. An old custom there holds that no man needs to die "whilst sage grows in his garden."

Sage has also been used for years to treat a variety of throat and lung ailments, including symptoms of tuberculosis.

Sage's magical properties make it ideal for smudging to clear a space, object, or person of negative or otherwise unwanted energies. It is particularly good for dealing with the energies of grief and loss, helping to dispel energy that might otherwise get trapped within the grieving person and prolong the grieving process.

Other magical uses include longevity, wisdom, protection, and wish fulfillment.

Aside from being used as a smudge or an incense ingredient, sage can be added to sachets for both wisdom and healing from grief. For the fulfillment of a wish, write the wish on a sage leaf and sleep with it under your pillow for three days. Then, bury the leaf outside of your home.

Note: a non-culinary, non-ingestible species of sage is used by Native Americans in smudging rituals and other spiritual practices. Usually called "white sage" (Salvia apiana), this variety is in danger of becoming extinct. While common sage grows easily and robustly almost anywhere, white sage grows only in the American Southwest.

Increased interest in both Native American and Western Witchcraft traditions across the globe have led to over-harvesting in the wild. Because common sage works just as well for all purposes described above, this guide recommends avoiding purchasing white sage, as doing so will only increase the likelihood of extinction.

Thyme

In contrast to the long, broad pale green leaves of garden sage, thyme leaves are very small, oval-shaped and dark green, with tiny pink flowers that bloom in spring and summer.

This hardy perennial is popular in kitchen herb gardens, but can also be found in dried form in the spice aisle of any grocery store. Thyme also grows in the wild, though wild thyme is not thought to be as potent as the cultivated variety.

Once you've worked with thyme, whether through cooking or through magick, its pungent scent is unmistakable.

Originating in the Mediterranean and spread throughout Europe by the Romans, thyme was used in Sumer as early as 3000 BC for its antiseptic properties. It was likely used by the Greeks as a smudging herb—the word "thyme" comes from the Greek for "fumigate."

Like rosemary, thyme was used as an embalming herb in ancient Egypt and placed into the coffins of the recently deceased in Europe. Roman soldiers placed thyme in their bathwater to increase their strength and bravery—an association that continued into the Middle Ages, when knights wore sprigs of thyme embroidered into their scarves.

Likewise, Scottish Highlanders drank thyme tea to keep nightmares at bay. Medicinally, thyme has been most widely used in cough remedies, but it can also help with skin inflammation, digestive problems, and rheumatism.

Thyme's magical properties make it ideal for workings focused on healing, purification, love, and psychic knowledge.

Wearing a sprig of thyme is still a way of drawing courage during difficult experiences, as is adding an infusion of thyme to the bath. Those who struggle with nightmares can try adding thyme to a dream pillow for more restful sleep.

Hang a sprig of dried thyme in the home to purify the energies and attract good health to all who live there. When you're working on a project or other goal that feels impossible, use thyme in a spell for staying upbeat and positive as you see it through to the end.

To attract faeries to your garden, plant thyme around the edges. Smudging with thyme can dispel feelings of melancholy, hopelessness, and other negative vibrations, particularly when you're just coming out of a long illness or experiencing some other prolonged struggle.

Chapter 5: Spells used for Wicca

Spells for Personal Empowerment

➤ **Earth and Sky Spell**

Ingredients:

- Bay leaf

- Basil

- Lemon balm

- A small rock of obsidian

- A small rock of tiger's eye

- A small cloth pouch (or you can sew your own if the latter then include needle, thread, and scissors in the items before you cast the circle)

- White tealight or short taper candle

Instructions:

1. Do this spell at night. Cast your circle, then raise your arms up, fingertips towards the ceiling. Feel the energy of the night sky, all its planets, moons, and stars, channeling down into your circle, swirling around until your circle fills with energy like water fills a glass. When your circle is full, imagine the energy glowing bright white, then allow your arms to drop comfortably at your sides.

2. Light the candle. Place the bay leaf in the pouch and say, *"Tonight I give myself the gift of strength, and of endurance."*

3. Place the basil in the pouch and say, *"Tonight I give myself the gift of wealth, and of the courage to conquer my fears."*

4. Place the lemon balm in the pouch and say, *"Tonight I give myself the gift of love, and of success."*

5. Place the obsidian in the pouch and say, *"Tonight I give myself the gift of protection from negativity."*

6. Place the tiger's eye in the pouch and say, *"Tonight I give myself the gift of clarity, and of integrity."*

7. Tie the pouch, or sew it closed if it's handmade. Hold the pouch in your hands and slowly move it clockwise (called "sunwise" in Wicca), above the candle. (Don't burn your hands).

8. Say: *"Tonight I cast this spell for me, to reach for the stars and cast my net to the sea, to walk the Earth in discovery, to live my life happily."*

9. Focus on the bag of charms, and imagine yourself in scenarios where you are happy, successful, and powerful. When you are ready, recite the Casting Words.

➤ **Inner Power Candle Spell**

Ingredients:

- A white, brown, or blue taper candle

- A mixture of clove, juniper, and rose oils to anoint the candle. Handle the clove oil with care—only one or two drops of each are needed.

- A small, thin, paintbrush.

- A small dish on which to burn the candle.

- Pink or kosher salt.

Instructions:

1. Matches to light the candle—preferable over a lighter, as metal should not strike a holy flame, but in a pinch, use what's available.

2. Cast your circle and draw the energy down from the universe. With the paintbrush, anoint the candle in the oil mixture, using brushstrokes that move from the back of the candle towards the front, and you. Work from the base of the candle towards the wick. Imagine yourself in moments of great personal power.

3. Light the candle and say: *"As it burns, so I learn. As it dances, so I turn. As it flickers, so I grow. As it melts, so my troubles go."*

4. Move your hands above the candle as if you were drawing the healing energy of the flame towards you. Do this as you repeat:

5. *"Flame of power, imbue me with your strength."*

6. Sit in quiet contemplation for as long as you're comfortable, imagining yourself overcoming obstacles, and obtaining happiness, and a peaceful heart. When you're ready, open the circle and allow the candle to burn down. After the candle is burned you can dispose of the

wax and salt either by tossing them in a crossroads, or by burying them.

➢ **Spell to Nourish the Heart**

Ingredients:

- Pink quartz
- Rose petals
- Lemon balm
- Lemon essential oil
- Do this spell on a new, waxing, or full moon.

Instructions:

1. Cast your circle in the bathroom. Fill a bath and add five drops of the lemon essential oil to it. Add the rose petals and lemon balm. After you've gotten into the bath, add the pink quartz. As you sit in the bath, close your eyes and imagine a pink, healing light gleaming on the water. Imagine your body soaking up this healing energy. Feel your heart glowing with happiness and warmth that radiates throughout your entire body.

2. When you are ready, repeat these words: *"I am worthy of love, and I am capable of love. I am worthy of peace, and I am capable of peace. I am worthy of happiness, and I am capable of happiness."*

3. All good things are possible. May they come into my life as blessings."

4. When you're finished with the bath, allow the water to drain and pat yourself dry (do not rub or wipe) with a towel from your feet up to your head. Discard the herbs and return to the quartz to your altar.

➢ Spell for Personal Success and Achievement

Ingredients:

- A piece of sunstone
- An orange candle
- Pink or kosher salt
- Juniper berries
- Some soil
- A small bowl, or cauldron

- Benzoin incense
- Myrrh oil
- Small, slim paintbrush
- Matches

Instructions:

1. Cast your circle, and anoint the candle with the myrrh oil. Light the incense. In the bowl or cauldron, place the salt, soil, sunstone, and juniper berries. Mix these with your athame or wand, in a sunwise direction.

2. As you stir the ingredients, say: *"As the Sun warms the Earth and encourages the harvest, so does my ability for success grow every day. I will achieve my goals and dreams, step by step, as sure as the sunflower and the wheat grows tall."*

3. Picture the sun shining down on a field of wheat and sunflowers: these represent your success and finances. Picture the wind swaying the tall stalks. See how the field spans out endlessly towards the horizon. This is your success; it is tangible and real.

   Say: *"As the candle burns its flame, so does my success increase."*

4. When you are ready, open the circle and allow the candle to continue burning down. Sprinkle the spell ingredients except for the sunstone in an open field at your earliest convenience.

➢ Tiger's Eye Self-Esteem Spell

Ingredients:

- A piece of tiger's eye
- A yellow, white, or orange candle
- Matches
- A small plate or candleholder
- Solar oil: three drops of rosemary, cedar, and orange oil mixed
- A small, thin paintbrush

Instructions:

1. Anoint the candle with the solar oil, then light the candle. Stand before it holding the tiger's eye in your hands. Look to the ceiling and imagine the sun. Close your eyes.

2. Imagine the sun's rays filling the space of your sacred circle. Picture their warmth filling you, soothing every limb, filling you with passion, and with courage. Know that whenever you face a difficult situation, the sun's energy will be there to keep you strong.

   Say these words:

   "I call upon the energy of the Sun to imbue this crystal with your power. May it be a constant reminder of my self-worth, each day I spend on Earth."

3. Lift your hand with the crystal and allow the sun to fill the tiger's eye with its bold, confident energy. When you're ready, open the circle and allow the candle to burn down. Keep the tiger's eye in your pocket throughout your days or place it on your altar for daily meditation.

➢ A Spell to Reclaim Power

Ingredients:

- White quarts
- A piece of onyx
- One white and one black candle

- Matches

- Sacred oil blend: rosemary, myrrh, frankincense

- A small, thin paintbrush

- Florida water, or holy water

- Bundle of sweet grass or hand-picked wildflowers

- A vase or glass half-filled with water

Instructions:

1. Do this spell on a waning or dark moon. After the circle is cast, anoint both candles and set them on your altar or workspace. Place the onyx and the quartz between them so that from left to right they look like this: black candle, onyx, white quartz, white candle. Take the bundle of wildflowers and lightly sprinkle them with Florida or holy water then shake the water onto yourself using the bundle of wildflowers, from head to toe. Once you've done this, place the wildflowers in the vase on your altar.

2. Now take the stones and hold them, one in each hand: hold the onyx in your right hand and the white quartz in your left.

Say:

> "I take back that which belongs to me,
> by the darkness of night and the bright light of day.
> I call upon the dark moon's energy,
> to guide my thoughts and light the way.
> What was stolen is now restored,
> and the balance of my mind returned.
> By the magick within these stones,
> and by the flame of the candle that burns."

3. Lift your arms, still holding the stones, and feel the energies of your life in perfect balance. Feel your power course through you like the infinity symbol, a figure eight—endless. No one can alter or stop this.

4. When you are ready, return the stones to their places on the altar, and open the circle.

➢ Simple Spell to Overcome an Obstacle

Ingredients:

- Small gathered sticks (you will need at least ten) from the woods: each stick should be approximately 5" long

- Dragon's blood incense

- A red candle

- Clove oil

- A small, thin paintbrush

- Matches

- A candleholder or plate

Instructions:

1. Cast the circle, anoint the candle, and light the incense. Take the sticks and one by one, build a small structure. The design is up to you: it can be a little house, a pyramid, or you can stack the sticks five across going one way, five across the other. Make sure the structure is as tall as you can get it.

2. While you work on this, describe the obstacle or problem you're wanting to overcome. With each placement of a new stick, describe one facet or fact of the obstacle.

    When you're finished with this work, say:

    "By the fiery flame of this candle, so I ignite my courage."

3. With one, strong sweep of your hand, knock the structure you've built off of your altar. As you're doing so, imagine your victory in overcoming the obstacle you described.

   Say: *"And so it is done."*

4. After you've opened the circle and allowed the candle to burn down, discard the sticks in the woods, a field, or at a crossroads.

Spells for Wealth and Abundance

Changing Your Mind About Money

Before you embark on casting a money spell, take some time to examine your attitude towards money. Unfortunately, many of us have a negative attitude towards money—even if we love getting money and enjoy shopping with it! Those of us who have a scarcity mentality are always worried about money running out, and who wouldn't be? Remember that magick is the exercise of will to create change. You can change your financial situation through magick, but you have to stop worrying about money being scarce.

Start changing your outlook today. Every time you spend money, be thankful for it. Actively thank your money for working hard for you—tell it to bring back its friends to you a hundred-fold. Even if you're just paying your phone bill, thank the universe for allowing you to pay it, and thank your money for being there when you needed it.

Bad ways of thinking to get rid of right now:

- I don't deserve to have a lot of money.
- I never make enough money.
- I don't possess the proper education, skills, or talents to make the money I want.

Remember, never ask "how". The universe knows how—you only have to trust in your strong connection to the universe. If you contradict your magical work, it will fail, plain and simple. You have to change your beliefs first so that your will can create miracles through magick.

Practice affirmations. Anywhere from a full lunar cycle, to a week before you want to cast your money magick spell, take a few minutes each day to repeat a money-related affirmation, such as:

"I deserve to have the money I desire."

"I am good at making money."

"I attract abundance every day."

"Money is coming to me every day."

Try to stay in the present when you recite affirmations; don't make statements that pertain to the future. Stay in the now. And even if you don't yet believe these affirmations, saying them every day will change your thinking, in time. You can choose to light a candle and cast a circle when you recite one or several of these affirmations.

Practice gratitude. When your thinking is gratitude-based, you will stop dwelling on what you lack and start focusing on what you have. Take time every day to say out loud or write down something you're thankful for having. BELIEVE what you're saying.

Counter negativity with a question. If you catch yourself slipping back into the old habit of thinking negatively about money, try this exercise. If you find yourself thinking, "I never have enough money," turn it into a question: *"Why do I feel as if I never have enough money?"*

Take time to meditate on the question, let it remain in your thinking as you go about your days. Eventually, you will answer the question subconsciously and the doubt itself will disappear and will no longer rooted in reality. That old, negative belief will no longer haunt you.

➢ **Orange Money Spell**

Ingredients:

- An orange
- A golden or silver dollar
- A small piece of paper and a pencil
- Powdered cinnamon
- Basil

- Patchouli (herb), or patchouli oil

- Orange zest, powdered or crumbled

- Vervain

- A brown or green candle

- Abundance oil: a mixture of honey, patchouli oil, lemon oil, and sandalwood

- Matches

- A dish on which to burn the candle

- A small, sharp knife

Instructions:

1. Perform this spell on a new, waxing, or full moon. Anoint the candle with the abundance oil and light it.

2. Write on the piece of paper: money come, money grow, money dance, money flow. Place the coin onto the middle of the paper and sprinkle the cinnamon, basil, patchouli, orange zest, and vervain onto it.

3. Fold the paper towards you, then turn it sunwise and fold it once more. Do this as many times as you need to make it small enough to fit inside the orange. Make a small,

deep cut in the orange and place the folded spell inside. Place the orange on your altar and keep it there for seven days. After the seventh day, remove the coin and donate it to a charity. Discard the orange and paper.

➢ A Simple Spell for Abundance

Ingredients:

- Your cauldron or a silver bowl
- Three silver dollars
- Collected rain or river water

Instructions:

1. Perform this spell only on a full moon. Fill the cauldron or bowl halfway with the collected water. As you drop each coin into the water, say:

   "Abundance, come to me,
   by river, road, air or sea.
   I am grateful for this abundance, eternally."

2. Place the cauldron or bowl where the moon's light can reflect upon the water's surface. The next day, remove

the coins and keep them in your pocket, billfold, or purse. Never spend them.

➢ A Treasure Chest

Ingredients:

- A wooden box with a latch
- A coin of every denomination, some foreign coins, and a paper bill of each denomination
- Green jade
- Pyrite
- Clear quartz
- Rose quartz
- A bundle of alfalfa, tied with green string
- Freshly picked basil leaves
- Three bay leaves
- A piece of ginger root
- Abundance oil
- Florida water or orange blossom water

- A spray bottle
- A bundle of sage
- Matches

Instructions:

1. Perform this spell under a full moon. A blue moon (the second full moon in a month) is a particularly good time for this spell.

2. This is an expensive spell, obviously, but a powerful one. Save it for a time when things are going well, or—save up for it to build up your abundance and help keep it going strong. In the spray bottle, mix some Florida or orange blossom water with a few drops of the abundance oil.

3. Light the sage bundle and gently smudge each coin, bill, and stone. Take the spray bottle and lightly mist each coin, bill, and stone, setting each one inside the box as you do so. As you place each object into the box, say:

4. *"By the power of three times three, this treasure box brings abundance to me."*

5. When you're finished placing all the objects in the box, close the box and place your hand upon it. Say:

"This box is now a magnet for wealth and prosperity

which then flows from this box to me,

that it harm none,

so mote it be."

6. Set the box in the light of the moon, either outside (where it won't be detected or stolen), or on a windowsill, and say:

"Bella Luna,

cast your light

upon this treasure box tonight

and let my magick take flight."

7. Recharge the box every full moon for continued flow of wealth and abundance. Note: if you ever find you're in a situation where you must spend the money in the box, do not worry over it. Use the stones in new ways for continued prosperity, and when you're able, refill and recharge the box.

➢ **Red Cloth Money Bag**

Ingredients:

- A red cloth bag or pouch (small); you can also sew your own

- Needle, red thread, scissors if you're using a bag you've sewn yourself
- Three golden dollars
- A small mirror—small enough to fit easily into the pouch
- A green candle
- Abundance oil
- A small, thin paintbrush
- Matches
- A candleholder or small dish

Instructions:

1. Do this spell only on a full moon. Anoint the candle and light it. Take time to draw down the power of the moon; holding your hands high, say:

   "Bella Luna,
   come on down,
   so lovely, with your silvery crown,
   grace this circle with your light
   bless my magical work this night."

2. Feel the powerful, lunar energy coursing down into your circle, filling the space with white light. Drop your hands when you feel the circle is full.

3. Place the three coins and the mirror into the pouch, then either sew or tie it shut. Hold the bag in your hand while focusing your gaze at the candle's light.

Say:

"Paper and coin,
abundance and wealth,
for joy, for freedom, and in good health,
is mine tonight, and forever on,
beneath the moon's light and the sun's,
to bring me no harm, nor to harm anyone."

4. Raise the bag up to the moon's light and say*: "So mote it be, and so it is done."*

5. After you open the circle, allow the candle to burn down. Carry the bag with you or let it remain on your altar. Additionally, you can place it on top of your wallet when you're at home.

➢ **A Simple Candle Money Spell**

Ingredients:

- A green candle
- Matches
- A dish on which to burn the candle

Instructions:

1. Do this spell on the full or waxing moon. Light the candle and very carefully, place you're the back of your hand above it, just high enough so that you can feel it warming your hand. Turn your hand in sunwise circles, and say:

   "God and Goddess, bring to me $500."

➢ **Seven Day Money Spell**

Ingredients:

- A green candle
- A white candle
- Two candleholders or dishes

- Abundance oil or Wealth oil: cedar, frankincense, and rose

- Matches

- A small, thin paintbrush

Instructions:

1. Do this spell on a waxing or full moon. Anoint both candles and place them approximately seven inches apart from each other and light them. Bring down the power of the moon, raising your arms to the ceiling and saying:

"Mother Goddess, grant me your powerful, lunar energy. Fill this circle with your light."

2. Imagine the lunar light filling your circle like rushing water. Drop your arms when the space is full.

3. Each time you say the following chant, move the white candle, representing yourself, one step closer to the green candle. Say this chant seven times:

"Riches and wealth, come to me,
by the power of three times three,
to bring harm to no one nor to bring harm to me,
Abundance is mine, so mote it be."

4. Allow the candles to burn for seven minutes, then snuff them out by pinching the flame. Burn them for seven minutes a day, for seven days. On the seventh day allow the candles to continue burning down until they're finished.

Spells for Love, Happiness, and Relationships

➢ The Heart of the Ocean Love Spell

Ingredients:

- A blue, green, or white bowl

- Seven seashells

- Seven pearls (you can buy a strand of pearls at a craft store—they can be freshwater or saltwater, either is fine for this purpose)

- Ocean sand (easy to find in the floral department of many large stores)

- A blue, green, or white candle

- Matches

- A dish or candleholder

- Pure Love oil: rose, sandalwood, jasmine

- A small, thin paintbrush

- Saltwater (you can make your own with collected rainwater and pink salt, use a teaspoon of salt in this case)

- A piece of green jade, or a moonstone

Instructions:

1. This is a spell if you believe that you are ready for a healthy, loving, long-term romantic relationship. You are ready to be open to receiving love as well as giving love, unconditionally. Perform this spell on a new, waxing, or full moon. Take time for this spell, do not rush through it. Have a soothing shower or relaxing bath before you begin.

2. Anoint the candle with the oil and light it. Pour the rainwater into the bowl, and slowly pour in the salt, stirring sunwise as you focus on your open, loving heart. Raise your arms toward the sky and feel the loving, peaceful energy of the moon pour down and fill your sacred circle. Once the energy glows the brightest, let your arms drop. It is time to begin.

3. Drop the gemstone into the bowl.

4. Pour the sand into the bowl so that it covers the bottom of the bowl but does not rise above the water. Say:

    "Life is change, like the shifting tides.

    I am ready for love."

5. Pick up one of the seashells, imagine yourself filling it with loving patience. Drop it into the water and say:

> "*Life is a test, and requires patience.*
> *I am ready for love.*"

6. Pick up a second seashell. Imagine filling it with laughter and delight. Drop it into the water and say:

> "*Life is fun, and filled with friendship.*
> *I am ready for love.*"

7. Pick up a third seashell, and imagine filling it with peaceful solitude. Drop it into the water and say:

> "*Life is sometimes a journey alone until we reunite again.*
> *I am ready for love.*"

8. Pick up a fourth shell and imagine filling it with passion. Picture embracing your true love, and if you're comfortable, picture kissing them. Drop the shell into the water and say:

> "*Life will make me hunger for the one I adore the most.*
> *I am ready for love.*"

9. Pick up a fifth shell, and imagine filling it with gentle calm. Picture holding hands with your true love, in silence, watching a sunset. Drop the shell into the water and say:

> "*Life is reflection, together with my equal in life.*
> *I am ready for love.*"

10. Pick up a sixth shell, and imagine filling it with strength. Imagine hearing words you do not like, and meeting those darker emotions with a renewed sense of love. Drop the shell into the water and say:

"Life is an occasional struggle, yet I rise to this with even greater love.

I am ready for love."

11. Pick up the last shell and hold it in your hands clasped. Imagine a lifetime in moving images, happy scenes, scenes of togetherness, scenes of disagreements with loving resolutions, scenes of travel, scenes of accomplishment. Say:

"Life is a winding road that I will walk together with my true love.

I am ready for love."

12. Drop the last shell into the water. With your hand, or with your wand, trace a sunwise circle above the bowl. Say:

"These ingredients I invest in thee, like all the treasures in the sea, to one day bless us, you and me, together in love, successfully."

13. Reach into the bowl and remove the stone you dropped in the beginning of the spell. Keep it on your altar or carry it with you as a beacon to your true love that they

easily find you in the world. Remember true love takes time. Allow the spell to send its message into the universe, and when the time is right, your true love will appear.

➢ **Attracting Love Sachet**

Ingredients:

- Lavender
- Red or pink rose petals
- A cinnamon stick
- Rosemary
- Yarrow
- Calendula
- Rue
- Lemongrass
- A small piece of paper
- A pencil
- A cloth pouch or bag, in red, orange, purple, or pink, long enough to hold a cinnamon stick

- Red string or yarn

- Three drops of Pure Love oil

Instructions:

1. In a bowl, mix the ingredients except for the cinnamon stick. On the slip of paper, write this sentence without lifting the pencil (don't worry if it looks sloppy, just do your best): True Love, come to me. Tightly roll the paper towards you. Place it against the cinnamon stick, and wrap the string or yarn around it tightly, three times. Say the Casting Words.

2. Place the herbs in the bowl into the pouch, carefully, then place the cinnamon stick wrapped with the paper. Add three drops of Pure Love oil and tie up the pouch.

3. Carry the pouch with you, or tie it to your bedpost for one lunar cycle.

➤ A Warm Heart in Winter Spell

Ingredients:

- Two pinecones

- Red string

- A fireplace or bonfire

Instructions:

1. Perform this spell on a waxing or full moon. Tie the pinecones together with the red string, and say "May I be united with my love by the next full moon." Say the Casting Words, then toss the pinecones into the fire to release the spell's energy into the universe.

➢ The Heart's Choice Divination Spell

Ingredients:

- Two onions
- Two pots and some potting soil
- A small, sharp knife
- Collected rainwater
- A pink candle
- A candleholder or a small dish
- Matches
- Pure Love oil
- A small, thin paintbrush

Instructions:

1. Do this on a new moon. After casting your circle, anoint the candle with the oil and light it. Take the knife and carefully inscribe the name of the two lovers you need guidance about—one in one onion, one in the other. As you carefully plant each onion, say the name of the lover in question.

2. Put one hand on each pot and call to the Goddess:

   "Wise and loving Goddess, my heart is confused.
   Help me know which lover I should choose.
   With the first that grows, I will know."

3. Allow the candle to burn down, and once it has, water the soil well, then place the two pots where they can get the most sun. Whichever onion sprouts first, that is the lover you should choose.

➤ **Rose Water Recipe**

Ingredients:

- Rose petals, enough to fill a mason jar
- Collected rain or river water

- Cheesecloth
- A pink candle
- Pure Love oil
- A small, thin paintbrush
- Matches
- A candleholder or small dish
- Pink and white quartz
- A teaspoon of honey
- Lemongrass
- Honeysuckle blossoms
- One mint leaf

Instructions:

1. Do this spell on a new or waxing moon and finish it on a full moon. Anoint and light the pink candle. Place the lemongrass, mint leaf, honeysuckle blossoms, white and pink quartz and rose petals into the mason jar then fill to the brim with the collected water. Seal the jar.

2. Draw down the power of the moon and let it fill your circle as you hold the jar in your hands. Open your eyes when you imagine the moon energy glowing bright.

Say:

"A gentle brew I make for you,
to heal the heart and bring love true."

3. Imagine the loving energy from your own heart pouring into the jar. Give it three, firm shakes, then set it beside the candle.

4. Once the moon is visible, place the jar in a windowsill or outside where it can bask in the moon's light. On the night of the full moon, return the jar to your sacred workspace or altar. Say:

"By the light of the Goddess moon,
I consecrate this spell to bring
true love soon."

5. Place it once again in the moonlight. The next day, carefully strain the rose water through a cheesecloth, setting the quartz stones aside to return to your altar for future use. Bottle the rose water to use in future love spells, to sprinkle on yourself before leaving the house if you seek true love, or to give as a gift to a friend who is looking for true love.

➢ Union of Love Spell Bag

Ingredients:

- White bag
- Apple peel
- Beeswax
- Wine cork
- White lily petals

Instructions:

1. Mix the ingredients together and place it into the bag. This should be used as a part of a handfasting ceremony to make sure that the union is blessed with happiness and love.

➢ A Spell to Strengthen Unconditional Love

Ingredients:

- A black, pink, and white candle
- Sacred Oil blend: myrrh, frankincense, patchouli
- A small, thin paintbrush

- Three small dishes or candleholders
- Matches
- Pink salt
- Rose incense

Instructions:

1. After you cast your circle, anoint all three candles and set the pink candle in between the black and the white candles. Light them, then light the incense.

2. Draw a figure eight, beginning with the black candle, so that it crosses over the pink candle and encircles the black and white candles. Say:

"Balance divine, yours and mine
never-ending, not pretending
strong and true, me and you
in this love, pure and fine."

3. Set the incense stick to burn in a holder, watch the smoke drift over the candles' flames as you imagine your love strengthening, becoming more balanced and stable. When you are ready, open the circle and allow the candles to burn down.

➤ **Spell for Welcoming the Start of a Relationship**

If you're an intuitive person, you've almost certainly been in this situation at least once: you meet someone new, notice a spark between the two of you, and can just tell that something is about to happen.

For most of us, this sets in motion a period of heightened awareness, a bit (or a lot!) of fantasizing about the other person, butterflies in the stomach, and many other signs and symptoms of an oncoming romantic relationship.

This period of time can be fun, but also truly challenging, especially when you just really want to know how it's all going to turn out. It can be very tempting to try to help things along with a little magick.

The less enlightened magical practitioners among us might simply cast a spell to make sure that the initial spark turns into an exciting romance. However, the all-important principle of "harm none" comes into play here.

It is actually harmful to interfere with someone else's free will by casting love spells that attempt to control how they feel. If you think about it, you probably wouldn't want the same done to you!

What's more, relationships that arise from successful manipulative love spells are doomed to fall apart sooner or later, since the feelings they are based on are not true and pure. Who wants to deal with the drama of a magically manipulated relationship when authentic, healthy and honest relationships are so much better?

This spell provides an alternative method for making the most of the spark you've recently discovered, without getting into less-than-ethical territory. The intention is to declare to the Universe that 1) you are receptive and ready for a romantic relationship, and 2) you desire that the connection with this new person manifests according to the highest good for all involved.

Of course, this means that you're open to the possibility that this spark will not evolve into a relationship. But since welcoming the start of a relationship is the focus of this spell, you are still setting an intention to find new romance. You never know—it could be that this new person actually ends up introducing you to your next love, who ignites an even bigger spark! The point is to focus on what you want, rather than who you want, and let the Universe take care of the details.

Ingredients:

- 3 sprigs of basil

- 1 pink ribbon

- Small vase

- Cup of water

Instructions:

1. Visualize yourself confident and at ease around the person with whom you are hoping to start a relationship. Imagine the two of you in as much detail as possible, sitting side by side in a sunny location.

2. Breathe deeply and summon a feeling of peace and ease around this person.

3. Pour water from the cup into the vase.

4. Now take one sprig of basil and place it into the vase and say: *"My authentic self-shines through in this new connection."*

5. Place the second sprig of basil in the vase and say: *"My authentic self resonates with the authentic self of the one I love."*

6. Place the final sprig of basil in the vase and say: *"This new connection serves the highest good of all involved."*

7. Now, wrap the pink ribbon around the three sprigs of basil.

8. Spend a few moments imagining how you want to feel in your next relationship, but keep the focus on yourself, rather than on the person you're hoping to be with.

9. Hold the vase in your hands and say: *"I welcome the start of this new relationship, for the good of all and harm to none."*

10. Make sure the vase has plenty of fresh water each day.

11. When the sprigs begin to droop or turn brown, take them outside and scatter them over the Earth.

Spells for Healing and Wellness

➢ White Light Healing Spell

Ingredients:

- A wall mirror
- A white pillar candle
- A dish or candleholder
- Matches
- Five white quartz pieces

Instructions:

1. You can do this spell at any time. The mirror doesn't have to be particularly large, just big enough that when you set it on the floor, against a wall, you can see your reflection if you're seated in front of it.

2. Place the mirror against a wall. Place the dish in front of it and set the candle on the dish; light the candle. Sit comfortably in front of the candle. Place the five quartz pieces around you on the floor so that you are surrounded by them. Allow your gaze to shift out of focus and watch your reflection in the mirror bathed in the light of the candle. Take deep, even breaths from your

center—your shoulders should not move up and down, your belly should move in and out. Sit with good posture.

3. See the white, healing light combine with the natural aura of your body. Picture the white light brightening your aura, drawing out any negativity of illness from your body. Feel the healing, cool, white light comfort your body. Watch the new, white aura shimmer and glow. Stay in this state of mind for as long as it's comfortable.

4. When you are done, extinguish the candle by pinching the flame, and return the mirror to its place. You can do this as a simple meditation, or cast a circle to do it as a magical affirmation.

➤ **Winter Healing Salve**

Ingredients:

- 15 to 20 drops grapefruit oil
- One-ounce beeswax
- One-part dried rose
- Two parts dried calendula
- One-part lavender

- One cup coconut oil

Instructions:

1. Using a double boiler; put all ingredients into the top pot or bowl except beeswax. Bring the water in the bottom pot to a boil. Once boiling, turn the stove down and simmer to allow the oils and herbs to infuse for at least an hour. Make sure you don't get water into the herbal infusion.

2. When the infusion is made, take off the heat and place to the side. Put three layers of cheesecloth on top of a bowl or funnel. Pour the oils over the cheesecloth to keep the oil and herbs separated. When you have completely drained the oil, gather the cheesecloth with dry hands that are clean and squeeze all the oil out.

3. Put the shaved beeswax into a pan on low heat, pour the infused oils you just made over top and allow to melt together. When the oil and beeswax have combined, pour into jars. Put into the refrigerator for 15 minutes to see how solid your salve will get. If you use less beeswax, you will have creamier salve. Using more beeswax will make a harder salve.

➢ **<u>Calming Waters Spell</u>**

Ingredients:

- A blue candle or bouquet of blue or white flowers

Instructions:

1. This is a spell that can be done in several places. You can perform it in the bathtub in your home, or in a lake, creek, river, or in the ocean. You don't need any spell ingredients but a candle for focus or a gift of flowers, and yourself, a body of water, and the elementals of water.

2. If taking a bath, cast a circle and light the candle for divine focus. If bathing in a natural body of water, leave the bouquet of flowers by the shore as thanks to the elementals of water.

3. This spell should be done on a dark or waning moon. Once submerged in the water, relax, take deep breaths. You can be standing or floating, or if in the bathtub, laying down. Once you've found that your mind is in a calm, healing place, say these words:

"Elementals of water, guardians of the rain
Elementals of water, fair spirits of the stream,
Elementals of water, children of Yemaya,

Elementals of water, shepherds of the sea,

Help me release all the worry, the stress,

the negative thoughts that trouble me.

Here in your safe, calming currents, I swim peacefully."

4. Feel the gentle embrace of the water, the push and pull of currents if you are in a natural body of water. Feel the cool, healing of the goddess and her elementals, surrounding you, comforting you, healing your pains, and worries. Remember that the goddess can handle all of the pain you release to her, she is infinite. Allow the stress to be taken from you. You are a child of the Goddess, and she is a loving mother to all her children.

5. Take some of the water and wet the top of your head with it, thus anointing yourself. Feel the coolness of the water refresh your third eye and your crown chakra.

6. When you are ready, leave the water and allow the air to dry you, or pat yourself dry—do not wipe the healing water away.

➤ **Healing Candle Spell**

Ingredients:

- A blue, white, or yellow candle

- Healing Oil: angelica, comfrey, and chamomile
- A small, thin paintbrush
- A dish or candleholder
- An incense holder
- A small knife, or screw

Instructions:

1. Cast your circle and anoint the candle. With the small knife or screw tip, carve the words "heal me" in both sides of the candle, then light the candle. Light the incense and allow the smoke to drift across the candle flame, filling the room with a healing scent. (Place the incense far enough away from you so that you are not directly breathing the line of smoke). Allow your mind to drift into an alpha state: your gaze is out of focus, your mind is calm, thoughts are discarded as they enter the space of your mind. As the candle burns, know that you are in the right place for healing of the spirit, mind, body, and soul. Feel the benevolent energy fill your circle. Feel the power of the universe filling your circle with healing light.

2. When you are ready, open the circle and ground. Allow the candle and incense to burn down.

➤ Earth Cord Spell

This spell is a simple but powerfully effective one. On a full moon, find space to work unbothered and unobserved out of doors. Stand barefoot if you can but if the weather is cold or the ground too rough, shoes are fine.

Cast the circle around you and look up to the sky. Call the power of the sun or the moon into your circle, silently or out loud, and feel the energy of the universe slowly fill your sacred space until the space is completely filled with divine power.

Stand straight, with good posture, and breathe deeply, keeping your arms relaxed at your sides. Imagine a silver cord of energy going from your solar plexus, to your belly, down through your feet and deep into the Earth. Feel the exchange of energy from your body to the body of the goddess. With each breath, feel the healing coming up from the ground into your body.

At the same time, feel the negativity, stress, weariness, and worry leave your body through the silver cord, to be carried down into the Earth where it will be dissipated and cleansed, and renewed as bright, healing energy. Stay in this stance for as long as you need, allowing the goddess to heal your body, heart, and spirit.

➢ **Burying a Bad Habit Healing Spell**

Ingredients:

- An egg
- A brown candle
- Tibetan healing incense
- Healing Oil
- A small, thin paintbrush
- A small dish or candleholder
- A shovel
- A brown paper bag
- A pencil

Instructions:

1. On a dark or waning moon, prepare your body first by bathing or showering. Cast your circle, and anoint the candle with Healing Oil. Light the candle as well as the

Tibetan healing incense. Raise your hands to the sky and ask the God and Goddess to grace your sacred circle with their healing energy. Imagine the circle filling with divine energy, and open your eyes when the energy glows the brightest.

2. Write on the paper bag the habit you wish to get rid of; be specific and detailed. Next, take the egg, and say:

"Little egg, a vehicle be
to remove the habit which vexes me,
so that I may see that habit undone
by the rise and set of the burning sun."

3. Now, take the egg, and slowly and gently rub it against you (careful not to break it!), starting with the top of your head, down to your face and neck, your shoulders and arms, your chest, ribs, and stomach, your lower back and buttocks, each leg and ankle, down to your feet and out over your toes. Place the egg carefully in the brown paper bag, and fold the bag so that it forms a small package. Move this package carefully and slowly, widdershins (counterclockwise), above the candle, careful not to get so close that the bag begins to burn. Say the Casting Words.

4. Open the circle and allow the candle and the incense to burn down while you go outside with the parcel and a shovel. Dig a small hole and bury the egg in the paper bag, and forget about it. In 24 hours, your bad habit should begin to dissipate, until it vanishes forever.

➢ Sunrise Affirmation Spell

Perform this spell on a waxing, new, or full moon. Research at what time the sun will rise at your location. Make sure you get plenty of sleep the night before this spell. Set your alarm to wake you up with enough time to shower, drink some water, and feel refreshed and ready.

Stand facing East, preferably outdoors, but in front of an east-facing window is also permitted. As the sun rises, say:

"Like the sun,
each day I rise,
I will not stop,
nor compromise.
With each breathe,
I live and grow,
I will not stop,
onward, I go."

Feel the energy of the rising sun imbue you with strength, hope, and vitality. Make a commitment to do a sunrise affirmation once a month. The sunrise is a magical time, and being awake during it can be very healing for anyone, but especially those in the creative or healing arts. The dawn is a great source of inspiration, and of hope.

Spells for The Home and Garden

➢ House Blessings Jar

Ingredients:

- A mason jar

- Collected water such as rainwater or water from a river

- An Amethyst, white quartz, jade, and sunstone

- Vervain

- Comfrey

- Rosemary

- Alfalfa

- Juniper berries

- Any wildflowers that are growing on the property, such as dandelions

- Honey

- Some soil from outside the property, or the nearest park if the home is an apartment

- A coin of each denomination, including a silver dollar

- Sage, Palo Santo, rosemary, or holy water (collected water and salt)

- Sweet incense

- A yellow or green candle

- Matches

Instructions:

1. Perform this spell on a new, waxing, or full moon. Especially powerful when performed on a blue moon (a second full moon in a month). Cast your circle around the entire home: if this is a house, you can walk around the outside of the house, or walk from room to room going north, east, south, then west.

2. Next, purge any negativity from the rooms using sage, Palo Santo wood, rosemary, or holy water. The holy water should be sprinkled in each room, walking widdershins about each room, all other ingredients should be lit so they smoke, and by holding them, making widdershins hand motions with the smoke in each room.

3. When you are finished cleansing the house, open the windows and doors, keeping an eye on small children and pets.

4. After a few minutes, close the windows and doors, and walk the house with the sweet incense, making sunwise hand movements to bless each room.

5. Finally, return to your altar and begin assembling the jar. Add the ingredients: soil and stones first, then coins, honey (save a little bit of the honey to anoint the candle), herbs, wildflowers, and last, water. Seal the jar.

6. Melt the bottom of the candle to affix it to the lid of the mason jar. Anoint the candle with the remaining honey, then light the candle.

Say:

"Bless this house,
this cozy home,
a place of peace,
back home to come,
let good luck grow
and bless these rooms,
let happiness flow,
often and soon,

*peace to this home,
and who dwell within,
where love and light,
come pouring in,
by day and night,
through thick and thin,
this house is blessed,
and all within."*

7. Allow the candle to burn down, and open the circle. Light another candle on the jar whenever you wish to reactivate it, on a full or new moon, reciting the words.

➢ Vacuum Your Home to Purification Spell Bag

Ingredients:

- Bag of any color
- Juniper sprigs
- Bay leaves
- Rosemary sprigs
- Sage leaves

Instructions:

1. Mix all of the herbs together and place into the bag. Tie the bag up and then place it in your vacuum. This can be in the bag or next to the filter. This will help to purify your home every time you vacuum and it will also give you a magical scent as you do so.

➤ House Cleansing Ritual

Ingredients:

- A household broom or magick besom
- Florida or holy water
- Kosher salt and pepper

Instructions:

1. On a dark or waxing moon, and after securing all pets and small children, open the exterior doors of your house. Sprinkle Florida water or holy water lightly on the floor in front of you, and sweep it towards the doors, beginning in the center of the house. You can put the water in a spray bottle to lightly mist the floors, especially if there is carpet.

2. Do this in each room until you're in the rooms that lead to the outside, and continue sweeping until you reach the thresholds. Sprinkle a small amount of salt and pepper on the thresholds, then sweep the water, salt and pepper outside, taking with it all the negative energy that's been tracked in.

3. Take care to thoroughly sweep the salt and pepper so nobody tracks it back in, and pets don't carry it on their paws. Another approach is to sew small cloth packets of salt and pepper mixture and place these on the thresholds to ceremoniously collect the negative energy to sweep out of the house.

➤ Garden Blessing Spell

Ingredients:

- White quartz flakes

Instructions:

1. Do this spell on a new, waxing, or full moon. It is best done in the morning or in the evening, whenever your garden is in shade and when you typically water your plants. At your altar, set a pitcher of water and light a white candle. Cast your circle and call down the energies

of the sun and the moon, and ask them to fill the water with their healing light. Open the circle and carry your pitcher out to the garden, bringing with you a pocket of quartz flakes. Water your plants as you would, then take each flake and set it a couple of inches into the soil among your plants, pouring the blessed water on top of it as you work. When you are finished, say:

"With blessings of the moon and sun,
my garden grows, one by one."

Spells for Protection

➢ Front Door Protection Charm

Ingredients:

- A clove of garlic
- Red cloth bag
- Three needles or pins
- Rosemary
- Sage
- Crown of Success oil or Dragon's Blood oil
- African violet petals
- Twine
- Scissors

Instructions:

1. On a Tuesday or Saturday of a dark or waning moon, cast your circle and press the pins carefully through the clove of garlic. Carefully place the garlic into the cloth bag, and add to this the rosemary, sage, garlic, African violet petals, and six drops of oil. Close the bag and wrap it

three times in twine, making a loop from which you can hang the bag on or near the front door.

2. Hold the bag towards the moon, and say:

"From this moment, from this hour,

trouble keep far from my door,

I use my cunning and my power,

to keep that which would harm me far away, forevermore."

3. Say the Casting Words. Affix the bag to the front door, or close to it. Recharge it twice a year with six additional drops of oil, and repeat the incantation.

Witch's Jar

Ingredients:

- A mason jar or any household food jar that once held something sour, such as pickles, or sauerkraut

- A collection of rusted, metal objects: screws, nails, hooks, etc.

- Broken glass (not mirrors)

- Vinegar

- A lock of your own hair, and some of your fingernail clippings

- A black candle

- Matches

- A candleholder or small plate

Instructions:

1. A witch's jar performs a simple function. Interestingly, it was once believed that one could trap a witch within such a jar—today, however, the witch's jar is a way to trap negativity, ill will, and animosity that's directed towards you.

2. On a dark or waning moon, light the black candle and place everything from the list inside the jar. Seal the jar and drip some of the wax from the candle on the lid, and say:

   "All that serves to harm me, come inside this jar and stay."

3. Snuff out the candle and take the jar outside to bury it. Some witches make four jars in total, one for each side of the house. If you rent or live in an apartment or any home without a yard, you can place the witch's jar in a

pot of gardening soil. You can even place a live plant in the pot—perfect camouflage for your jar!

➢ Four Corners House Protection Spell

Ingredients:

- Four black cloth bags
- Four small, circular mirrors
- Twine
- Kosher salt
- Black peppercorns

Instructions:

1. Remember that black is an important color in protection magick and should not be considered "evil" or "dark." Just as the darkness of night protects animals who need protection against predators so we do sometimes use the color black to keep us hidden from our enemies.

2. Cast a circle on a dark or waning moon. Place inside each cloth bag a mirror, a pinch of kosher salt and a pinch of black peppercorns. Tie up the bags and bind them each

three times with twine, making a loop in one of the binds so the bag can be hung, if you choose. Hold each bag in your hand and say for each one:

"Invisible to misfortune,
my home remains a safe haven.
Invisible to trouble,
my home remains safe,
behind a black wing, like the raven."

3. Place one bag on each side of your house. You can hang it from a window or place it on the ground, whichever you prefer.

➢ **Invisible from Harm Personal Protection Spell**

Ingredients:

- A fresh basil leaf
- A dime
- A piece of onyx
- White yarn, or any thick, white thread.
- Crown of Success oil

- A small, sharp knife or boline
- A black candle
- A white candle
- Two candleholders or two small dishes
- Matches

Instructions:

1. On a dark, new, or waning moon, cast your circle. Carefully carve the words "Trouble do not see me" on each candle. Place the candles on your altar, one candle to each side of you, and the ingredients in the middle. Take the basil leaf and place the dime upon it, then the piece of onyx upon that. Carefully wrap the three items together with the yarn or thread, concentrating on being able to walk about in the world, free from harm, not troubled by others. When you are finished, tie three knots while you say:

   "Trouble do not see me." Say the Casting Words.

2. Carry this charm in your pocket, backpack, briefcase or purse to keep harm from finding you.

➢ Quit a Bad Habit Spell Bag

Ingredients:

- White or black bag
- Pinch of cayenne
- Eucalyptus
- Cactus needles

Instructions:

1. Mix all of the ingredients in the bag and tie it closed. Keep the bag with you to help you get rid of a bad habit.

➢ Restful Sleep Spell Bag

Ingredients:

- White bag
- Jasmine flowers
- Chamomile heads
- Dried lavender

Instructions:

1. Mix all of the ingredients in the bag and tie it up. Tuck into your pillow to help promote restful sleep and pleasant dreams.

Springtime Blessings Spell Bag

Ingredients:

- Bag of any color
- Pen or pencil
- Paper

Instructions:

1. Assortment of dried sage, moss, dried clover, dried chamomile, tarragon, thyme, dried rosebuds, and lavender

2. Write down at least five blessings in your life on the piece of paper and tear it into small pieces and add them to the bag. Add in your choice of the above herbs into the bag. Tie up the bag and them place it in some place that is safe to keep your blessings close and to attract more blessings.

➤ Travel Protection Spell Bag

Ingredients:

- Bag of any color
- Oak leaves
- Chamomile heads

Instructions:

1. Quince seeds, fresh mugwort, comfrey, bergamot tea leaves – optional

2. Add the oak leaves and chamomile heads in a bag and ask the Goddess Fortuna Redux, or any other Goddess of good fortune when traveling, for protection and a watchful eye. If you are using the option herbs, mix them in the bag as well. Keep the spell bag hanging from your rearview mirror, tucked into your luggage, or you can carry it in your purse.

➤ Safe Journeys Spell

Ingredients:

- A white rose (only the flower, removes the stem)

- A white feather
- A white cloth bag
- A lodestone
- Nag champa incense
- Matches

Instructions:

1. A lodestone can be purchased in a pagan supplies shop or online. Do this spell during any lunar phase but the dark moon. After you cast your circle, light the incense. Hold the white rose blossom and circle it sunwise with the incense, then place it in the bag. Do the same for the white feather, and for the lodestone. Tie up the bag and hold it up, then circle it three more times with the incense. Say:

   "May this blessed charm, filled with light,
   bring safe travels, day and night."

2. You can make this charm for a loved one or friend who's planning on traveling, or for yourself before a trip. You can also keep it in your car to keep you safe while you drive on daily errands or your commute.

3. As with all charms, you can recharge this one under a full moon when you feel the need to.

➢ **Invisible Ward Spell**

Ingredients:

- Kosher salt
- Collected water, such as rainwater or river water.
- Obsidian
- A black candle
- Crown of Success oil
- A small, thin paintbrush
- A small glass, or your cauldron or cup
- A small knife or your boline

Instructions:

1. Do this spell under a dark moon. After you cast the circle, carve a figure eight symbol in the black candle, and anoint it with the Crown of Success oil. Fill the container you've chosen to use with the collected water, then add a

teaspoon of salt. Take the piece of obsidian, and make a figure eight symbol in the air directly above the container of water.

Say:

"Infinity circles, day and night,
charge this water
to keep me out of sight."

2. Drop the obsidian into the water. Place the cup outside or in the windowsill to soak up the dark moon's energy. Allow the candle to burn down.

3. Keep the invisibility water in a bottle or spill-proof container. When you want to use it, either paint a small figure eight on your body (good places are your chest or stomach, anywhere where the salt residue won't be seen), or on your front door, or vehicle, depending upon the context of your need for invisibility.

Spells for Luck

➤ Birthday Blessings Spell

Ingredients:

- A tall white pillar or taper candle
- A small, sharp knife or your boline
- Altar oil: frankincense, rose, lemongrass
- Florida water
- A small, thin paintbrush
- A small dish or candleholder
- Matches

Instructions:

1. Do this spell on your birthday, regardless of lunar phase. If it occurs on a waning moon, be prepared for unnecessary or harmful things to begin to move out of your life, so that the happiness can move in.

2. Cast your circle and carefully carve two-word wishes into the candle, such as: "gentle love," "happy home," or "satisfying work." Use your imagination and carve what you truly want for the coming year. Anoint the candle

with the altar oil. Light the candle. Take the Florida water and place a small amount on the top of your head, your forehead, the back of your neck, and on the back of your hands.

3. Gaze at the candle's flame, and imagine scenes in which the things you've carved occur, or could occur. Take deep, calming breaths from your stomach, and sit with a straight posture. Take some time in this sacred space, breathing, and meditating on the happy year you have in front of you. Even if you've recently suffered a trauma or loss, imagine the year bringing you healing, and solace from the pain.

4. When you are ready, open the circle and ground, but allow the candle to burn down on its own.

➢ **Nutmeg Spell**

Ingredients:

- A whole nutmeg
- Frankincense oil
- A dollar bill
- Red string or yarn

Instructions:

1. Do this spell on a full moon. Cast your circle, and hold the nutmeg in your hand as you call upon the energy of the moon to fill your sacred spice with lunar energy. Dab a bit of frankincense oil on the nutmeg, then wrap it in the dollar bill. Next, bind the wrapped nutmeg in red string, seven times. Tie the knot three times, and say:

   "Lucky charm, bold and bright,
   bring me luck both day and night."

2. Allow the charm to bask in the light of the full moon, then carry it on your person, bag, car, or altar.

➢ Seven Berries Spell

Ingredients:

- Seven juniper berries
- A small green or white bag

Instructions:

1. Begin this spell on a Sunday during a waxing moon—making sure that the full moon is at least seven days away. Cast your circle and place the juniper berries in the

bag. Hold it in your hands and allow the power of the sun and the moon to fill your circle, and charge the berries.

2. Carry the berries on you for seven days. After that, discard them in running water. You will then have a very lucky week.

Spell for Attracting Money into Your Life

Sometimes, no matter how well we plan, emergencies happen and ends don't quite meet. Unexpected medical costs, family emergencies, a change in employment... life can definitely throw the occasional wrench in our finances!

This simple spell helps boost your money-attracting powers to smooth out any financial wrinkles caused by unexpected events, but it's useful for any time you feel you need a little bit of extra cash. The basil leaf, with its money-attracting energies, lends its power to your personal energy.

The work begins with a quick clearing of the mind, allowing any negative thoughts that may be lurking there to be released so that they don't block your intentions from manifesting. Of course, this is a good step to take before working any magick, but it's specifically called for here in case you're actively worrying about the situation at hand, which would definitely interfere with the energy of the spell.

Ingredients:

- 1 fresh basil leaf
- 1 green candle
- Purse or wallet

Instructions:

1. Begin by taking three deep breaths. Inhale slowly through your nose, and exhale fully, releasing any negative thoughts or emotions.

2. Light the candle and place your purse or wallet in front of you on your altar or workspace.

3. Hold the basil leaf between your palms and visualize a green light surrounding your purse or wallet. Let the green light wash over you as well.

4. Imagine your purse or wallet full of money. See yourself opening your purse or wallet to find it full of coins and bills. When you have this image firmly in your mind, say the following (or similar) words:

"Sweet basil, with energy divine,
bring the money I need to me, right on time."

5. Now, open your purse or wallet and gently place the basil leaf inside.

6. Gently extinguish the candle by waving your hand over it or using a candle snuffer. You can reuse the candle for general atmospheric lighting, or to repeat this specific spell at a later date.

7. Let the leaf remain in your purse or wallet for up to one week.

8. Be careful not to stress about how the money will show up in your life, as this interferes with the manifestation. Let the Universe sort out the "how" for you!

➢ **Help with Legal Issues Spell**

Ingredients:

- Red jasper
- Hematite
- Small white cloth bag
- High John the Conqueror root
- Success oil: basil, myrrh, dragon's blood, rosemary
- Small, thin paintbrush
- The Justice tarot card
- The World tarot card
- The Empress tarot card
- A small, yellow candle

- Matches

- A candleholder or small dish

- A red apple

Instructions:

1. Do this spell on a waxing or full moon, on a Monday or a Friday. Before you begin, thoroughly cleanse yourself both physically and spiritually. Smudge your altar space and tools.

2. Anoint the candle and light it. Allow its warm glow to soothe your anxiety about the upcoming court case or legal issue.

3. Take the High John root, which can be purchased online or in a magical supply store, and consecrate it with the success oil. Hold it to your forehead and say:

   "Justice be gentle, and favor me,
   Empress be loving, and comfort me,
   World be open for me to journey,
   may things go my way, successfully."

4. Place the High John root in the bag. Stand the three cards up behind the candle or on the altar so you can gaze at them. Take the red jasper in your left hand, the hematite in your right, and look at the cards, one at a time, as you repeat:

"Justice be gentle, and favor me,
Empress be loving, and comfort me,
World be open for me to journey,
may things go my way, successfully."

5. Place the jasper and hematite in the bag and tie it securely. Now take the Justice card and place it on top of the bag. Say:

"Justice, find all in favor of me that I will be successful in my endeavors." Return that card to the altar.

Take the Empress card and place it on top of the bag. Say:

"Empress, mother goddess, soothe my fears and let those who I deal with have mercy on me." Return that card to the altar.

Take the World card and place it on top of the bag. Say:

"Universe, enable it so that I keep my liberty and dignity, and am allowed to walk my path uninhibited in this World." Return that card to the altar.

6. When you are finished, allow the candle to burn down. Take the remaining wax and the apple and place in a crossroads at your earliest convenience.

Chapter 6: Application of wicca spells in everyday life

For the beginner, practicing and evolving your understanding of what makes a good spell and what makes good practice can be a difficult journey. With mixed results at first and a steep learning curve, it would be disingenuous to suggest that perfecting the art of Wicca is as simple as reading out the words in a book. Rather, those who dedicate themselves to learning the best practices and those who strive to extend their knowledge will inevitably see the best results.

There different ways in which the wicca spells can be applied in our everyday life. Such spells include the ones listed below:

- Love Spells
- An enchantment for healing fractured relationships
- Increasing libido with a Wiccan spell

- A spell to conjure romantic interest
- Using tarot to locate a soul mate
- Winning another's love with an incantation
- Wealth spells
- A simple gambling spell
- Simple Wiccan Money Spell
- A spell for bringing success to your workplace
- Protective spells
- Guarding against negative spirits
- Cleansing
- Communication
- An incantation for the banishment of spirits
- General tips and tricks for protection using Wicca
- Healing spells
- A spell for healing
- A cleansing ritual with the power to heal

- A spell for the release of negativity
- A healing spell that uses light
- An incantation for self-healing
- Bringing harmony and peace to an infected space
- Distance Healing Spell
- Divination spells
- The construction of a scrying mirror
- Candle spells

Conclusion

Herbal magick is one of the most practical ways for you to begin creating magick and casting spells in a very practical way. Many witches use herbal magick as a way to have a holistic approach to healing through magick, as herbs heal on an emotional, mental, spiritual, and physical level. Modern science has proven the power of magical healing herbs, making them an excellent contender when it comes to casting practical magick.

I hope that through reading this book, you feel confident in having your magical needs met through the art of herbal magick. There is a lot to learn, and it is truly important that you learn the foundation as deeply as you learn the rest. Many Wiccans get excited to begin spellcasting and forget that a large part of the magick comes from within, meaning that they need to have a full understanding of the magick that they are accessing.

Equipping yourself with this knowledge ensures that you are practicing your magical rituals in a way that is deeply grounded and sacred, allowing you to fully harness the energy. Overlooking just how deep and sacred each ritual is can lead to lower quality spells and can potentially disrupt your results.

You might find that your spells are not as powerful, or that you have strange or unwanted outcomes because you are not honoring the sacred power of the magick enough. Learning the full depth of magick and all of the power that comes with it ensures that you are prepared to harness that power and use it in the right way to ensure the highest good of everyone is met with every spell that you do.

As you go forward, I encourage you to discover where you can source high-quality herbs from so that you can begin casting herbal spells on your own. This way, you can start harnessing the real power of the entirety of existence through your magick. Remember, plants are connected into all of the elements, making them extremely powerful. Using just one plant gives you the power of water, fire, earth, and air all in one, plus the properties of that particular plant. Herbal magick truly is a powerfully holistic and practical magick source that will earn you plenty of power in exchange!

Thanks for choosing this book! If you enjoyed it, let me know what you think and leave me a quick review on Amazon, I'd be really happy, thanks!

Wicca Moon Magic

*How does the Moon Affect Nature, Animals and People?
Find out How to Understand Moon's Magical Properties According to
the Philosophy of Wicca, With Rituals and Spells*

Justine J. Scott

Introduction

Congratulations on purchasing *Wicca Moon Magic* and thank you for doing so.

The following chapters will discuss the basics of Wicca and its connection to the Moon. They will also cover the way the Moon moves, how these changes affect its connection to Wicca, and the history of Moon worship in the British Isles. Finally, this book will also provide several rituals based on the Moon and discuss how to tailor your magical practice to align with the Moon's energies.

There are plenty of books on this subject on the market, so thanks again for choosing this one! Every effort was made to ensure it is full of as much useful information as possible and I would be really happy if you left me a quick review on Amazon. Enjoy the reading!

Chapter 1: Wicca and the Moon

To understand Wiccan Moon Magic, one must first understand Wicca. At its core, it is an earth-based religion that worships nature alongside both a Goddess and a God. Wiccans believe all thing in nature are filled with magic and Divine power. Every tree, rock, star, and drop of water are part of the Divine, as are humans and animals. But in all the natural world, nothing holds as much Divine energy as both the Sun and the Moon.

Wiccans view the Sun as the embodiment of their God. It does not matter what name they apply to Him or what form He takes. The Sun is His emblem. It shines with His light and brings the heat of His energy into our lives.

The Moon is the opposite side of the coin. She represents the Goddess and Her calm, soothing energy. As the Moon waxes and wanes, it represents different aspects of the Goddess. And this is because the Wiccan Goddess has three aspects: The Maiden, The Mother, and the Crone.

These three aspects – which are referred to as the Triple Goddess or the Three-Faced Goddess when spoken of collectively – are a common motif in Wiccan practices. She is represented in everything from the phase of the Moon to the changing of the seasons.

But the Moon and the Triple Goddess are far more than just representations. Many Wiccan rituals call on the power the Goddess and the Moon. Female practitioners perform rites to connect with the Moon's energy. And all Wiccans, no matter their gender, incorporate the Moon and Her energy into spells and rituals.

Wiccans seek balance in all things. Light to dark, warm to cold, life to death. But even though they seek balance, the Moon is such a prevalent symbol that it appears much more often than the Sun. Triple Goddess pendants are one of the most identifiable Wiccan icons.

The History of Moon Worship

The practice of Moon worship goes back much further than the current incarnation of Wicca. Wicca, as it stands today, was created in 1954 by Gerald Gardner. And though Gardner created the modern Wiccan religion, he rooted it in English and

Irish beliefs that predated the presence of Christians on either island.

Moon worship has existed across cultures and continents for millennia. It has likely existed since humans first looked up at the Moon and felt the same awe that people still feel when they gaze up at Her today. But Gardner modeled Wicca largely on the practices of the ancient English, Welsh, Scottish, and Irish. This makes sense, given that Gardner himself was British.

Unfortunately, many of the pre-Christian religious rites in both Britain and Ireland have been lost over time. This was, in part, due to intentional action by Christian conquerors that invaded the islands long ago. Many pre-Christian traditions were seen as threats to the power of the Catholic church. In order to remove the threat, Catholic conquerors outlawed most of the practices.

This was not restricted to Britain and Ireland, of course. It was the standard practice of the day. As Bishop Elegius of Noyon, in what is now present-day Western Europe said in a sermon, "Let no Christian take note... of the Moon, before commencing any work." Elegius went on to say that people should no longer "shout at eclipses" nor refer to the Sun and Moon as Lords or make oaths using their names.

Elegius railed against many things in that same sermon. But none appeared as often or in as many different contexts, than the Moon. Ancient Celts even dedicated an entire festival to the power of the Moon, known as Samhain. It was held at the beginning of November, around what is now All Saint's Day for many people. Ancient Celts would light bonfires and pour out offerings to spirits and gods so that evil would pass the village by during the coming winter.

Samhain was also the night when the spirits of the dead rose from their graves to visit the living. Plates of food were set out for these lost loved ones. And, in some cases, people used the thin veil between the living and the dead to communicate with those that had passed on.

The Sun also had its own holiday, known as Beltaine or Bel-Tane. These two holidays were the largest in any given year. They were so important to ancient Celts that blessings were often phrased as "the blessing of Bel-Tane and Samhain." Which, to worshipers, meant the same thing as saying "the blessing of the Sun and the Moon."

Gardner adapted all of this into the Wiccan religion. Both Samhain and Beltaine appear on the Wiccan Wheel of the Year. This Wheel marks all eight major holidays of the religion. And, even to this day, Samhain is one of the largest and most widely celebrated.

The Moon and the Goddess

Wiccans seek balance, this is true. But they also understand that change is inevitable. Hours, days, and seasons all spin on regardless of what humans do. Rather than rebel against this, Wiccans try to move with the flow of change and find their balance in the change. They try to celebrate it. And this is part of why the Triple Goddess and her connection to the phases of the Moon are so important to Wiccans.

Each face of the Triple Goddess is reflected in the phases of the Moon. The Moon's fourth phase, known as either the New Moon or the Dark Moon, represents the absence of the Goddess. And just as each phase relates to an aspect of the Goddess, each phase also brings a different kind of energy that practitioners use in their spells and rituals.

Because the Moon's phases run on cycles, it is hard to say which is the Moon's "first" phase. But many Wiccans start with the waxing Moon, since it is connected to the Goddess' Maiden aspect. The Maiden Goddess represents all new growth. She guards newborns regardless if they're plant, animal, or human.

And She watches over all new endeavors. It doesn't matter if the new venture is a business plan, a relationship, or a piece of art. The Maiden looks over the fresh wellspring of energy that guides nearly every new venture.

The Maiden also represents the eager vitality of youth. Giddy energy, the promise of growth, and abundant optimism are all Her trademarks. And if practitioners want to bring this energy into their spells, they should aim for the Moon's waxing phase. Spells can be cast any time while the Moon is waxing to receive the Maiden Goddess' energy. Any time, that is, other than the day before the full Moon. That day – as well as the day of the full Moon and the day after – belong to the Mother Goddess.

Unlike the Maiden, the Mother Goddess has only a few short days to bestow her energy on Wiccan magical workings. But what She is not given in time, she more than makes up for in the abundance of Her energy. The Mother Goddess is the most fertile face of the Triple Goddess. To Wiccans, the fullness of the Moon represents the fullness of a pregnant belly.

But the fertility of the Mother Goddess is not limited to the specific act of carrying a life or giving birth. Rather, the Mother represents all that is fertile and all that nurtures life. If the Maiden is the eager beginning of a thing – whether that is life or a creative project – then the mother is the patient middle point. The Mother has seen the benefits of optimism, but has also known failure. She has grown and matured. And along the way she has learned how to nurture.

The energy of the full Moon is best suited for spells that help people through a tough time. Maybe someone is running out of steam on a painting or they're struggling to finish a lengthy work project. Perhaps life has been unkind or someone is out of options and needs help. The Mother Goddess' energy can help all of these situations and more.

She can be called on during the full Moon, as well as the day before and day after. Spells cast in Her light are those that leave people feeling safer, more secure, and more confident in themselves. They are the spells that seek to lift up and nurture, as well as those that urge people to complete their goals.

That is not to say that the Mother Goddess does not have her sharper side, of course. Anyone who has threatened a mother's child knows what sort of fury a mother can call down. And the Mother Goddess is no different. Although, because of the Wiccan Rede's order to "Harm None," the fury of the Mother Goddess is less about retaliating during an attack and more about protection.

Full Moons are the best time to set wards and protections. These protective spells can be for people or homes, or they can be for ventures either magical or mundane. With the energy of the Mother goddess, Wiccan protections spells are awesomely powerful and fearsome for those who try to cross them.

But what of spells that seek to banish or remove things from a person's life? Neither the Maiden nor the Mother, in their eagerness and their fullness, have energy suited to banishing. They are still young, still learning that there are some things that cannot be healed, cannot be completed. For those situations, Wiccans call upon the Crone Goddess during the waning Moon.

The Crone represents the last phase of the Moon, known as the waning Moon. She also represents the later years of life, when mot adventures have already been completed and wisdom is in more abundance than energy. The Crone is the calmest of the goddesses, content to sit with her knowledge and consider all possibilities before making a choice. She has lived her brash years. Now is the time for her caution and introspection.

With this introspection also comes the knowledge that some things should not be borne. While the Maiden seeks to explore and the Mother seeks to nurture, the Crone seeks to protect. She has seen the darkness in the world and has lived through enough of it that she has learned when and how to end something.

Wiccans call on the Crone during the waning Moon when they must banish something or someone from their lives. They also call upon Her when an end is near. This could mean the passing of a loved one, at which time the Crone can act as a guide for the beloved's soul to reach the afterlife. Or it could mean the end of a project when the Crone's wisdom can help practitioners overcome any final hurdles and reach their goals.

Finally, there is the new Moon which is also referred to as the Dark Moon or Dark of the Moon. There is no aspect of the Goddess associated with this lunar phase. Instead, this is the phase that reflects the absence of the Goddess. Spells cast during this time either call on the unknown that comes after death, as this phase comes after the phase of the Crone. Or, viewed the other way, the new Moon is also a time of unknowable potential because it precedes the birth of the Maiden Goddess.

Each phase of the Moon brings unique energy to Wiccan spell work. This is true whether the phase calls on the unknown space between lives or on the power of a Goddess aspect. Every night is a new opportunity for Wiccans to bring the power of the Moon into their work. And, as with all energy, this lunar boost can take their spells to new heights.

The Tides and Ocean Witches

All Wiccans see the Triple Goddess' aspects in the phases of the Moon. But, for some, the Moon has an even deeper effect on their magical practices. As an earth-based religion, Wicca encourages its practitioners to connect with the planet. For some Wiccans, this becomes a deep bond that influences the nature and direction of the magic.

Some become mountain witches, who draw their energy from massive peaks of stone beneath their feet, the dizzying elevation, and the wild forests that coat most mountains. Others become desert witches who feel most comfortable among sand dunes and cacti, where the scorching days and frigid nights present a balance they rely on. But there is one group of magic workers that are more affected by the Moon than most. And they are ocean witches.

Every school child knows that the Moon controls the tides. When the Moon draws close, its gravitational pull causes Earth's water to rise on the side closest – and oddly, the side furthest – from the Moon. Where these waters rise, it is high tide. As Earth spins, this tidal force moves, bringing high tide to new shores and letting once-high tides recede.

Ocean witches feel the pull of these tides in their bones. Their magic ebbs and flows with the movement of the ocean they have connected to. Some may experience this as feeling low-energy when it is low tide and "amped up" when it is high tide. Others may find that certain kinds of spells work best during high tide, but barely work at all during low tide.

Though it may seem harsh that ocean witches must consider the Moon twice in all their workings, this is actually an asset. Ocean witches can channel all the same lunar energy as other witches. But, with a little bit of extra knowledge, they can also channel the power the tides as dictated by the Moon.

Shadow Work and the Dark of the Moon

The Dark of the Moon has already been touched on. But shadow work is its own field entirely separate from the Triple Goddess. And, as such, it must be discussed separately. The Goddess can be involved, of course. But shadow work is much more about the practitioner than the powers around them. This is why it is more easily done during the Dark of the Moon.

Wiccans foster connections to the world around them. And, most of the time, this means nurturing new connections. But there is always deeper work to be done. And one such form of work is called shadow work. This term refers to magical soul searching. It is the process by which Wiccans and witches look at the connections they already have and try to understand them fully. This could mean intense meditation, self-reflection spells, or mundane research to discover the who and where of their roots.

No magic should be undertaken lightly. But this is truer of shadow work than nearly any other magical field. Witches who undertake shadow work must be prepared to learn things – about themselves, about others, and about the world – that may challenge their world view. They may expose secrets that are hard to process and upend beliefs they have held onto their entire lives. Shadow work is about **knowing**. And sometimes knowledge can hurt.

But knowledge can also heal. And this is why so many witches choose to undertake shadow work. Everyone has small thoughts in the back of their minds that they don't want to face head-on. Shadow work requires practitioners do just that. And, in the end, they come out knowing themselves better than they ever would have otherwise.

The nature of shadow work means that it is best suited for the Dark of the Moon, or the new Moon. Though some practitioners may want the aid of the Goddess, shadow work is ultimately something that must be undertaken alone. And the new Moon, when the Goddess is either leaving this life or waiting to be born back into it, is a time when practitioners are most alone.

Shadow work is considered advanced magic, due to the possible repercussions. It should not be undertaken lightly. And no summary can do it justice. But when the Moon is dark in the sky and there is no moonlight to be found, all witches know of shadow work and its potential. It is another journey, another path, waiting in the dark space between one Moon and the next.

Chapter 2: Lunar Cycles and Events

Long before the modern calendar, humans measured time by the phases of the Moon. This meant a different number of weeks and months in any given year, all of them based on the movement of the Moon. Humans now use the Gregorian Calendar almost exclusively. And this means that few bothers to track lunar cycles anymore. But many Wiccans are among those who do.

Moon Signs

There are many reasons Wiccans track lunar cycles. And Moon signs are one of the most common. Moon signs, like the more well-known idea of birth signs, tell Wiccans which astrological house the Moon rests in. Some practitioners even go so far as to mind out what house the Moon was in at the time of their birth. Like sun signs, this information is believed to affect a person's behavior, fortune, and future.

While the sun takes roughly thirty days to move from one sign to the next, the Moon takes only two. And, like the sun, it progresses from one house to the next in a predictable cycle. These houses – such as Libra, Virgo, or Taurus – all have their own correspondences, traits, and affiliations.

Because the sun and Moon move through the astrological houses at different speeds, a person's sun sign may be very different from their Moon sign. A fiery solar Aries may find that their Moon sign is the calm Pisces. Wiccans who believe in astrology find that Moon signs change exactly how someone presents in their solar sign.

Libras, for example, are often so preoccupied with balance that they forget to look at the bigger picture. A solar Libra with a Virgo Moon, however, is much more grounded since Virgo is an earth sign. This combination allows the person to draw back more easily and remember that small details are not the only part of balance that matters.

Some practitioners also feel their magic is strongest when the Moon is in "their" house. Someone born under a Gemini Moon, for example, might find that their Gemini nature is stronger. At the same time, they will find that their energy flows more easily and their spells are more effective. This effect is even stronger when the sun and Moon are both aligned with a practitioner's particular combination.

Lunar Events

The Moon usually follows an orderly progression through the sky. Everyone – magical and mundane – can glance up and see the same reassuring globe glowing with light reflected from the sun. Every now and then, however, something changes. The lunar calendar doesn't quite sync up with the Gregorian Calendar or something causes the Moon's light to glow an unusual color. Most people just shrug it off when these things happen. But some people, Wiccans in particular, place great importance on these occurrences. Their exact reaction differs from event to event, however.

The Blue Moon

There are two kinds of blue moons. One of them happens when the air is so heavy with smoke or dust that the Moon visibly turns blue. This is most common after heavy forest fires or volcanic eruptions. So, it's not surprising that many cultures have fearsome lore surrounding a visibly blue Moon.

Some cultures believed that sleeping under the light of a blue Moon would drive a person insane. Others believed that falling ill during a blue Moon meant a person would die in eight days. And others believed that if any person died under a blue Moon, three more members of their family would soon follow.

But not all myths around this type of blue Moon were so dire. Wives who saw a blue Moon in the sky were told turn over their mattresses, as it would make them more fertile. And anyone with a coin in their pocket when a blue Moon rose in the sky was supposed to turn it over to increase their wealth. Similarly, picking flowers and berries under the light of a blue Moon called abundance and plenty into a person's life.

But this is only one type of blue Moon. And, although there is a lot of lore surrounding it, visibly blue Moons don't have much effect on Wiccan magic. The second type of blue Moon, however, does. Even though it is visibly normal, the second full Moon in any given month is also known as a Blue Moon.

Lunar cycles are either twenty-seven or twenty-nine days long, depending on the metric. Earth's Moon takes a little over twenty-seven days to make one full orbit, but it takes twenty-nine days to make it through one full cycle from waxing Moon to full Moon. Because a lunar cycle is so close to the full length of most Gregorian months, a Blue Moon only happens roughly once every two and a half years.

The rarity of a Blue Moon is enough that it usually makes headlines when it rolls around. But as interesting as it is to the mundane world, magical communities find it even more important. Blue Moons are a sort of "super Moon." It takes the energies of the full Moon and doubles them.

It is also the Moon of "long shot chances." If practitioners cast to a spell to reach an unlikely goal, they stand a better chance of success during the Blue Moon. A Blue Moon is, as the saying goes, rare. What better time is there to reach for the stars that would normally seem much too far away?

The Violet Moon

Unlike the Blue Moon, the Violet Moon is not widely recognized in scientific or mundane circles, despite the fact that they are more or less polar opposites. While the Blue Moon is the second full Moon in a Gregorian calendar month, Violent Moons are the second new Moon. This time frame means they are about as rare as Blue Moons.

There is no visible form of a Violet Moon, however. Any Moon that comes close to a violet color is usually referred to as a Blue Moon with all the same lore. Violet Moons also have fewer pop culture appearances, though they are the subject of a few songs that are very popular in Wiccan circles.

Just as the Violet Moon is the exact opposite of a Blue Moon in terms of the Moon's phase, it is also opposite in the energy that it brings. If the new Moon is a time for shadow work, then the Violet Moon is the time when Wiccans can reach the deepest levels of introspection.

Should the practitioner need to banish something, the Violet Moon holds the deepest void of any lunar event. And should a magic user want to tap into the potential that precedes any birth, the Violet Moon may be the greatest source of potential energy they could hope to encounter.

The Blood Moon

While both the Blue Moon and the Violet Moon hold potential positive energy, the Blood Moon is usually seen as a purely negative event. There is a Christian prophecy placing the Blood Moon as part of an approaching Armageddon. But Wiccans take a slightly less drastic view of the phenomena.

A Blood Moon occurs when the earth moves between the Moon and the sun, placing the Moon into the earth's shadow. This usually leads to an eclipse. But, before the eclipse, the Moon takes on a deep reddish tint. It is easy to see why this occurrence can make even the most literal-minded person a little bit uncomfortable. The Moon is supposed to reflect bright, cool light. By contrast, the light of a Blood Moon feels hot and uncomfortable, too much like the way anger feels hot under the skin.

Though Wiccans do not see a Blood Moon as part of an End Times prophecy, they still take a dim view of the event. Because many Wiccans track the movement of the Moon, they usually know when an eclipse is scheduled to take place. Many Wiccans will work heavy layers of protective magic in the days and weeks leading up to the eclipse to protect them from a potential Blood Moon.

Even if Wiccans don't take magical precautions, they will take mundane steps to avoid the negative energy around the Blood Moon. They will become more introspective so as to avoid conflict. Some will avoid going out as much as possible and others may avoid the light of a Blood Moon altogether.

Is it important to note that not all cultures view Blood Moons as bad omens. Some view them as reminders to let go of grudges or to strengthen ties within the community. But Wicca is based on the lore and practices of Pre-Christian Britain and Ireland. Because of this, Wiccans tend to stick with the lore from those locations. And the lore than has survived to present day paint Blood Moons in a very negative light.

Blood on The Moon

Blood on the Moon is a random phenomenon, unlike a Blood Moon which has at least some regularity to it. When blood appears on the Moon, it is because of smoke or particles in the air, much like a visible Blue Moon. Instead of turning the Moon a single, uniform shade, however, it does one of two things. It either creates a red ring around the Moon or brownish-red spots across the Moon's face.

Either version of Blood on the Moon is a bad sign. Wiccans believe that it is a sign of bad things to come. Many Wiccans will ward themselves with protective spells that draw on energies other than those of the Moon. Some will stock up on protective stones such as quartz, which cleanses energy, and hematite, which ground someone and reflects negative energy back to its source.

The Harvest Moon

Unlike the other lunar events in this chapter, the Harvest Moon happens every year, without fail. It does not rely on an eclipse or atmospheric conditions. And, unlike most other lunar events, the Harvest Moon is closely tied to the motion of the earth itself. The Harvest Moon is the last full Moon before the Autumnal Equinox.

To fully understand the importance of the Harvest Moon, one must understand the importance of the equinox. There are two equinoxes each year, one in September and one in May. For those in the northern hemisphere, the March equinox is known as the Vernal Equinox while the event in September is known as the Autumnal Equinox. The titles are reversed for those in the southern hemisphere.

During each equinox, the visible center of the sun is directly over the equator. At first glance, this information might not seem particularly important. But these two days are the closest the earth comes to having perfect balance between night and day. And this makes both days particularly important for Wiccans. Their search for balance and their connection to nature mean that the equinoxes are ideal days for specific rituals and spells.

In addition to the near-perfect balance between light and dark, the Autumnal Equinox has also long been associated with the largest fall harvest throughout Europe, Britain, and Ireland. Long before the Gregorian Calendar – or any single unified calendar for that matter – farmers knew that the change in weather and daylight meant that it was time to bring in the last of their summer crops. The idea of harvest, combined with the equinox's sense of balance, create the specific energy that makes the Harvest Moon so important in the Wiccan faith.

The full Moon is always a time of nurture and abundance. And those traits are magnified ten-fold when they coincide when the Autumnal Equinox and the fall harvest. As farmers bring in the crops that they have nurtured all summer – crops that will, in turn, nurture them through the winter – in from the fields, Wiccans can cast spells to call forward safety and abundance during the cold months to come.

It is one of the last summer-like lunar events before deep autumn sets in as well. Many if the autumn holidays are meant to remember the dead and honor nature as much of it dies or goes dormant in preparation for winter. The Harvest Moon is one final hurrah for life and the ecstatic energy of summer before the tone of the world's energy shifts into a more subdued, sustainable frequency.

Eclipses

Eclipses stand separate from other lunar events because they are just as dependent on the sun and the earth as they are on the Moon. Both lunar and solar eclipses are laden with magical lore. And both affect magic in their own unique ways. Further complicating matters is that there are several schools of thought on how each type of eclipse affects magic users. Each magic user might have to stay attuned to their personal energies during eclipses to see how the events affect them personally.

The Lunar Eclipse

There are several types of Lunar Eclipses. They range from partial to total and, for some, depend on how exactly they are obscured. Some eclipses are total, meaning the earth passes between the sun and the Moon, blocking the Moon's access to solar light. Others occur when the Moon falls – partially or entirely – into the Earth's shadow although the Earth itself is not in the way of the Sun's light.

Lunar eclipse lore does not readily distinguish between the different types of eclipses. And this might be why there are so many different ways eclipses are said to affect magic users. Practitioners should track eclipses as they come and go to see how they are affected by each one. They can then track these affects in their journal or Book of Shadows, which is also known as a Grimoire. Because the timing of an eclipse can varies depending on where a person lives, magic users should try and get their eclipse information from a space-monitoring organization, just to ensure the accuracy of their data.

There is no hard and fast rule to determine how an eclipse will affect someone. But there are a few very specific pieces of lore that surround the events and how they alter magical energy. The two most common schools of thought are either than the energy of the Moon is blotted out entirely or that it is much more potent than it is at any other time.

Those who feel that Lunar Eclipses blot out the energy of the Moon point to the fact that the Moon is no longer shining in the sky. These practitioners feel that, without the light the Moon, their lunar spells simply have no power. Some people balk at this claim because the Moon's light is reflected from the Sun and, as such, should not be seen as the only mark of lunar power. But that is a deep-seated argument in the Wiccan community that is not easily solved in one book.

Practitioners who feel that the Lunar Eclipse boosts the Moon's energy find support for their belief in the way the Earth, Sun, and Moon are in alignment. Pop culture likes to make jokes about when "the planets align." But there is really power to be had when different energies line up and point to the same goal. In the event of an eclipse, some magic users find that the Moon's energy intertwines with that of the Earth and the Sun. During the brief duration of the eclipse, this energy can fuel incredibly powerful spells and affect massive change.

Among those who find the Moon's power increased during eclipses are those who feel that an eclipse creates an entire lunar cycle in one short span. As the Moon moves either behind the Earth or into its shadow, it begins to wane. Then, when the Sun's light is completely blocked, the Moon is in its new or dark phase. And, finally, the Moon waxes as it moves back into the Sun's light, until it is once again full.

Running through an entire lunar phase in the course of one day generates a huge amount of energy, or some magic users believe. Sort of like winding up an antique engine or spinning a top so fast it become a blur. This shortened "super phase" spins up a ton of energy that magic users can then siphon into powerful spells.

Even those who feel an increase in energy during this time should be careful, however. Energy generated during the eclipse is likely to be explosive and hot, unlike the cooler, more gentle energy most Moon magic relies on. Spells cast with eclipse energy are not going to manifest patiently. They will burst into action and the change they bring will be swift and, often, massive. Practitioners should be prepared to act quickly, lest the sudden changes overwhelm them.

The Solar Eclipse

Despite their name, Solar Eclipses are just as dependent on the Moon as they are the sun. Unlike Lunar Eclipses, however, they don't directly involve the Earth. This changes the way the eclipse affects magical energy, though only slightly.

As with the Lunar Eclipse, there are some who feel that magical energy is essentially paused during a Solar Eclipse. Energy drawn from the Earth, the spirits, and the Divine is still available, of course. But celestial energy is locked down while the Moon blocks the sun from earth's view. Unlike Lunar Eclipses, however, this is not simply a case of one heavenly body blocking the light of another. In the case of Solar Eclipses, the Moon passes between the Earth and the Sun. This blocked out nearly all of the sun's light, creating a darkened sky in sickly shades of brown and red. And that is if the sky does not darken completely.

But as the Moon blocks the sun from the sky, it too goes dark, it is backlit but a thin corona of sun, since it cannot block the sun's light entirely. But it is unable to shine from Earth's point of view. All the energy of the Sun and Moon are trapped between the two until the Moon moves out of the Sun's path.

And, just as with Lunar Eclipses, there are people who find that Solar Eclipses have the completely opposite effect. For some, this is due to the fact that Solar Eclipses can only happen during new Moons and, as such, the Moon and Sun are the same astrological house or zodiac sign. The energy of that sign or house is then increased. This, in turn, expands the energy and power of people born in the same house or under that same sign, whether it is their Sun or Moon sign.

Another school of thought is that equinoxes are a sign of rapid change. The Moon covers the sun entirely, effectively swallowing it whole. But, before too long, the Sun re-emerges, triumphant and unharmed. This makes the energy of the Solar Eclipse especially well-suited for spells that want to enact quick change. Or, of course, spells intended to help someone come through a difficult situation unharmed.

A fourth and final group of magic users find that Solar Eclipses provide all the energy of a one-day cycle and a full seasonal cycle in the span of just a few minutes. Thanks to the eclipse, the sun goes from a bright high-noon energy level through its normal daily waning to the dark of night, only to "rise" again as the Moon moves out from in front of it.

This high speed "rising" and "setting" can also represent the sun's movement through the sky during the seasons of the year. And thus, an eclipse provides the energy of not only a whole day in just a few minutes, but the energy of an entire season as well. All of this energy is ideal for enacting sudden change or powering a powerful spell.

Folklore and Science

Many people understand the way Wiccans look at the Moon. Yes, much of folklore was a way for early humans to explain planetary workings when they did not have the tools to find the actual sources. And despite what some people think, Wiccans are well aware of this. They know that the sun is not really being swallowed by the Moon. And they're well aware that atmospheric debris causes Blood on the Moon, not direct Divine intervention.

Instead of ignoring either science or folklore, Wiccans tend to blend the two. Yes, smoke from a forest fire might be causing the visible blue color of the moon. But that does not mean that the Goddess did not stir the winds Herself so that magic users would receive the signs they needed. Likewise, eclipses happen because of the way Earth moves in relation to the sun and the Moon. But that does not change how an eclipse affects magical energy.

It is entirely possible – and important – for Wiccans to honor both folklore and science. Blended together, the two offer a deeper understanding of the world around us than either could hope to achieve on its own.

Humans have long looked up at the sky and told stories about the great orbs hanging there. Every culture has their myth and every myth has its own story. But now, today, Wiccans are taking those stories and the newest scientific research, then combining the two to create lasting change. Moon magic does not fly in the face of science. Rather, it embraces it. And as it does, it brings a whole new level of energy to Wiccan spells that rely on the power and might of the Moon.

Chapter 3: Ritual and Spell Basics

There are, quite literally, millions of spells. That might actually be a low number, depending on how distinct each spell needs to be. Most involve herbs, crystals, or stones. The spells in this book do occasionally call for additional items. But each additional item is just an extra that helps set the tone of a spell or more finely focus its energy. The spells and rituals can be performed without anything extra at all. But the one thing they cannot function without is the magic of the Moon.

Before diving into the magic itself, it is important that practitioners understand the difference between rituals and spells. Rituals are rites during which Wiccans honor the Moon, the Goddess, and Her energy. There are several different kinds of rituals for each phase of the Moon. This book focuses on one piece.

Spells, on the other hand, are meant to tap into the energy of the Moon and use it to enact the will of the magic use. It is possible to honor the Goddess and the Moon while doing this, of course. But honoring the source of the energy is not the main intent of a spell.

It is also important to note that practitioners should only do spells and rituals they are comfortable with. Some practitioners prefer to perform their work Sky clad. Or, in other words, nude. Other practitioners practice certain rites from the very beginning of Wicca such as the Five Fold Kiss.

None of this is required, however. Practitioners do not have to engage in rituals or spells that make them uncomfortable in any way. It does not matter if the discomfort stems from as aspect of the rite or from the rite as a whole. Wicca is a religion that connects the individual to nature and the Divine. There is no reason that discomfort need be a part of that.

The spells and rituals in this book are meant to be largely accessible to most people. They are written for solitary practitioners but can easily be adapted to fit groups of magic users, which are sometimes known as covens. The only steadfast requirement is that they must be performed during the appropriate phase of the Moon or lunar event. Otherwise they may not work or, if they do work, they may create unintended outcomes.

Each ritual listed below begins with an outline for a ritual bath that includes some herbs, potential candles scents and colors, as well as a chant or short song that practitioners can sing while bathing. The ritual then moves into ideal ritual clothing as well as a few alternatives. The clothing is largely gender neutral as robes and tunics have been through much of early history. Each description then moves into the ritual itself, followed by steps to take once the rite is completed. And, finally, each section is rounded out with spells that are ideal for each phase of the Moon.

Although each component of the ritual can be fine-tuned or – in many cases – dropped altogether, there are specific reasons each step has been included. From ritual bathing to cleaning up afterward, practitioners are advised to at least understand the purpose of a step before they alter the rituals from their presented formats.

Preparing for After the Ritual

Rituals and spell work require a lot of energy. Some people can channel or offer this energy with absolutely no concerns. They come out the other side of a rite feeling refreshed and blessed. Some people, on the other hand, come out feeling drained. It all depends on how a magic user relates to their own energy.

Regardless of which category a magic user falls into, they should expect to come out of a ritual needing food, water, and rest. Even people who find rites energizing may come across one that leaves them more exhausted than usual. It is always a good idea to have snacks and drinks waiting for everyone who participates in a rite.

Though some groups suggest alcohol, as it is a traditional celebratory drink, this is not required. Water is ideal, as many magic users find themselves parched after the exertion of a rite. Other good options are fruit juices, flavored waters, and teas. Artificial drinks are less popular, as they belong more to the mundane world and less to a world where humans connect deeply with nature.

Ideal snacks for post-ritual fuel include nuts, fruit slices, and cut vegetables. If the ritual is particularly important, such as for a holiday, personal celebration, or rare lunar occurrence, some Wiccans prefer to have whole meals waiting. Whichever route a practitioner takes should keep in mind the idea of staying connected with the world around them. And, as the ritual is meant to honor the Divine, refreshments after the ritual should honor the practitioners. This means opting for healthier options and ensuring there is something for everyone, regardless of dietary restrictions.

Ritual Bathing

Not all practitioners perform ritual baths. The concept may be new even to experienced magic users. But it is an ancient concept that spans multiple cultures and magical practices.

At the base level, a ritual bath is a way for magic users to get themselves into the right frame of mind. Even if they bathed only that morning, a ritual bath changes the tone of their energies. They leave behind the stress and pressures of their mundane day. In their stead, practitioners can accept the calm, purposeful energy they will need during a ritual.

Ritual baths also help magic users wash away any unwanted energy. Everyone picks up stray bits of energy throughout the day, some good and some bad. And, for the most part, that energy remains part of people until they next ground, center, or bathe. Magic users shake this energy off more readily because they know how to handle it. But a ritual bath helps them clear out unwanted energy much more easily.

And though it is called a ritual bath, many practitioners who engage in this step prefer to take a ritual shower. "Ritual bath" just has a more esoteric ring to it for most people. And though the reason for the name change might be a bit silly, the purpose of a shower versus a bath is not.

When most people bathe, they do it in a small tub of standing water. That water is derived from pipes in their home and is not rooted in a natural source that can cleanse the water as they bathe. Few people have access to a clean body of water in which to wash away errant energy. Ritual baths in a standard bathtub would remove energy from the practitioner, of course. But the energy would just stay in the water until the practitioner drained the tub. At that point, much of the energy would just reattach itself to the magic user.

Showers, on the other hand, wash all the unwanted energy down the drain. Rather than swirling around the person only to reattach, errant energy is swept away before it can find its way back to the magic user. It also helps that these showers wash away the dirt and grime of a day in the mundane world, leaving the magic user feeling refreshed for their ritual.

Ritual bathing does not stop at the shower itself. Many practitioners take it a step further by continuing their chant or mindful self-awareness while they apply lotions, fix their hair, and – in some cases – apply makeup. Most people continue this focus into the next step, which is putting on ritual clothing, also known as ritual garb.

Ritual Garb

Most people have seen movies with magic users in them. Each movie involves long cloaks, hooded robes, and maybe even some sort of slipper. These costumes give the magic users the aura of medieval monks calling on powers greater than they truly understand in order to work some unseen or unknowable purpose.

While actual ritual garb lacks much of pop culture's melodrama, there are a few things that costume designers get right. Most ritual garb is based on the style and clothing of pre-Christian Britain and Ireland. This is slowly changing, however, as practitioners with more diverse heritages join the religion and more people create their own version of Neo-Wicca.

Before a Wiccan can design their own ritual garb, however, it is important that they understand the basic requirements for such clothing. These requirements, as well as the cultural roots of

Wicca, have shaped what is now known as traditional Wiccan ritual garb.

The most important aspect of ritual clothing is that it is comfortable. It shouldn't be too tight or cut poorly. And the material should be comfortable against the practitioner's skin. Uncomfortable ritual clothing will only serve to distract the magic user. At best, this will interrupt their ability to properly honor the being at the center of their ritual. At worst, this can cause a spell to lose power or go astray.

Ritual garb must also be safe. This means that, while flowing robes are popular, sleeves should be relatively snug against the wrists and arms so they do not dip into a candle flame accidentally. A robe's hem should also be an inch or so above the ground so that practitioners don't trip on it when moving around during a ritual.

Safety is just as important when selecting footwear for a ritual. If the ritual is held indoors or on soft grass inside the bounds of private property, magic users can go barefoot or opt for soft-bottom slippers. If the ritual is held outdoors, particularly on land that other people have used, hard-bottom shoes are recommended. Rituals performed in the woods almost always require boots or modern shoes to protect the wearer's feet from rocks, sharps sticks, and any garbage other people might have left behind.

And while most ritual garb is made to resemble clothing from bygone eras, it is entirely possible to wear modern clothing for rituals. If a magic user chooses to go this route, they should set aside an outfit that is solely for ritual use. This prevents the clothing from picking up any errant energy and ensures that the clothing is always clean when it is time for rituals. And, on that note, it is important to keep ritual clothing clean. If something spills on a ritual garment, it should be cleaned up right away. Stains not only make the garment seem less important, but they can carry energy from one ritual into another.

Practitioners who want to make their own ritual garb should start simple and work their way up to more complex garments and decorations. It is perfectly acceptable to start with a "street clothes" outfit with only a few pieces of ritual jewelry, then slowly substitute handmade alternatives. Practitioners do not need to have a lifelong ritual outfit ready before their first ritual. They can start with what they have and change things as the need and possibility arises.

Wiccans who perform a lot of rituals or for whom religion is a central pillar of their lives may have specific clothing for each type of ritual. The ritual garb subheadings for each ritual will include suggestions for every level mentioned above. From those who wear street clothes and simply need a small trinket to those who have clothing specific to each ritual.

Creating a Circle

Once the practitioner is ready to begin their ritual, they must cast a protective circle. These are energetic barriers that protect a magic user from outside energy – and keep their own energy focused on the ritual – until they have completed their rite. They are raised at the beginning of any spell or ritual, then are released as the last act of the rite.

There are several ways to cast a protective circle. Some practitioners choose to etch a permanent circle into the floor where whey perform spells and rituals. Others prefer to use a large loop of string that can be laid out before a rite and collected up afterward. Still others use material like salt or chalk to create a temporary and disposable circle. And yet others rely solely on visualization.

Each variation on the circle has its pros and cons. Most Wiccans choose the version that works best to suit their needs. They consider whether or not they can practice openly, how much space they have, where the practice, and how often they are likely to perform a rite. With these criteria in mind, they decide which circle marking technique best suits their needs and they practice it until they are adept at raising their energy.

Protective circles should be large enough to encompass all magic users involved in a ritual or spell, a central altar, and any markers used to indicate the cardinal directions. Regardless of the material used to lay the circle – or if the circle is made using visualization alone – practitioners should walk the inner perimeter of their circle before raising its energy. This should be done in a clockwise direction, which is also known as Deosil. Walking in this direction puts the magic user more in tune with the energy of the Earth, as it is the same direction that the Sun travels through the sky each day.

Once the outline has been placed around all of these components, the person in charge of the ritual closes their eyes and visualizes the circle as a ring of energy. They then imagine this circle becoming a sphere, closing the ritual in on all sides and protecting those within from harm.

No energy can pass back and forth across the barrier unless it is invited. A physical being can cross the circle, however, and this may break the energetic barrier. For this reason, it is important that anyone participating in a spell or ritual should stay inside the circle from start to finish unless there is an emergency. In this case, if only one person needs to leave, the practitioner leading the ritual can create a door by which the person can leave. If everyone needs to leave, the leaders can drop the magical barrier, releasing all the energy at once.

Bugs and pets can also break the shield of a protective circle but it is not as easy for them to do, since they carry less energy than a human. Still, if possible, practitioners should keep their pets in a separate area from their ritual space. This will prevent any unintentional breaks in the circle and allow the ritual or spell to be completed in peace.

Some practitioners use chants to focus their energy while they raise their circles. Each ritual in this book includes its own specialty chant for those who wish to use them. Spells, on the other hand, rarely require chants since the protective circle is often smaller and containing lower energy levels. Magic users can raise circles in these instances much more easily, so no chants have been written for the included spells.

Calling the Quarters

As the Moon and sun are important in Wicca, so are the four cardinal directions. North, south, east, and west are often referred to as the Four Quarters or the Four Watchtowers. They are called before every ritual or spell so that their energy can support whatever work the magic user wants to do. Then, at the end of the rite, the energy is released before the protective circle is lowered. Unlike most energy, the energy of the Watchtowers is neutral and so is not stopped by things like protective circles.

Not only do each of the directions have their own energies, but they have elements that they alone relate to. North is the direction of Earth, the most stable of the elements. It is strong, subdued, and sturdy. South, conversely, is fire. It is bright and hot, energetic and chaotic. East represents air, which is the softest of the elements. It easily changes direction, carries only that which is light as a feather, and brings breath to every lung though it is the most intangible of the elements. Finally, there is west, the watchtower of water. Water, too, can change direction. But it usually takes more time, particularly deep water. Water changes and shapes things gradually, and can carry just about anything if respected.

Each element connects to the phases of the Moon and the faces of the Triple Goddess in its own way. Because of this, the incantations used to summon the Watchtowers tend to change from ritual to ritual depending on the phase of the Moon being honored. Spells are a little more lenient, since the Moon is aiding the spell rather than the focal point of it. As such, a general call to each Watchtower will suffice, regardless of the Moon's phase.

Performing the Ritual

The majority of energy in a ritual or spell is used in the core performance. In rituals, it is used to when interacting with the energy of the being honored. When casting a spell, the energy it put into the spell itself, sort of like fuel being added to a car. It is the thing that makes the spell go.

Because each spell and ritual are a little bit different, the details will only be given in the subsections dedicated to each ritual or the selection of spells. Many of them follow a standard format, which is intentional. Having consistent formats for spells and rituals allows practitioners to learn the framework by heart. Once they do this, they can move within that framework without thinking, allowing them to devote more energy and attention to the ritual itself.

Practitioners new to magic are advised to follow the rituals as they are laid out in this book. Because these rituals were developed by an experienced magic user, they effectively utilize as much energy as possible. As practitioners gain more experience and confidence with their energy and their magic, they can change things as they see fit. If part of a ritual is not possible due to personal limitations, whether they be space or capability, small modifications are absolutely acceptable. Just be sure that the changes honor the flow and pace of the ritual.

Ending the Ritual

As energy is called into a protective circle at the beginning of a ritual, so it must be released at the end. This is usually done by thanking whatever entity is being honored – in this case, various phases of the Moon and their corresponding aspects of the Triple Goddess – and then bidding them farewell.

From there, the magic user moves to the Watchtowers. They release these energies in the reverse order they were summoned. If, for example, the practitioner summoned the energies of the Watchtowers in the order of north, east, south, and west, they would release the energies starting with west and working backward through the list.

This allows the practitioner to move in a counterclockwise direction, otherwise known as Widdershins. Though this direction is considered unlucky in some situations, it is simply a way to balance the energy of a ritual. It functions as a way to "unwind" the energy that the practitioner "wound up" by walking Deosil at the beginning of the ritual

Cleaning Up

The Wiccan appreciate for balance and a sense of connection goes beyond the metaphysical and metaphorical. Wicca encourages both of these traits while also focusing on a sense of personal responsibility, all of which is particularly important for those who perform magical works. And this is why it is vital that all magic users clean up when they are done with a ritual.

Because each ritual is different, the cleanup will always look a little different. If a ritual call for a practitioner to put something on their altar, there is no reason to take the item down unless that's what the practitioner wants to do. Similarly, if a magic user drew a chalk circle on their floor and it is safe for them to leave it in place, they don't have to wipe it away when the ritual is over.

Many rituals involve things like flowers, herbs, and food. And though some practitioners enjoy leaving these things on their altar as offerings to the Goddess and the God, they can quickly sour. If someone chooses to leave offerings on their altar, they should check on those offerings a few times a day to make sure that no bugs or rot have set in. At that point the Divine beings have taken all the energy they want or need from the offering. It is safe to dispose of it as any other plant waste.

Cleaning up after a ritual is especially important if it was held outdoors. Even dried plants can drop seeds that may or may not be invasive to the area. Animals may get into offerings of food that then make the animals sick. And it goes without saying that no member of a religion focused on nature worship should be comfortable littering.

If the practitioner is wearing ritual garb, now is the time to take it off. They should do so slowly and with focused intent. As they do this, they should also feel for any differences in the energy of the garment from when it was put on. If there are vast differences or if the garment feels heavy or dirty, it may need to be laundered and cleansed before it is worn again. Cleansing is usually a simple affair in which Wiccans leave items out in the light of a full Moon so that all unwanted energy can be washed away.

Differences Between Spells and Rituals

Though both spells and rituals use magic – and, by extension, the magic user's personal store of energy in addition to Divine and natural energy – the two practices are very different. Their differences lie in the way they are performed and the intention of those performing them. Though pop culture has long confused the two, they are distinct practices.

Differences in Form

On a surface level, rituals and spells look very similar. Both require a protective circle. And, in the case of large spells, both require that the practitioner call forth the energy of the Watchtowers. But spells are, generally, much less formal than rituals. Smaller spells are especially distinct from rituals in that they do not require the calling of the Quarters. Magic users are free to do so, of course. But unlike rituals and large spells, the act is not required.

Many practitioners also forgo ritual bathing and ritual garb for spells. Though both the bathing and the ritual clothing help Wiccans focus their minds on the spiritual rather than the mundane, such narrow focus is not required for most spells. And this is where spells and rituals differ on the basis of intent.

Differences in Intent

The purpose of a ritual is to honor a specific entity. For Wiccans, these entities are might be natural energy sources such as the sun, the Moon, mountains, or oceans. Or they might be Divine beings such as the God or any aspect of the Triple Goddess. In some cases, rituals might even honor spirits such as ancestors, Faeries, ghosts, or land spirits.

Honoring these energies is believed to bring their blessing on those involved in the ritual. The blessings might even extend to families or communities the practitioners are part of. There are no express requests made during rituals. Rather, energy and respect are offered to the entity in question with the understanding that, should it please them, they will bestow blessings in return. In that way, Wiccan rituals are like rituals from any other organized religion.

Spells, on the other hand, use energy to enact the will of the person casting the spell. This will cannot be harmful, as dictated by the Wiccan Rede's mandate "An' it Harm None, Do What Ye Will." But there is no mandate against a spell to banish an illness, help someone succeed in academic or professional settings, or to attract love into a person's life.

Accomplishing these goals takes a great deal of energy. And few humans possess that kind of power on their own. So, to boost the energy of the magic user, they call on the Watchtowers, the Divine, and various spirits that they feel safe working with. The spells in this book specifically call on the different energies offered by the Moon.

The type of energy called upon also dictates how well a spell will perform. If the spell is meant to banish an illness, it wouldn't make sense to power it with the energy of the waxing Moon. The waxing Moon belongs to the Maiden goddess and she is not one who has suffered much illness. Nor is she of the mind to banish anything, given her curious and abiding nature. The spell would be better served by the energies of the waning Moon or the new Moon, if lunar energies are required.

This book is focused on lunar magic. And, as such, all of the included spells and rituals are written with the Moon's energies in mind. Nearly any spell can be adapted, however. Once a practitioner has enough experience, they can change the energy they call upon and the ingredients they use. But, for now, the Moon's energies will provide more than enough power for the following spells and rituals.

It is also important to note that, for the sake of clarity, all the spells and rituals are written as if dictated directly to the reader. This should allow for a smoother read and a deeper understanding of the magical works.

Chapter 4: The Lunar Grimoire – The Full Moon

The Full Moon Ritual

Most Wiccans celebrate the full Moon more than any other phase of the Moon. As such, it is only fitting to begin with a full Moon ritual. This particular rite is intended to honor the Mother Goddess as well as the abundant and nurturing energy She brings when the Moon is full.

Before you begin this ritual, you will want to make sure your altar is clean. Most Wiccans keep a chalice and incense on their altar at all times. Both will be used during this ritual. Other materials will include some sort of drink to pour into your chalice (please be sure your chalice is safe to drink from), clear quartz, and a small offering of plant material or food that does not include rosemary. You may also want to bring anything that needs cleansing or charging into the circle so that you can include that in the ritual.

Much of the ritual is written with the assumption that the incantations and prayers will be spoken aloud. If you are shy or are not in a place where you can say them out loud, you can simply recite them in your head or mouth them without sound. The Divine will hear you and understand, regardless of whether or not you emit sound.

The Ritual Bath

Begin you shower as you would any normal shower. If possible, keep the lights dim, but do not turn them off entirely. As with all things in magic, safety is key. Should you feel inclined to light candles, choose neutral or soothing colors and a scent that reminds you of home. And home could mean the place you grew up or your idea of home.

For some, this might be the scent of freshly baked cookies. For others, it might be the sharp scent of pine needles to represent the mountains. The full Moon belongs to the Mother Goddess and She is the utter embodiment of Home.

Ritual baths are essentially normal showers but with a little more mindfulness. To this end, you should either opt for unscented soaps or soaps with rich scents like sandalwood, dragon's blood, or coffee. The Mother Goddess is a goddess with experience who still delights in the beautiful. Scented soaps allow you to honor her fullness and wisdom while indulging in a small act of luxury.

As you bathe, try and be mindful of all that the full Moon represents. Think on things that are full and ripe with possibility. Imagine possibilities that you would like to see manifest in your own life. Focus your mind on those things you would like to nurture or grow. You can be as literal or as metaphorical as you want. The Goddess will see your intent when you bring it into the ritual circle.

When you are ready to end your ritual shower, close your eyes and envision the water washing away any stray pieces of energy. You can imagine these as tiny bits of thread stuck to your skin. As the water washes over you, imagine them swept away down the drain, leaving you only with your own focused energies. Before you turn off the water, you can opt for a small prayer to the Mother Goddess, thanking her for the abundance you already have and the fullness of energy you feel.

Ritual Garb

If you are the type to wear street clothes to a ritual, you can attune your clothing to the full Moon by adding small trinkets or pieces of jewelry. A ceramic full Moon charm is easily added to a bracelet and worn around the wrist. Larger charms can be threaded on cord or ribbon, then tied around the neck. Even these small symbols help connect you to the energy of the full Moon.

For those who have a single set of ritual clothes, there are larger additions to focus your energy on the ritual at hand. You can add a sash or belt embroidered with images of the full Moon. Or, if you want to purchase a specialty item, you can find scarves printed with photographs of the Moon taken by various spacefaring craft.

If you want to create a set of ritual clothing specific to the full Moon, try to use colors associated with the Moon and motherhood. Pale grey for the color of the Moon or white to symbolize the cool light She shines down upon us. Red indicates the blood of womanhood as well as the vitality of life and birth. Light blue is another color associated with the mother goddess, as it is soothing and can also resemble the color of the Moon itself.

Anyone can paint full Moons on their face with the appropriate makeup. You may also want to consider drawing full Moons on your arm in non-toxic or cosmetic markers. Trinkets may also be worn on belts or in your hair, should your hair texture and length support them.

The Ritual

Begin the ritual by raising your protective circle. Then stand facing west. For the full Moon ritual, the Quarters are called beginning with west because west corresponds to water. And the water of the womb is what brings forth all life, as the Mother Goddess knows better than anyone.

Raise your hands and tip your face up the Moon, your eyes closed. Recite the following incantation:

Oh, waters of the west

See my circle and hear my plea

Join me now, on this night

To honor the Mother Goddess

Who turns the fullness of her face upon us?

Walk around the perimeter of the circle – or, if casting from the center, turn in place – until you are facing north. This is the next cardinal direction when moving clockwise or Deosil around the circle. The next three incantations are given in order of the directions they represent. Be sure to move or turn toward the proper direction before reciting each incantation.

Stable Earth of the north

May the roots of your energy weave together beneath me

And join me this night in my circle

I ask your support as we honor the Mother Goddess

In whom all things grow

Gentle wind in the east

Dance around me as I honor our Mother

As her fullness hangs above us

I ask that you lend yourself this night

To the powers within my circle

Mighty fire to the south

The burning agent of passion and change

I plead, lend me your fierce energy

That my voice be lifted to the Mother herself

Full and high in the sky above us

Lower your hands and return to your altar or the center of the circle. Tip your face back toward the full Moon and let yourself sink to your knees. This is a position of veneration and shows the Mother Goddess that you wish to honor Her.

When you are settled on your knees, spend some time in thoughtful meditation. Think first of the things that have come to fullness since the last full Moon. If you can't think of anything in particular, think of times when you felt content or nurtured. Let yourself smile as you think of the positive events you have encountered or the uplifting emotions you have felt.

While still on your knees, shift your thoughts to things you would like to nurture. This can be personal achievements, professional goals, or even relationships you would like to see grow stronger. If it helps, you can visualize smoke or wind carrying these desires up to the Mother in the Moon, that she may look at them and help as she can.

After you have spent some time in contemplation, rise to your feet and open your eyes. Move to your altar and light the incense, bringing together the elements of air and fire. For the full Moon ritual, you can use incense similar in scent to the soap you used for your ritual bath. As you light the incense, recite these words:

Mother Goddess

This night you bless us with your light

As you hang brilliant and full in the sky

In this circle we honor you, the elements and I

Fire and air breathe life together

As the smoke rises towards your light

I pray they will carry my voice to you

High above me in the night sky

Pick up your drink in one hand and your chalice in the other, then continue with the next section of the prayer.

Water honors you

As it ebbs and flows

Bringing life as you do

I share this ebb and flow with you

And offer of my own energy and my own libations

Take a sip of your drink, then pour some into your chalice until it is about half-full. If your usual chalice is not safe to drink from – which is something you should be absolutely certain about – use a glass in place of your chalice.

Now set down the liquids and pick up the clear quartz.

Earth, as it supports us all, joins me in honoring you

With this stone it joins me in my circle

Together we offer our enduring devotion

And seek to nurture, as you do, the goodness of life

If you have brought something into the circle to be charged or cleansed, now is the time to arrange them. Anything that you want to cleanse should be laid out in direct light from the full Moon. These items do not need to stay on your altar, but you should not leave your protective circle.

Items that need to be charged should fit on your altar. If it is something too large, like a bag or a garment, you can lay it out in front of your altar. The charging will work best if they too are in the light of the full Moon but they should not touch the items being cleansed. As you lay out the items, be sure and say a small prayer to the Goddess so that she knows you do not assume she will help, but are asking for her aid instead.

Mother Goddess

Who nurtures all things great and small?

If it pleases you

Lend your energy to (name the item or items)

That they may aid me in honoring you

And nurturing the world around me
As you nurture and guide us all

The final step of the ritual is to take stock of all you have set before the Goddess, then turn your face up to the sky once more. Think again on all the ways you have felt the Mother Goddess' presence since the last full Moon and fill yourself with gratitude. Visualize your vibrant feelings rising up to the Moon, carried by the smoke of your incense. Know that the Mother Goddess sees your gratitude and your appreciation, and let it gladden your heart a little more.

If you have been having a hard time, return to your knees and bow your head. Imagine the presence of the Mother Goddess' hand on the back of your head as you let yourself feel the frustration and sadness that has been building up. With the Moon full and bright in the sky, let your own heart be cleansed as the items laid out in the moonlight are cleansed. Though the Mother Goddess might not offer an immediate solution, let her bring you comfort and solace so that she can guide you to a place of peace.

This step may be an emotionally heavy one. Some practitioners may find that they cry or physically react in other ways. These reactions are normal and should be accepted as part of the solace offered by the Divine. So long as they do not hurt you or anyone else, let the reactions take their natural course. You may feel more drained at the end of the ritual. But there is a strong chance that you will also feel more peace.

Finishing the Ritual

There is no rush to finish this ritual. You can sit in the energy and emotion of it for as long as you need to. The Mother Goddess is patient above all else. When you feel it is time to end the ritual, rise to your feet. Quietly thank the Goddess for the time she has spent with you and anything else you felt during your ritual. There is no codified wording for this, as every experience will vary. But it is important to name the things you felt, so as to open your own awareness and ensure the Goddess feels acknowledged.

Next you must release the energy of the Watchtowers. Start in the south, as that was the last quarter called at the beginning of the ritual. Move through each direction in a counterclockwise or Widdershins fashion. As you do, recite the following incantation but tailor it to fit each of the directions and their elements:

Southern Fire

Thank you

For lending me your power this night

May you go in peace

Protected by the Mother's light

When you have released all of the quarters, return to the center of your circle. Close your eyes and summon forth the visualization of your circle. Lower the energy until it is no longer a sphere by a flat circle on the ground. Then walk the perimeter of it, one hand out over the circle so that you can gather up your energy as you go. Walk counterclockwise and collect your energy, effectively breaking the circle.

Now is the time to clean up any remaining debris from the ritual. The drink in your chalice can either be drunk, as the Goddess has had her fill of it, or you can pour it out. You can also leave it on your altar overnight, but it may spoil or attract bugs depending on the drink you used.

As you clean, try to focus your energies on filling up any drained or empty spots within yourself. You may feel exhausted after the ritual and centering will help alleviate some of that. Food and water will also help, as well sleeping or working quietly on something you find soothing. Now is the time to fill up your soul with good things that you want to see grow in your life, starting with a little bit of self-care.

General Full Moon Spells

Spells are like rituals in that you must cast a protective circle and call in the appropriate entities before you can cast a spell. For the spells in this chapter, each one should begin with raising a protective circle and at least calling in the energy of the full Moon with the following incantation:

Oh, Mother Moon

Please join me in my circle

Lend your energy to my working

That I may taste success with your aid

You can also call in the Watchtowers if you feel so inclined. But these spells are all relatively small so calling the quarters isn't entirely necessary.

Creative Abundance Spell

Artists run dry. It's a fact that every artist, no matter their medium, has cursed since humans first invented art. This spell seeks to refill the well of inspiration when it seems empty.

You do not need to be at your altar for this spell, though you will need a surface to write on. If you're flexible you can cast this circle anywhere and simply put your paper on the floor. A clipboard or other hard surface might also help. And if you can cast your circle around a table, that may be ideal.

Whatever surface you choose to use, bear in mind that you will be folding your paper and pouring wax on it to seal it shut. There is a strong possibility of dripping wax onto the surface under your paper. Please plan accordingly.

You will need:
- A pencil or pen
- Several blank sheets of paper
- A candle in either grey, pale blue, or red
- A match
- A candle holder
- Access to a safe moonlit location to store your paper overnight

Once you have raised your circle and called in the energy of the full Moon, settle yourself wherever you intend to write. Place your writing utensil on top of the paper, then place your dominant hand on top of both. Close your eyes and turn your face up to the Moon. Focus your thoughts on the spell at hand. If other thoughts keep crowding in, simply acknowledge them and then remind yourself that you are focusing on the spell.

When your energy is focused and your breathing is as even as possible, light the candle and recite these words:
Though it feels my muse has fled
I shall not fear and I shall not dread
For the Mother does Nurture us in all things
And with Her aid, my dreams take wing

As you say the incantation, you should feel the energy of the Mother filling you up. It might not feel like the electric fervor of creative inspiration. But it should feel like a determined sense of purpose. You should feel as if you have set your sights on something and you know with absolute resolve that you will do your best to reach that goal. It makes take a few recitations and some visualization before you can maintain this sense of purpose.

When you are full of Her energy, open your eyes and pick up your writing utensil. On the paper in front of you, write down a description of the project you want to work on. Be as vague or specific as you like. You may find that you start vague and move into incredible detail as you go. For example, a composer might start with "a song that evoke wonder when looking at fireworks" and end up with the instruments they want to use, sections of music, and possibly even follow-up pieces.

Write until you cannot write any more. You may write on the front and back of the sheets or use multiple pieces of paper. Or you may find that you only write one or two lines before you can no longer put until words what you are thinking of. Both are acceptable, it is simply a difference from one person to another. When you are ready to set down your pen or pencil, take a deep breath and add one final line. At the very end, under the last thing you wrote, add "Aided by the Mother Goddess, I am determined and I Will Succeed."

Now set aside your writing tool and begin folding the paper. Try folding it into thirds or into sixths so that the opening is in the center of the page rather than only at the edges. The more pages you have written on, the more difficult this will be, but try at least for a tri-fold such as they use for letters sent through the post.

Carefully pick up the candle and, with an eye on the flame so you don't burn yourself, pour the wax over the seal. Imagine the Mother Goddess' hand over yours, guiding where the wax goes so that you are sealing all that creative energy into the packet together. The wax may run and the flame will always tip so as to point up, so be very careful not to burn yourself.

Now set aside the letter and let the wax cool. As this may take some time, you can release the energies from your circle and open it, then go about your normal business. Once the wax is hardened, however, take the letter to a place where it will stay safe and dry while bathed in light from the full Moon. Leave it there overnight, then retrieve it in the morning.

When you're ready to work on whatever project you described in your packet, crack the wax seal and open the pages. Breathe deeply and let the determination of the Mother fill you once more. If you have to wait before you can work on your project, leave the letter on your altar or under your pillow so that it either remains charged by proximity to the Divine or remains close to your thoughts.

Full Moon Contentment Spell

The Mother Goddess is a being of contentment. She is content to wait for the birth of her child. She is content to ready her home for the new life it is about to receive. And She is content to share that peace of mind with those who believe in her.

This spell charges a small stone with that aspect of the Mother Goddess' energy. Whenever you feel anxious or suffer from stress, simply hold the stone and rub it with your thumb. Any stone will do, but there are a few types of stones that work best. Hematite and clear quartz are excellent options. If you do not want to purchase a large enough chunk of either to hold firmly in your palm, you can use any stone you pick up from nature in a moment of relative calm.

You Will Need:
- Your chosen stone
- A stick of incense in a soothing scent such as lavender
- A match or lighter
- A place in full moonlight to leave the stone overnight

Raise your circle and invite the full Moon and Her energy into your circle. Though you *can* call the Quarters, it is actually advised that you don't. This spell is meant to focus the energy of the Moon into your chosen stone. If you call in other energy sources, the effect on the stone might become muddled.

When the energy in your circle has settled, light the incense. As the incense settles into steady burn, close your eyes and focus your thoughts. As with the last spell, you do not have to banish all other thoughts. Simply acknowledge any that are not related to the spell, then let them go and return your focus to the magical work at hand.

After your thoughts are focused, take the stone in your dominant hand. With your palm down, so the stone is exposed to the smoke, slowly pass the stone back and forth over the incense. As you do, recite the incantation:

Great Mother of All
Shining high above the world
Wellspring of peace and home
I beg three, reach out to me
Fill this stone with your loving comfort
That I may carry You with me
And soothe my aching soul

Repeat the incantation a few times, until the stone grows noticeably warmer in your hands. At that point, set the stone aside and tamp out the ember against a hard, non-flammable surface other than the stone. Make sure the ember is entirely snuffed out, then put the incense back into its holder and set down your stone.

Release all the energy from your circle. Take extra care to thank the Mother Goddess for joining in this spell and lending her energy to the stone. Once the energy is released and the circle opened, clean up any ash from the incense and retrieve your stone. Set it in place where it will stay safe and dry overnight while it soaks up the light of the full Moon.

In the morning, retrieve your stone once more. You may want to find a small pouch to put it in so that it does not get lost in the bottom of your bag or confused with another stone. Make sure you always have this stone close at hand, even if it's just on a table nearby when you're working. Whenever your stress levels start to rise, take the stone in your hand and rub your thumb across it as you focus on the warmth and comfort housed within the stone.

If you use your stone frequently, it will need regular cleansing and recharging. You can cleanse your stone under the new Moon and charge it under the following full Moon. If you do not want to go that long without a Soothing Stone, you can charge two in one night and use one while you're cleansing the other. And while it is true that you can cleanse items under the full Moon as well as the new Moon, you cannot cleanse and charge an item at the same time.

You will also want to make sure you have a fairly good idea which type of stone you're using. Most stones found on the ground are sedimentary rocks and, for the most part, can handle things like water and mild heat. But certain stones such as hematite react badly to water. Hematite can rust and some – albeit rare – crystals can even have explosive reactions. If you're not sure your stone is safe in water, put it aside when you're bathing or swimming. It is always better to err on the side of safety.

Chapter 5: The Lunar Grimoire – The New Moon

The new Moon stands as the polar opposite of the full Moon. It is not a time of fullness and abundance. Rather, it is a time of emptiness. But this does not have to be a negative thing. There is potential in emptiness. Nothing much eventually becomes something. Or, conversely, a sense of nothing offers peace after a long stretch of activity. Everyone has been through a stressful time where they wanted only to go home and do nothing. That is exactly the sort of rest offered by the new Moon.

New Moon rituals have very different energy from full Moon rituals, which is only to be expected. While the full Moon brings a sense of warm determination and contentment, a new Moon ritual focuses on the chill calm of reflection. Whether you feel the new Moon is the end of something or the beginning, it is a time for calm. A time when you can sit comfortably in the cool darkness, without fear or anxiety.

Before starting this ritual, you will have to gather a few things. You should have your journal, Grimoire, or Book of Shadows on-hand. If you don't want to write in those, you can bring a sheaf of paper or common notebook into the circle. You will also want something to write with and a hand mirror large enough to see your whole face in. If you practice any form of divination, bring your tools with you into the circle. Because this ritual may take some time, you will also want a comfortable place to sit and a surface on which you can write for some length of time.

This ritual focuses on self-reflection, which may also be known as Shadow Work. More experienced practitioners may actually delve into the spirit realm while conducting Shadow Work. But, for now, you will start with self-reflection. You will use your mirror – and any divination tools you may have – to reflect upon yourself, your thoughts, and any questions you may have. Then you will write down what you learn and any new questions you may want to explore in the next new Moon ritual.

Ritual Bath

As with the last ritual, you want the lights dim. If it is safe to bathe only be candlelight, you might want to give that a try. Those who opt for candles will want to try dark grey or black candles, though these might hard to find in scented versions.

Should you find scented versions – or opt for scent over color – try to go for light scents that aren't too floral. Things like juniper or mulberry. These scents are sweet, but they do not evoke the bright growth of the waxing Moon.

Sandalwood is still a good scent for this ritual bath, because sandalwood is widely accepted as a cleansing scent. If you want to differ from your full Moon ritual bath, however, opt for something sweet. This will give you a little energy boost without taking your energy to a warmer level.

You should also opt for a shower that is room temperature or slightly cooler. Always be mindful of the weather and the ritual's location, however. If you're going to be outside on a cold night, you don't want to drop your body temperature too low beforehand. If you're inside or can put on layers, however, a slightly cool shower is a good way to keep your mind focused on the coolness of the new Moon's energy.

As you bathe, focus your thoughts on things that have ended since the last new Moon. Try not to dwell on any one thing too long. This will be difficult if the ending was recent or particularly painful. And if you have lost a love one, you may want to address that loss in its own ritual. But for general endings, simply acknowledge each one and then move to the next.

When you have gone through them all, think of the things that you want to start before the next new Moon. This could be someone you want to start talking to, a project you want to undertake, or a holiday that is coming up in the next twenty-nine days. Let each one sit for a moment before moving on to the next. In this way, you can acknowledge that the new Moon is about both endings and beginnings, as it ends one lunar cycle and begins the next.

Focus your thoughts once again on the energy that you have collected throughout the day. The people you encountered, the experiences you had. Envision all of this as loose thread stuck on your skin. Not envision them washed away by the falling water. Imagine all of the random bits of energy swirling down the drain before it can settle on your skin once more. Start at your head and hair and work your way down until even your toes are clear of energy that is not yours.

Turn off the water, all the while imagining the cool starlight washing over your skin in place of moonlight. There is no Goddess in the sky this night. Instead it is you and the stars, and the infinite possibilities that can rise out of nothing.

Ritual Garb

Street clothes for this ritual should be in shades of dark grey or black. You can emulate the stars, whose light is the only light in the night sky during this ritual, by wearing small rhinestones or pieces of metal. Small, shiny black beads can represent the new Moon as well. These are easily strung into bracelets or necklaces, or worn on belts. Some people might even braid them into their hair, depending on hair length and texture.

If you have a set of ritual clothes, add a black or dark grey sash. Black sashes with strands of glittery thread are especially suited to new Moon rituals. You may also want to wear a cloak with a hood, depending on the weather and where the ritual is being conducted. This not only puts your face into shadows as the Moon is in shadow, but it allows you a little bit more solitude in a group setting.

For those who want to make specific robes for new Moon rituals, a tunic or shift in black is an excellent choice. You can embroider it with tiny stars to simulate a moonless sky. Small silver accents such as jewelry or small baubles sewn onto the fabric also make for excellent representations.

Although a hood may hide your face in shadows, you generally want to be fresh faced for this ritual. The new Moon is a time of reflection and, while some people feel more comfortable in makeup or face paint than without it, reflection is best done when we are most our natural selves.

The Ritual

Set your protective circle, ensuring that it surrounds a place where you can sit and write. You do not need to have your altar in the circle for this ritual, though you may feel more anchored if you include it.

Once your circle is raised, it is time to call the Watchtowers. Unlike the full Moon ritual, the new Moon ritual is about connecting to your own energy and the energies around you that you can call on when the Goddess is not present. Because of this, the motions to call the Watchtowers are much more specific and attuned to the elements of each direction.

To begin, move to the northern point of your circle. North is earth and the earth's energy is, largely, calm and cool much like the energy of the new Moon. Because their energies are so similar, the new Moon will ease your ability to call on the powers of the north. Hold your hands palm-down toward the ground, then recite this incantation:

Immovable Earth of the North

As no light shines in the deep cool calm of your caverns

So, no light shines from the Moon this night

I seek your steadfast guidance

As I walk in the shadows

Beneath the Moon's covered face

Move next to the east and hold your hands out to either side. Be sure and keep your eyes open while you summon the energy of the Watchtowers. Though there is no moonlight, the nights of the new Moon are times when we can see the most clearly. With your hands out and your eyes open, speak the incantation:

Breath of Wind and Air residing in the East

Whisper your secrets to me

On this the night of the new Moon

Fill my lungs that I may breathe life

Into truth hidden among the shadows

South is the next Quarter as you move clockwise around your circle. When you stand at the southern edge of your circle, hold your hands in front of you. Turn your palms out as though you are warming them at a fire. To summon the fiery energy of the south, call out these words:

Brilliant fires of the South
I call upon your light this night
As the Moon does not shine
So, the light of your flames will dance among the stars
I ask that, together, you guide me through the shadows
To learn and explore
And to return home safely

Finally stand at the western edge of your circle. Unlike the previous directions, your hands will be in motion as you call this Watchtower. Hold your hands down at your side and gently sway them as if you are stirring your fingertips through water that they just barely reach. The liquid energy of the west can be called forward with these words:

Life giving waters of the West
I call upon you this night
As you grow darker through your depths
So, this night grows darker as the Moon hides Her face
Tonight, I wander into the shadows
And pray that you help me rise back to the light
Before this night is over

If you cast your circle around your altar, stand in front of it. If you did not, kneel or sit in the center of your circle. Bow your head and close your eyes. Before you can begin Shadow Work, you must focus your mind. Many people are told that focusing on themselves is selfish. And, in some situations, this is true. But this ritual is about self-reflection and, in this instance, focusing on yourself is the only way to learn more about who you truly are.

Observe your thoughts for a little while. If there are thoughts that continuously crop up or dominate your mind, make a note of them but do not judge them. Tonight, is not a night for judgment. The new Moon is a time to observe and to learn, which you must set aside judgment to do.

You don't have to sit too long with your thoughts. It will be hard to tell time when you are being introspective, but a good rule of thumb is to stop when you notice your thoughts are on a loop. This either means you have sat with your thoughts for a very long time or your mind is preoccupied with a few specific things and it is time to dig into them.

Settle yourself into a comfortable position where you can write. This portion of the ritual will take quite some time, so sitting on the floor with a clipboard might get uncomfortable. Make sure you're sitting in a place where you have your mirror close at hand. And if you have Divination tools, ensure you have room to use them.

Once comfortable, place your dominant hand over your writing utensil and the paper you're going to use. With your eyes open and your gaze focused on a spot somewhere in the distance, recite this incantation:

Tonight, I walk among the shadows

Tonight, I will learn and grow

But as I walk in the darkness, I will not fear

For I am grounded in earth

My lungs are filled with mighty wind

Fire lights my path

And the deep waters of life will guide me home

It is normal to be nervous before undertaking Shadow Work. But always remember that the energy of the Watchtowers and their elements are protecting you as you undertake your journey. You can also repeat this incantation – or parts of it – as you progress through the Shadow Work.

There isn't a hard and fast structure for the rest of the ritual. You may find Shadow Work uncomfortable and feel that you're ready to stop after only a few minutes. Or you may find that digging into your questions is fascinating and freeing. If this is the case, you may find yourself leaving the ritual hours after starting. In either case, make sure you have refreshments ready to replenish you after the fact.

Shadow Work does begin with a few specific steps, however. Earlier, when focusing your thoughts, you made note of any that appeared repeatedly or seemed to dominate your inner monologue. The first thing you will do is write down these thoughts. You can be as vague or descriptive as you like. So long as you understand what your notes are referring to, whatever you write is enough.

You might not delve into those thoughts during your first round of Shadow Work. But it is good to keep a record of them. Over time you may notice patterns in your thoughts that can act as guides for future Shadow Work.

After you write down those thoughts, write down any questions that have been on your mind. These questions are not limited to any topic. They can be religious, personal, or simply matters of curiosity. And though this might not seem like an effective form of self-reflection at first, the direction of your curiosity says a lot about you. If you find yourself frequently thinking about a certain topic and are simultaneously seeking creative inspiration, you may find the two work together. Or if you struggle in a certain personal area and find your thoughts dominated by large changes you want to make; one is likely to affect the other.

Take your time with these questions. Write down any branching ideas or new questions that arise. If you use Divination, you might want to ask for guidance in which branches to follow as you explore your thoughts. Some Divination forms may also provide simple answers that can help you resolve some questions or simplify others.

Eventually you will reach a natural stopping point. Either the energy of water will call you home, you will run low on your own energy, or your thoughts will simply go quiet. Do not push yourself past these points. These are your cues that it is time to leave the shadows and return to the light with all the knowledge and questions you now carry.

Finishing the Ritual

Take a moment to orient yourself when you return from your journey in the shadows. Set down your pen, shake out your hands, and take several deep breaths. After walking so long in your thoughts, it is a good idea to reconnect with your body.

Start with your toes and really listen to the signals your body is sending. Feel the way they press against the socks or shoes or the floor. Notice the way they settle one against another. Then move your awareness to your foot, maintaining the same level of detail.

Move up from your feet to your knees to your legs to your hips. Take special care with joints such as knees, ankles, hips, and shoulders. These are some of the most vulnerable yet important places on your body. Notice any discomfort and make the decision to address those feelings as soon as the ritual is complete. Then, when the ritual is complete, follow through on these decisions.

As you move up through your body take stock of your energy levels. Do you feel refreshed or exhausted? Are you hungry or thirsty? All of these issues can be addressed once the ritual is complete, but first you must be consciously aware of them so you can approach them in a deliberate manner.

As your awareness reaches your face, pick up the mirror. Hold it in front of you and slowly take in the features of your face. Try and think a positive thing about each feature. This may seem vain or frivolous, but you just spent time taking in your own thoughts with compassion and curiosity. As your face is the aspect of yourself you turn out into the world, it is only right that you give it the same respect if only for a few minutes.

It may be difficult to take this step at first. Many people have features they dislike or tend to glaze over. But the new Moon is a time of potential and of walking with yourself. Use this opportunity to plant the seeds of self-love and self-respect.

When you have touched on each of your features, give yourself a kind smile and set aside the mirror. Rise from your seat but do it slowly. You might feel weak or slightly disoriented, even after taking the time to reconnect with your physical self. Once on your feet, move to the western point of your circle and begin to release the energy of the Watchtowers.

Hold your hands as you did when calling the Quarters. Recite each of the following incantations while standing at the appropriate edge of the circle. You should be moving in a counterclockwise direction so you can "unwind" the energy that you called forth earlier.

Thank you, oh guiding waters of the West

I wandered far from home but did not fear

For I knew you would call me back

Up through the depths and into the light

Thank you, brilliant flames of the South
You were my guide through the darkness
And lit my path home
I stand here now aglow in your warmth

Thank you, wise air of the East
You filled my lungs with breath and my ears with secrets
All I have learned I carry forward
And will speak with the winds of my breath

Thank you, steadfast earth of the North
For holding me fast in your cool darkness
And being the place upon which
My feet rest
To ground me back into the here and the now.

Walk the perimeter of your circle counterclockwise, one hand extended over the circle so you can gather your energy back into yourself. This is especially important when you perform Shadow Work under the new Moon. Such magical work requires a lot of energy, even if it does not feel like it at the time.

Once you have gathered up your energy, put everything back where it belongs. If you wrote your shadow work directly into a journal or Grimoire, return it to its usual storage place. If you opted for loose paper or a common notebook, you can put these into a binder and either store them in a private location or keep them with your Grimoire.

It is especially important that you eat and drink water after Shadow Work. Though you spent most of your energy on your own thoughts, it is still a taxing process. This is even more true if your focus was on emotionally heavy topics. Though it might be tempting to reach for junk food, you might want to opt for a full meal. If that is not an option, at least go for something with protein, fat, and some nutrients. Once you have met those marks and had some water, it's perfectly acceptable – and even encouraged – that you indulge in some kind of sweet treat or junk food.

If your work took you into emotionally heavy territory, you might want to engage in some self-care using comfort items. For some people this is a specific childhood toy. For others it is a particular piece of clothing or a scent that they keep a candle of. You can also put on a movie or soothing music. Just be mindful that you will likely need rest soon after completing the ritual and its clean up.

Some Shadow Work leads to places of pure curiosity. If this is where your shadow work led, you might want to pull out your notes the in the next few days and do some mundane research. This will not damage the energy of your Shadow Work or pull you back into it. It's simply one of the many areas where your magical and mundane lives will intersect.

General New Moon Spells

The new Moon is the Moon of reflection and that was the focus of the ritual. But the new Moon also presents a chance to either rid yourself of things you absolutely never want to connect with again, or to plant seeds for exciting new possibilities. The following spells tap into one of these two possibilities.

Because there is no Goddess to call on, you must do one of two things. You must either call the Watchtowers into your circle or you have to ground and center before casting your spell. The Watchtowers will lend you any extra energy you need. Grounding and centering allow you to concentrate your own energy, however. Both options give you the power you need to cast the spells. You need only choose the energy balance that feels right for you.

If you do choose to call the Quarters, you should develop your own general summoning chant. New Moons are an opportunity for you to work more closely with energies other than the Moon. As such, you should interact with them on as personal a level as possible. While you will want to properly screen general spirit energy before connecting with it, the Quarters are always a safe energy to connect to.

New Moon Banishing Spell

Banishing spells are usually reserved for the waning Moon. As the Moon slowly vanishes from the sky, so the subject of the spell vanishes from your life. Some things, however, call for more intense and direct action. That is where a New Moon Banishing Spell comes in handy.

You must be careful within banishing spells. Because the Wiccan Rede specifies that you can do no harm, you must not cast the spell on a specific person or group of people. You can direct the spell to your bond with the people you want to avoid. But you cannot cast your spell directly upon them.

At best, the spell will not work. At worst, the negative intention of the spell will bounce back at your, increased threefold in accordance with the Threefold law. This is a magical law that states all energy you put out into the world will come back three times over. It is not something magic users should take lightly.

You must also be mindful of your intention when you cast a banishing spell, particularly this one. New Moon banishing spells call upon the void where the Moon would normally shine in the sky. All banished things are cast into this void and intention dictate how this is done. As you cast the spell, keep in mind the thought that you want to do no harm and that the banishment is simply a means of protection and growth for all parties involved.

The idea of doing no harm is also reflected in the materials listed for this spell. After the spell you will be disposing of the box. The hope is that a cardboard box tied with cotton string will decompose, thereby returning all the energy and components involved back to the earth where they can be reclaimed, cleansed, and returned to the world.

You will need:
- A small cardboard or paper box
- A scrap of paper
- A nearly-use pencil or nearly-empty pen
- Black cotton thread
- Either a garbage can or a place to bury the box
- Something to write on

Cast your protective circle before you call the Quarters or ground and center. No matter which energy option you choose, you want to be inside your protective circle when you begin. Once you have raised your circle and collected the energy you want to use, settle yourself in a comfortable position to write in.

Close your eyes and visualize the thing you want to banish. If you are having trouble with a specific person or group of people, focus on the bond that connects you to them. If it is a negative thought or habit, create a visual representation for the thing. You can also do this for an illness, though banishing an illness takes a great deal of power.

Hold the visualization firm in your mind. When you have a good grasp of it, open your eyes and place your dominant hand over the paper and whatever you have brought to write with. Surround the image in your head with glowing black bonds that reach up into the space where the Moon usually shines. These bonds are the call of the new Moon's void. As you progress through the spell, they will slowly pull the visualization into the void, effectively banishing the subject of your spell.

Once the bonds are firmly in place, raise your free hand up toward the sky and recite these words:

A scrap of paper

A stub to mark

A banishment that casts you

Into the dark

Not a care to give

Only scraps for will do

I sever now

My bonds to you

The void of the Moon shall hold you

And keep you far from me

This is my will, this is my cry

Upon the new Moon

So, mote it be

Lower your hand and pick up your writing utensil. On the scrap of paper, write down the thing you visualized. It can be "my bond with (name)" or "my habit of (habit)." It does not have to be more descriptive than that, as your visualization will have done much of the work.

Take a deep breath and then scribble over the words you have just written. Don't rip the paper, because you don't want to leave a mark on your writing surface that may tie the banished thing's energy to your space. Instead, scribble it out slowly and deliberately. This is not something to be done in anger, but rather a calculated choice that is in everyone's best interest.

Once you can no longer read the words – or the ink or lead has run out – set the writing tool aside. Fold up the piece of paper several times, until it is either hard to fold or too small to bother folding again. Place the scrap of paper into the cardboard box and put the lid in place. Do all of this slowly and with complete control. You want to reflect the new Moon's cool confidence.

When the lid is in place, tie it down with the string. You may want to bring a lot of string and tie it down several times. The more knots holding the lid in place, the tighter the barrier between you and the thing inside. As you tie each knot into place, imagine the bonds of the new Moon's energy pulling your visualization further and further away from you. Know that as it moves away from you, it sinks into the void.

Shake out your hands to rid yourself of any unwanted energy. Open the circle as you would do with any other spell, then pick up your box. Before you clean up the remainder of the spell, carry the box either to the garbage or to a spot where you can bury it without fear it will be disturbed. If you throw it in the garbage, immediately take the garbage bag out to the can so the energy of the spell – and the thing banished – is not sitting in your home.

Now you should go back and clean up the rest of the spell. Either throw away or recycle the remainder of whatever writing tool you used in the spell. To fully finish the spell, you can nurture something that stands in opposition to the thing you banished. If you banished a bad habit, perform an opposite positive behavior. It does not have to become a new habit. In this instance it is simply a mundane rejection of the thing you have magically banished.

Planting Seeds Under a New Moon

The new Moon might be darker than other phases of the Moon. But that does not mean that everything about it must be shrouded in darkness. Shadow Work can create wild positive change. Such is the nature of a Moon that hovers between the end of one cycle and the beginning of another.

To honor the liminal space the new Moon inhabits, you can just as easily plant the seeds of something new as banish something unwanted. This spell is meant to be cast on the new Moon using its undefined potential energy. Unlike the other spells thus far in this book, this spell then connects the new Moon to the next phase. So, as the waning Moon grows, so will the energy of this spell.

You will need:
- A piece of paper OR a printed visual representation of your goal
- A pen (if using blank paper)
- A small, soft drawstring pouch
- Your bed (after the spell has been cast)

Cast your circle and raise your energy. Because this spell calls on the energies of both the new Moon and the waxing Moon, it is best to ground and center rather than calling on the Quarters. This way your spell is powered by your own will and the dual Moon energies that will grow as the Moon does.

When you have settled the energies within the circle, place the image or piece of paper in front of you. If you have chosen to write down the goal you want to reach – or the thing you want to see grow – now is the time to write it down. You can use as much paper as you need. Just bear in mind that the paper will go into the pouch at the end of the spell. The pouch, in turn, will go under your pillow.

With this in mind, write out your goal or the nature of what you want to see grow. Visualize your energy flowing from your fingers and down into your writing utensil. Each stroke on the page will carry your energy and lock you intend to the thing being described.

If you have chosen a printed visual representation – or have chosen to print your goal's description – imagine your energy flowing into the tip of your pointer finger. Trace the shape of the image on the page. If the page contains printed words, trace your finger along the lines of text and read them out loud. Should you be unable to read them out loud, you can mouth the words instead. Both use your breath, which layers the work with additional energy.

When the description, the reading, or the tracing is complete, lay down your utensil and place your hand flat on the page. Close your eyes and envision your goal at its fullest. Imagine it fully grown and realized. Then, with image still in your mind, slowly funnel it through your hand and down into the page. Your hand will likely start to feel warm due to the amount of energy you're channeling. So long as it is not painful, keep going until the entire image has been siphoned into the page.

Once the image has been locked to the page, recite the following incantation

New Moon in the sky

Devoid of light

I call upon you

This quiet night

Soon you will grow

So big and so bright

I ask you now

Please lend me your might

As you grow with each night

Larger and brighter you'll seem

Please lend such vibrancy

So, this, my seedling dream

Let it grow in your power

Till it is as I have seen

By the powers of the Moon

Both new and waxing

So, mote it be

Pick up the paper and slowly fold it until it will fit into the drawstring pouch. Slip the paper inside and pull the drawstring shut. Set the pouch aside and release the energies from your circle as you normally would. After you have released the energies and opened the circle, take a few minutes to clean up the spell.

After the spell has been cleaned up, take the pouch to your room and place it under your pillow. If this is not a secure location, you can also place it between your box spring and your mattress or under one of the slats beneath your bed. So long as it is near you when you are dreaming, any location will do. Each night before you fall asleep, summon forth the image of your goal. If you have a large goal, turn your thoughts to the first step – or next step, in some cases – that you need to take.

Chapter 6: The Lunar Grimoire – Eclipse Magic

Because eclipses do not usually last long – and their appearance varies depending on where in the world you might be located – it is easier to cast spells during an eclipse than perform an entire ritual. The type of spells you will want to cast also vary depending on the type of eclipse that is in effect. And, of course, you may find that your magical energies are blocked during an eclipse. If this happens, take the time to ground and center so that you hold onto the energy you do have.

If you find that you energized by eclipses rather than drained, you may find eclipse magic to be useful. The term "eclipse magic" is used specifically because it is possible adapt nearly any spell to the energy of an eclipse. There is a framework that you must work within. But once you have the basic guidelines memorized, the rest is up to your comfort and creativity.

To adapt spells for eclipse magic, you must first know what kind of eclipse it is. If it is a lunar eclipse, you may be seeing an entire lunar cycle in one day. This will allow you to call upon the entire spectrum of lunar energies as outlined earlier in this book. You might also be seeing a blood Moon, which presents its own specific complications.

If the eclipse is solar in nature, you will witness the sun covering over the Moon. The smaller celestial body will entirely block out the larger, which can also signify lunar energies reaching a fever pitch of intensity as they are backed by the full might of the sun. Solar eclipses may also provide you with all the energy of a daily or seasonal cycle in the span of only one day. But that is more in line with solar magic and therefore outside the scope of this book.

Both types of eclipse bring the energies of the sun, Moon, and earth into alignment. The biggest differences between them are which energies are amplified, which are reduced, and how exactly those amplifications play out.

Lunar Eclipse

If you are going to work with the energy of the lunar eclipse, be prepared to call on every facet of the Moon's power. This means that your spells should call on the energies of all three Triple Goddess aspects as well as the void of the new Moon. While this may seem like an energy overload – and if you're new to magic, it might be – your spells will be able to reach intensities otherwise unimaginable.

A banishing spell, for instance, can start before the eclipse begins. As the Moon passes out of sight, so does the subject of the banishment. When the Moon reappears, it is as if an entire lunar cycle as passed, severing your ties to the unwanted thing as surely as an entire month of time could.

Creativity spells, on the other hand, will lead to intense creative fervors. These should only be cast if you will have immediate access to your creative medium. While a spell to boost creativity will usually leave you feeling tired, the energy of eclipse is so potent that you may feel a bit like someone over-charged your battery.

Solar Eclipse

Solar eclipses only happen during new Moons. Because of this, the lunar energy that is supercharged through the Moon's alignment with the sun is the energy of the new Moon. Thankfully the new Moon has the most diverse and flexible energy of all the lunar phases. This gives you a lot of options to work with.

You should time your solar eclipse spells so that the take place during the fullness of the eclipse. Because eclipse appearances vary based on where you're located and how the earth is oriented during the eclipse, you might have to get the exact time from the website of a reputable space agency. Once you have the specific time, however, you can plan your spells accordingly.

It is also a good idea note the expected duration of an eclipse. The success of your spell depends on the energy it receives from the event itself. If your spell extends beyond the time frame of the eclipse, it might not absorb as much energy.

When calling on the Moon's energy during a solar eclipse, make sure you remain grounded. Because the new Moon is tied so heavily to the concept of the void – and it is now powered through alignment with the sun – there is a greater risk of getting lost among the shadows. There are several ways you can ground yourself so that this does not happen.

The easiest way is to ground and center before and after every spell. These are good practices to perform in a general sense. But during a solar eclipse they remind you that your power is your own and that you can always follow the tether of your energy back to your physical self.

You may also want to carry a stone in your pocket or your hand when working with the energy of the solar eclipse. Conversely, if you do not want to work with the energy of the eclipse and are, instead, trying to ward against it, the full Moon soothing stone spell in this book is an excellent option. Because the new Moon and the full Moon are opposites, the charged stone can act as a balance to keep you on an even footing until the eclipse passes. If you know a solar eclipse is coming up, you can charge several stones to either magnify the effect or to give to others who might react similarly to the eclipse's energy.

Eclipse Safety

If you are performing your magical works outside during an eclipse, always practice safety first. This is particularly important during a solar eclipse but applies to any eclipse event.

The first rule of working magic during an eclipse is that you never look directly at the eclipse. If you are working during a solar eclipse, even if you don't intend to look at the event, make sure you're wearing appropriate eye protection. General use sunglasses do not count as appropriate eye protection. You will want to get eclipse-specific eye wear. The glasses should be no more than three years old and should not be scratched.

Aside from possible eye damage, there is also the social impact of an eclipse to consider. There are many myths surrounding eclipses that may have people on edge. Such myths range from the impacts of eclipses on pregnancies to the idea that direct exposure to an eclipse can cause cancer. These myths have all been debunked. But if you plan on working in a group during the eclipse – or working outside where you might encounter other people – be aware that tensions may be higher than normal.

Chapter 7: The Lunar Grimoire – Moon Magic Spells

It is absolutely possible to perform rituals for both the waxing and the waning Moon. But they aren't particularly common. Rather, most Wiccans use the two longest phases of the Moon to perform a variety of spells.

The rest of this chapter is dedicated to spells that capitalize on the very specific – and very different – energies of the waxing Moon and the waning Moon. Both sections are rounded out with suggestions as to how experienced magic users can adapt other spells, they find to use these energies as well.

As with the previous chapters, all of the spells and suggestions are written as if they are spoken directly to you, the reader.

The Waxing Moon

The waxing Moon is a time of growth. As the Moon grows larger in the sky, so does the Moon's energy. But even at its smallest sliver, the Moon is laden with the energy of new life and of growing things. This means that any spells you cast during the waxing Moon will cause growth.

Ideal spells for the waxing Moon are things like hair growth spells, spells for increased creativity, and spells to help manifest your goals. Goal manifestation spells are particularly popular. Many Wiccans believe that, as the Moon grows larger in the sky, its energy brings their goals closer.

It is, of course, possible to cast spells with less positive outcomes. Such spells include increasing the distance between you and something you dislike. You must be careful with these spells as they must be cast in a way that does not run afoul of the rule to Harm None. But so long as the spell intends no harm, the waxing Moon can help bring about changes that some may see as neutral rather than positive.

The example spell in this chapter – one to promote hair growth – err on the positive side of the waxing Moon. Suggestions on tailoring any spell to the waxing Moon – including banishing spells – are at the very end of this section, after the spells.

Hair Growth Spell

Many hair growth spells require that you use a homemade salve on your hair. That can be a problem for some hair textures, however. This spell is written to be safe for all hair textures and focuses mainly on visualization.

You will be doing a little bit of drawing, particularly in setting up a "model head" to depict your ideal hair length on. But you don't have to get particularly detailed. Just a "u" shape for the head and a few lines for the shoulders will do. Your mental visualization is more important than the drawn image.

This spell also calls for a drawstring pouch. If you choose to reuse the pouch from previous spells in this book, please be sure you cleanse it first. Any tools that are used in a spell – pens, candles, lighters, and incense sticks included – should always be cleansed between uses. It doesn't matter if the next use is magical on mundane. If you didn't deliberately charge the item to carry out the spell, cleanse it before you use it again.

You will need:
- A sheet of paper
- A pencil
- A drawstring pouch

- A surface on which to draw
- A handheld mirror

Cast your circle and call on the energy of the waxing Moon. You can use any of the previous incantations in this book or write your own. Simply tailor it to fit the energies and Goddess aspect of the waxing Moon.

Once you have called the Maiden and her waxing Moon energy into your circle, settle yourself either at a table on your knees. Set aside your paper and your pencil, and pick up the handheld mirror. The first step of this spell is to acknowledge yourself with a kind smile. Spells to change your appearance do not mean that your current appearance is negative and it is important to reaffirm that.

With your smile in place, turn your attention to your hair. Take in its current length and find something to appreciate about it. You may like the color or the texture. Perhaps you like the way it currently frames your face or how easy it is to care for. All things grow best when they are treated positively and your hair is no different.

Now envision this positive aspect of your hair growing as you visualize your hair reaching the desired length. If you appreciate that your hair is easy to care for, imagine that it stays healthy as it grows longer. Should you appreciate the texture of your hair, imagine your longer hair with the same texture. Try to maintain your smile as you conjure this mental image.

Hold the visualization in your mind and set the mirror aside. Pick up your pencil and trace out a basic shape to represent your head and shoulders. You can make it as simple or complex as you like. If you do not feel comfortable drawing, you can print a simple head and shoulders outline from the Internet and use that.

Now draw in the hair you currently have. Again, this does not have to be very realistic. The imagine in your mind will carry the energy for this spell. Your physical drawing is just a way to carry that energy from the mental to the physical realm.

Pause for a moment and close your eyes. Focus on the mental image of your ideal hair length. With the refreshed image at the front of your thoughts, open your eyes and add hair to your drawing. Draw until the hair on your drawing more or less matches the hair in your image. When this is done, set down your pencil and place your dominant hand flat on the page.

Close your eyes and visualize an aura of energy around the image in your head. When the image is entirely surrounded in your energy, channel it from your mind and into your hand, where you will push it into the paper. As you do this, touch your hair with your free hand and say this incantation:

Maiden Goddess

Growing high above

I seek to grow in you

As you grow that which you love

My hair is my own

And I wish to see it grow

Nurtured by the energy

Of the waxing Moon's glow

Finish channeling your mental image into your drawing as the incantation draws to a close. Open your eyes, pick up the paper, and fold it until it will fit in the drawstring pouch. Once you have released the energy from your circle and cleaned up the spell, put this pouch under your pillow.

Be sure and hold the pouch whenever you are preparing to handle your hair. This could be before a shower, when you're about to comb or brush it, or when you plan on styling it. Part of the power in this spell is that the pouch acts as a physical reminder to take the best possible care of your hair. It is a spell that relies on real world action as much as it relies on Divine power.

You can also take this pouch with you if you go to get your hair cut or trimmed. If you feel comfortable, you can show your drawing to the stylist so they know the goal you have in mind. This will help them guide you in the direction of appropriate products and care tips for your hair.

Altering Spells for the Waxing Moon

Nearly any spell can be altered to benefit from the energy of the waxing Moon, though this should only be attempted by experienced magic users. Altering a spell without fully understanding magic may lead to impotent or misdirected spells.

If you have some magical experience, however, there are only a few things you must keep in mind when altering spells for the waxing Moon.

When adapting a spell to fit the energy of the new Moon, make sure you focus on an element of growth or exploration that relates to the spell. If you're trying to banish your connection to something, for example, you can focus on a growing space between you and the subject of your spell.

Spells to break bad habits are also easily adapted to the waxing Moon. You need only shift the focus from the bad habit to growing your resistance to the habit. Or, if you're replacing a bad habit with a good one, you should center your spell on growing the energy around the new habit.

So long as you shift the focus of your spell to growth, you can align it with the energy of the waxing Moon. Just remember that the Moon is growing throughout this phase. Unless you cast the spell toward the end of the waxing phase, the energy in your spell will continue to grow. A banishment spell cast at the beginning of the waxing phase will create a huge rift, rather than a small separation between you and spell's focus. Make sure you time your spells accordingly.

The Waning Moon

Once the brilliance of the full Moon has passed, the Moon begins to wane. And, as it grows smaller, the power of the Crone Goddess becomes more manifest. Despite pop culture's tendency to see crones as fearsome and dangerous, the Crone

Goddess is a wonderful protector. She has seen nearly all that life can offer and has lived through it all.

Spells cast during Her phase of the Moon are usually focused on the idea of endings. The Crone is a Goddess near the end of her Divine life. Yes, she will be reborn with the waxing Moon as a Maiden. But, for now, She is contemplating the life that she has lived and preparing to see it come to a close. Spells for this phase are, accordingly, focused on introspection and closure.

The waning Moon is a popular time for banishing spells. They are especially strong when cast at the very beginning of the phase so that, as the Moon grows smaller, so does your connection to the target of your spell.

You may also want to use the waning Moon as a time to say goodbye or ask for an ending. Perhaps you've have suffered a loss. Or maybe a creative venture just keeps going and you're ready to move on. Whatever the reason, the waning Moon is the perfect time to bring things to a close.

Saying Goodbye Spell

This is quite possibly the most emotionally taxing spell in this book. Shadow Work can be draining. But it is possible to do

Shadow Work without delving too deep into emotions. Depending on what it is you are saying goodbye to, this spell requires you to face those emotions head-on.

If you are saying goodbye to a loved one or something particularly close to your heart, you may find yourself expressing a range of emotions throughout this spell. It is important that you show yourself compassion and allow the emotions to manifest. So long as you do no harm, the emotions are a healthy reaction to saying goodbye.

You Will Need
- Something to represent that which you are bidding farewell
- A box or envelope large enough to hold your representation
- A dark grey or black candle
- A lighter or matches
- A candle holder

Raise your circle and call on the power of the waning Moon. Because this spell is particularly personal, you will want to create your own invocation. It does not have to be fancy and it does not have to rhyme. But it should call on the waning Moon as well as the Crone Goddess and appeal to her knowledge of endings and farewells.

The Crone's energy may be slower to answer than the energy of the other Goddess aspects. This does not mean that she has declined you. She simply needs a little more time to enter your circle. Her energy is cooler and calmer than other energy you may have worked with. It is more akin to the energy of the new Moon, though it is more reserved. Many practitioners feel Her presence as a calm sense of resolve, regardless of whatever emotions they have in that moment.

When Her energy has settled into the circle, seat yourself in a comfortable position. The more painful the goodbye, the more comfortable you will want to be. If you are prone to very strong emotions, you might want to include a comfortable place to sit, lay, or curl up in your circle.

Take up the representation of that which you are saying goodbye to. Run your hands or fingers over it, taking time to remember small details about the representation. When you have covered every inch of it, hold it in both hands and close your eyes. Imagine the thing you must bid farewell to.

You will likely begin feeling stronger emotions at this time. Imagine them as small waves around your feet, neither warm nor cold. You feel them but they do not distract you from the work at hand. In this moment, the calm energy of the waning Moon will help bolster your focus.

Unlike previous spells, there is no incantation for this spell. Instead, you must talk about the focus of your spell. If it is a person, you can recount memories with them. If you're saying goodbye to a project, you can speak on the details or the impact it had on your creative or professional outlook. This may take quite a bit of time and you might have to shift your position to keep going. If it is difficult to speak, you can simply recount the details in your thoughts. Just be sure you hold the representation.

Take all the time you need. This is not a spell to be rushed or taken lightly. Process your thoughts and feelings with as much compassion as you can summon. They are present for a reason. And you must trust in the power of the Crone Goddess that she will help you make sense of the things you're feeling and thinking.

When you are ready, settle yourself once again on your knees or in a seating position, if you moved. Take several deep breaths until your breathing returns to normal, if necessary. When you once again feel in control, create a mental visualization of the object in your hands. From this point, the spell varies depending on the nature of what you're saying goodbye to.

If you're saying goodbye to something that was a positive part of your life, you might not want to sever all ties to it. In this case, visualize tendrils of the Crone Goddess' power wrapping around the image in your mind. At the same time, connect a tendril of your own energy to it. This does not have to be a strong connection or a line by which you feel power to the image. It is simply a way to stay connected with the subject of your spell.

Visualize the Crone Goddess' energy carrying your visualization away as the Moon wanes over the next several days. Unlike with banishing spells, your visualization – and the thing it represents – will not be pulled into the void when the Moon vanishes from the sky. Instead it will travel with the Crone Goddess as she is reborn. It, too, will be reborn so that its energy can come back to the world, refreshed.

If, on the other hand, you are releasing something negative, you will want to avoid attaching your own energy to the visualization. Instead, imagine the bonds of the Goddess' energy wrapping tightly around it and holding it in a vice grip. You may want to tighten your hold on the physical representation as well, just to create a physical foundation for the energy's control.

Now imagine the energy of the Goddess carrying this thing away from you. When the Moon vanishes from the sky, the Goddess will release your visualization into the void before She moves on to her birth. It will stay in the void of the new Moon and go through a cleansing cycle over the next lunar cycle. When the next new Moon appears, the energy will find its way back into the world. At that point it will be cleansed of all connection to you.

Take another deep breath and open your eyes. Put the physical representation into whatever container you selected to house it. When it is secure, release the Crone's energy and open your circle. The next step, again, depends on your connection to the subject of your spell.

If the connection is positive, find a safe space to store the container. You may feel the urge to bring it out and look at it from time to time. This is perfectly fine, so long as you connection to it doesn't interfere with your daily life. If the connection is negative, however, you may want to discard or bury the representation and its container. Depending on the materials of either one, you can also burn it on the night of the new Moon to ensure all of its connection to you is sent into the void of the dark Moon.

Altering Spells for the Waning Moon

As with the farewell spell, anything you alter to fit the waning Moon must rely on the Moon's energy. It will be hard – if not impossible – to make things grow when you power a spell with waning Moon energy. Instead, focus on things you want to see diminish.

Take creativity spells as an example. Rather than trying to boost your creativity, which would run counter to the energy of the Moon, focus instead on reducing writer's block. If you want to form a new habit, focus your spell on reducing your resistance to that habit.

You may also find surprising success with spells that rely on calm energy. If you need consistent energy to carry out a project but the full Moon has already passed, you can call on the Crone's steadfast storehouse of energy to help see you through. Just be aware that the Crone is a goddess who knows her limits. She is not going to let you ignore yours.

A Final Word on Moon Energy

Moon energy is just one kind of energy. It is potent and readily available any night of the year. Even during the new Moon, there is a kind of lunar energy to be had.

But lunar energy is not required to perform magic. You can perform spells that run counter to the Moon's energy if you call upon the Watchtowers, spirits, or even your ancestors. The Moon is powerful but it does not dictate everything.

And this is part of the balance that sits at the core of Wicca. In order to fully work with Moon magic, you must understand its benefits and limitations. Magic, like any other tool, is guided by both. And as you explore various branches of magic, you will find one that works best for you. This can only happen when you've taken the time to fully understand each branch you've explored.

If Moon magic is where you find your magical home, embrace it. Bolster your spells with images of the Moon, songs in Her honor, and representations of all the Moon's phases. Call upon all aspects of the goddess and learn to walk in the shadows that fall when it is the dark of the Moon.

You may also find that studying Moon magic leads you as much to astronomy as astrology. Do not fight this pull. Understanding the Moon and the celestial bodies that move around it will only serve to enhance your power. In your studies you will find that Moon magic intersects with other branches of celestial magic, such as star magic and Sun magic. Go where your studies leads you.

Learn and grow within the Moon's light. She is always ready to guide you.

Conclusion

Thank you for making it through to the end of *Wicca Moon Magic: How does the Moon Affect Nature, Animals and People? Find out How to Understand Moon's Magical Properties According to the Philosophy of Wicca, With Rituals and Spells.* We hope it was informative and able to provide you with all of the tools you need to achieve your goals, whatever they may be.

The next step is to look into other branches of Wiccan magic. You may find that Moon magic suits you best. However, it is always a good idea to look into other magic variations to find the styles and combinations that best support your goals.

Finally, if you found this book useful in any way, a review on Amazon is always appreciated.

Wicca Crystal Magic

A Practical Guide on How to Improve your Life with the Magical Power of Crystals Used by Witches. Attract and Maintain Healthy Relationships, Reduce Anger, Stress and Anxiety

Justine J. Scott

Introduction

Just like other forms of magick, crystal magick plays a very critical role in directing a specific intention you have to the Universe. One thing you will note about crystal spells is that they use other magical tools like herbs, chants, candles, and charms among others. However, the main ingredient in this form of magick is one of more crystals.

Crystals are quite unique magical tools that naturally occur and unlike candles and wands, they are not made by the human hand. You can carve them into various shapes and they still will be effective like when they are used in their raw form. The thing about crystal stones is that they communicate ancient wisdom with us. However, we have to be open and receptive to their messages.

The powers that the crystal possess is similar to that of a wind blowing. In other words, it is naturally occurring. In fact, all matter that we can see and those that we cannot see possess a certain vibrational energy that is intertwined with one another.

Crystal magick works by following the concept of metaphysics and quantum energy. This is exactly how they are able to communicate and transform your reality. This explains the reason why you have to use the crystal together with the power of intentions to harness the interconnection with the Universe.

The crystals use the Hermetic principle of the Law of Attraction. This law states that although we may see certain things as being still, all matter is in constant motion. It also follows the Law of Mentalism that states that everything is mental. In other words, all of the creations arise from the mind of the Universe.

Therefore, we can harness the power of our thoughts and that of our intentions and channel that energy out into the universe through the energy of the crystals. In other words, the crystals serve as conduits of energy to bring us healing and send us positive energy that will manifest in various ways in our waking life.

The use of stones and crystals for magical reasons has grown in popularity in recent years. Many stones have planetary attributions and related herbs as well. These stones can be used for magical talismans, jewelry, offerings or even just carried around in your pocket for protection or other energetic uses. Our ancestors knew of these powerful stones and used them wisely for important magical endeavors. Whether for protection or to house energies or spirits, stones can add a nice dynamic to our practice, while also being beautiful aesthetically.

Consider our traditions of wedding rings and other meaningful jewelry. These metals and stones are used for distinct reasons, whether the general population knows it or not. Choosing stones and metals in your jewelry should be done with great care and not haphazardly carrying around energetic properties that won't benefit you. Diamonds are relatively universal, but the metal they are housed in and other added stones can potentially cause problems for some people especially if the stones are not properly cleansed.

Many New Age communities have been promoting the use of crystals for energetic cleansing and protective barriers for their homes. These techniques are often sold as a newly discovered practice, but we know the folly in this concept. Crystals and stones are formed over the course of thousands of years, comprising of one or many combinations of organic compounds. These crystals and stones all carry their own energetic signature that can be felt or harnessed by a skilled witch or magician. Along with the energetic signatures, these crystals also form physical patterns that are not only beautiful, but also affect their behavior and energy.

The stereotype of the fortune teller with their crystal ball like we see in movies and television shows is far removed from the reality of crystal healing and divination. Although you can very well use a crystal ball to divine and cast spells, it's not going to go over like the movies of course. Many people use the stones for scrying and divination, but there are many other uses too, from protection, planetary work, housing knowledge and even for casting spells or wands, stones and crystals have a lot to offer a Wiccan practitioner.

Not unlike plants and herbs, crystals are considered to be alive, maybe not in the scientific sense of life, but nonetheless alive in some way. Science has found that these crystals do give off measurable energy. Piezoelectricity is found in many stones and is readily used in many devices today, from cellular phones to electric guitar pickups. Striking stones with a hammer or exposing them to certain temperatures will release these electric charges. We know through science that humans are electrochemical in nature as well, this brings up the notion that everything is connected somehow, perhaps the electrical charges are the means that we share experience and existence with the rest of the universe.

There are many ways we can start a crystal magick practice as Wiccans. Crystals can not only be used on their own to house energy or spirits, but can be combined with other materials to create wands, scrying mirrors, fetishes, pentacles or even sculpted to create statues of deities. Crystals and stones also work really well with color correspondence magick. We know planets, herbs, deities and even certain holy days have color correspondences that align with the energy of certain things. There is no exception to this with stones, and in fact stones and crystals are a great way to bring color into your practice. Keep in mind that some stones are dyed a certain color, it will always be more effective to go the natural route, and there are plenty of colorful stones readily available.

Some people feel that for a full effect you have to use the most expensive crystals and stones. This is not particularly correct; you can have just as much success using a common red stone like carnelian as opposed to an expensive and pure ruby. Even a rough ruby works just as well. While diamonds, rubies, sapphires and emeralds are essentially the same chemical makeup, and tend to be purer with less compounds, they tend to be very expensive when they are cut and appraised. These expensive stones are usually harvested in negative ways as well. You do not need expensive stones to have a successful crystal magick practice.

There are thousands of different stones and almost all of them have been explored or used for spiritual or magical purposes. Just like many other practices some people are way more skilled in working with stones than others, be open-minded when approaching stones. And if you are having trouble opt for easy to use stones like clear quartz in your workings. We can't cover them all, but we can touch on a few of the more popular and readily available ones.

But before starting with the first chapter, I want to thank you for choosing this book and I'd really happy if you left me a quick review on Amazon. Enjoy reading!

Chapter 1: What is Wicca

Wicca is Pagan Witchcraft developed in England. It began in the first half of the 20th century, but became famous when Gerald Gardner, a retired British civil servant, introduced it to the world in 1954. Wicca uses 20th century and ancient pagan motifs for its ritual practices.

To help you identify which Wiccan practices and rituals will serve you best, and should, therefore, have a place in your Book of Shadows, it may be useful to run through what Wicca actually is. Different people have varying ideas about this, and that's partly down to the treatment of Wicca and witchcraft in movies and television shows. Also, because Wicca is such a flexible belief system, this can also influence practitioners' views on what they believe constitutes Wiccan practice. So, here's a brief rundown on what is known about Wicca.

Wicca is a belief system or religion – call it what you will, either is appropriate. Fundamentally, its many practitioners promote an organic system of living in harmony with the Universe and appreciating everything it provides for us, while other religions may take the bounties of Nature and the Universe for granted.

Wiccans take pleasure in the hope that dawns with the sunrise, and appreciate the unique beauty of the setting sun. They admire the light as it filters through the leaves of the trees in the forest, and honor the moon as it shines brightly through its phases in the evening sky. They marvel at the way a sleepy meadow blazes into vibrant life as the first rays of the sun strike the grass and flowers with the dawning of a new day.

Wicca is appreciating simple things like the delicate patterns of dewdrops on spider webs, and the way a gentle breeze will lovingly caress the skin on a warm day. Wicca is tuning into the breathtaking blaze of color as the leaves change with the turning of the seasons, and appreciating the softness of the snow in winter. It's working in harmony with Nature and the Universe, for the highest good of all, since we are all part of the One, the Creator, the Divine Spirit, or whatever you choose to identify with.

Wicca knows that you are in the perpetual presence of Mother Nature on all levels, and you realize and gratefully acknowledge your specific role in her enormous family. When you, as a Wiccan, dwell in Mother Nature's house, you are no longer susceptible to the influence of the ego.

Being a Wiccan practitioner means to aspire to be a healer, to help and teach others, to look for the Divine in everything and everyone. Wiccans are givers and protectors who tread their spiritual path with reverence, love, light and positivity of thought, word and deed.

Wicca is a spiritual lifestyle choice whose core tenets are founded in the revival of pre-Christian customs and beliefs originating in certain areas of modern-day Europe. Much of the available information on how the ancients lived and worshipped has unfortunately been eradicated by the determined efforts of the medieval Christian church. However, scholars are continuing to build a picture of Wicca and its earliest influences with the help of the sparse information that is available to them.

Archaeological excavations appear to date the origins of the Wiccan religion back as far as the Paleolithic cultures that revered a Hunter God and Fertility Goddess. 30,000-year-old cave paintings have been discovered in various areas of Europe. Often, they depict a human male with a stag's head, and a pregnant woman standing upright in a circle, surrounded by 11 additional figures. Clearly, the Goddess and the God were regarded as the creative force from around 28,000 years before the emergence of Christianity as a belief system.

The idea of using the term Wicca instead of witchcraft owes a lot to the violent history of witchcraft over the last thousand years, when innocent men and women were persecuted, tortured and murdered, purely for following their beliefs. Hollywood and the entertainment industry in general have also played a part in sensationalizing what is essentially a harmonious, peaceful way of worship and live. Now we know more about Wicca as a religion, let's consider which practices and prayers should be included in the Book of Shadows.

The three terms, witchcraft, pagan, and Wiccan, which are often erroneously used synonymously, but there are subtle differences amongst the three.

Pagan is a term that originally was used by Christians to separate Judaism, Islam, and Christianity from non-Abrahamic religions. Paganism can refer to a polytheistic belief in a pantheon of gods, or a monotheistic religion where the Goddess is the centerpiece or even the dualism of Wicca with both female and male parts. Thus, Pagan is a catchall phrase that denotes a large variety of religions, even including Buddhism and Hinduism. Typically, paganism refers to worshipers of a spiritual path that includes a revival of older religious practice and earth-worship. Neopagan refers to newer pagan practices.

Witchcraft is a tradition of practicing magick that dates back to ancient times. Witches are often pagan and/or Wiccan, but there is no requirement for them to be either. Witches can also have a wide variety of religious practices and/or worship different deities.

Wicca, on the other hand, is a form of witchcraft, but it does not follow all the conventions of witchcraft, and it is a pagan religion, but also does not follow all conventions of paganism.

Instead, Wicca is an organized religion of witches who follow basic rules and who worship the Goddess and God.

What Wicca Is Not

It is a popular belief among evangelical Christians that Wicca and paganism are devil worship or Satanism. Most likely this is due to the Christians being unable to separate Wicca and paganism from the duality of the Judeo-Christian God and Satan, which are the only two deities acknowledge by Christianity. It is thus difficult for them to differentiate, and so evangelicals usually lump the two groups in with Satanism. Knowing the difference becomes even murkier since the term paganism is derived from a Christian usage.

Not Black Magick

Wiccans are white witches instead of black witches, which are more common in other traditions of witchcraft. Black magick is not used by Wiccans because it goes against the Short Rede and often causes harm or danger to the practitioner or the target of the spell. Wiccans find black magick distasteful, as it does not promote harmony with the earth or spirits.

Black magick centers on the wants or needs of the practitioner without regard for how it might affect other people. Black magick includes necromancy, compulsions, and rituals that involve aggressive, dark, and dangerous malicious spirits such as demons and devils.

Wicca Spells

Wicca spells, or magick (with a 'k' so as not to be confused with magicians and illusionists), can be thought of as a type of prayer for those who practice Wicca. Where a Christian would say a prayer, a Wiccan would use a spell. Since Wicca is a religion that teaches its followers to live in peace with their neighbors and with the environment and to mind their own business. This means that the use of spells fits in nicely with the everyday life of a Wicca follower. The spells are used to hopefully arrange matters in their own lives to their liking.

Since the followers of Wicca believe in many different forms of theology, the spells differ from actual prayers as a Christian might make. The spells are more aligned with the meaning they want to convey, and they can be aimed at a particular deity. Wicca includes polytheists, duotheists, monotheists, and pantheists. Most follow the duotheistic system of worshiping Mother Goddess and the Horned God. Mother Goddess is thought of as an ideal role model for young women and is associated with springtime, fertility, and life. The Horned God is viewed as an ideal role model for young men and is associated with the afterlife, the natural life, and animals.

There are several different views of the use of spells, or magick, among the followers of Wicca. Some believe that magick is a force of manipulation that works through the practice of sorcery or witchcraft. Some feel that magick is the art and science of making change happen in conjunction with will. Some believe it is the controlling of the forces of nature that are generally kept secret. The most popular explanation of spells is that it is a law of nature, created through the superpowers that live in the natural, and using all of the five senses to create amazing results.

Spells are often performed as part of ritual practices which are sometimes performed in the sacred circle. Within the ritual, Wiccans will perform spells designed to affect a particular change in the real world. These spells can be used for gathering wealth, banishing negative influences, healing people, prompting fertility, or protecting the person, home, or family. These spells are sometimes referred to as white magick, not to be confused with the black magick of evil spells designed to cause harm to another person.

Wicca is a religion that calls for the affirmation of life. Followers are a force of positivity that works against the destructive powers that regularly threaten the greater world. They follow no ethical or moral code or particular dogma but instead adhere to the Wiccan Rede whose message states that followers should not harm other beings in their pursuit of life. This means that people are free to live the way they chose as long as their personal choices never infringe upon the rights of other people or life forces in nature. If this happens, then the Wiccan must be ready to take responsibility for their choices.

This is also why spells are generally used to better the person who is making the spell and not to overly affect the life of another person. When spells involve some effect to other people, then it must be a positive effect, because the Law of Threefold Return state that any action that a person performs that affects another person will return to the source three times, whether it is a positive effect or a negative effect. This means that the event will affect the spell-caster three times or will affect the three levels of the person, the mind, spirit, and body, once each. This idea is similar to the idea of karma.

Spells are not concerned with harming people or in turning people into animals or even in granting a specific wish for a person. Saying a spell is nothing more than using a set of prayers and actions in order to ask for help from the divine with some part of the person's life. They use charms, chanted verses, phrases, or words that are assumed to have special powers. They can be used to harm others, but most spells are used to better the person who is casting the spell. Casting spells is a matter of personal preference, and not all Wiccans do so.

Since Wiccans are forbidden from harming other people, this includes casting any spell that could control, manipulate, or dominate another person without their expressed desire, and this includes love spells. The intent of the spell determines whether it is harmful to others or not. A spell might be cast upon another person to make them fall in love with a specific person or just to fall in love with someone. This would be considered a manipulative spell because it is meant to change the life of another who might not want that particular change in their lives. If the target of the spell asked for the spell, then it would be allowable. And if a Wiccan cast a spell to make them seem more desirable and attractive to love in general, then that would be allowable. A spell to make themselves more desirable to a specific person would not be allowed because it could be seen as affecting that other person which is not allowed.

Spells can be a few simple phrases or sentences. Alternatively, they can be long, complex paragraphs that involve a full sacred circle and ritual. Most spells follow the same basic format:

- **Knowledge** – a person must begin with what they already know about their selves

- **Will** – a person needs to have a belief in their own skills and abilities, practices, and relationship with the Divine

- **Daring** – the person is willing and ready to make a particular change in their lives and they are asking for Divine assistance in reaching their goals

- **Silence** – a period of silence before and after the spell

So, a spell that someone casts to help them find a good job might look like this:

(Begin with a few moments of silence) A good employment is waiting for me, a great job awaits me, and I know it is out there. I have the skills they will need to fill this job, and I am the perfect person. Now is the time for me to accept this challenge, and I ask the Divine Ones to come to me and to bestow this job upon me. (End with a few moments of meditative silence).

There are hundreds of spells that have been passed down through history through people's spell books or by word of mouth. People often write their own spells so that the spell is personalized to that person. Many people who use spells feel that a spell will be more effective if it is modified to match the thoughts and personality of the person and the specific situation they are trying to change.

As long as people believe in the power of incantations, spells, and magick, there will be a need for them and a use for them in their culture and beliefs. These spells are kept by the individual in their own grimoire, their particular text of magick, also known as the Book of Shadows.

History

The history and exact date the Wiccan practice came into existence is highly controversial. Some people believe that the religion is immensely old, having been in existence for many centuries. This ideology is opined to the thought that due to the nature and sensitivity of the practice, it must have been kept hidden for many centuries, only coming into the limelight during the 19th century. The proponents assert that ancient times were immensely problematic. Pagans and people who followed religions that were deemed "unacceptable" were persecuted, and this essentially included all religions outside of Christianity. In as much as most people submitted to the mainstream religion, there were ritualists such as the Wiccans who managed to keep their practice hidden. Due to the extreme care taken, they were able to survive and avoid persecution. The practice started to be more commonly used in the modern era after there were laws put into place that protected freedom of expression and religion; thus, the Wiccan followers no longer had anything to be afraid of. Notably, this theory has no proof, although is amongst the most compelling explanations of the history of the practice.

Proper records of Wicca dates back to mid-20th century England, when an author and occultist known as Gerald Gardner suddenly became vocal about it and drew the attention of people to its existence. According to Gerald, the religion had been in existence for many years, even earlier than the onset of Christianity in Europe. This meant that the religion had been around for several years, and the reason as to why the followers weren't vocal about it was due to the fear of persecution. As per his claim, the practitioners had managed to successfully pass down the tradition from generation to generation. Wicca spread to the United States in the 1960s and is estimated to have quite a following in the country. Proponents consider the religion to be purely spiritual and different from conventional religions, which have no emphasis on nature. As of the 1980s, it was estimated that there were 50,000 Wiccans in both Europe and Northern America, a number that is estimated to keep growing exponentially as more people become accustomed to the practice.

Ever since Gerald introduced the religion to the world, it has changed in a number of ways. First, the tradition is no longer hidden and mysterious, and many people know about its existence. Therefore, if any person affirms to their various beliefs, they are likely to have an easier time joining it with absolutely no fear of persecution. Gardner also published his first book about the rituals, known as the Book of Shadows. The publication contains vital information about the practice, with spells and basic information that pertains to Wicca. Although the original idea was for the book to be a secret, it has since spread, and many people have gained access to it. Through the book, more people are privy of everything that pertains to the practice and if it appeals to them to join. To date, several versions of the publications have been published. However, it is important to note that reading the books may not really be enough to get all the vital information regarding the religion;

you may need to seek out various sources to get the full picture. Since the founding witches did not really write anything down concerning their religion, the knowledge of the real history is undoubtedly a little difficult to grasp.

Gardner receives credit for not only introducing the practice to the modern world but also for also founding the current Wicca movement, which still follows the tenets of the ancient practices. The practice is no longer considered to be secret and is open to any person who may want to be a member. The current Wicca tradition is still based on the reverence of nature, performing magick and the worship of the female deity known as the goddess. The practice also borrows the western witchcraft practices, with vital input from Doreen Valiente, a Wiccan enthusiast and follower. Doreen was also an established author, and most of the knowledge Gerald obtained is credited to her.

Despite the growing popularity, people from other religions continue to view Wicca in a negative light. The fact that the Wiccan describe themselves as witches is seen as Satanic, which creates a form of strife and division among them. Other religions may have difficulty even interacting with the Wiccans, as they are associated with demonic and satanic notions. Wiccans have continued to disassociate themselves with devil worship, although it is not easy. The Wiccans will often say that it is easier for them to associate with Hindus and other religions which are nature-oriented, as opposed to most religions which are deity-oriented.

Wicca Symbols

Symbols are considered to be some of the most powerful things that human beings have ever created. Though symbols are just drawings, the meaning derived from them is immense. Wicca uses symbols as signs and as parts of magick. Some symbols are regarded as elements while others are representations of very deep ideologies. Some of the basic symbols used by the Wicca are as follows:

Pentagram/Pentacle

In modern times, the pentagram is a highly controversial symbol that most people associate with devil worship. As illustrated, the pentagram consists of a five-pointed star which is within a circle. According to the Wiccan members, the five-pointed star is an illustration of the aspect of key energy-giving and protection properties. The star is a representation of the five key Wiccan elements - air, water, fire, earth, and spirit. The fact that the elements are enclosed together is considered to be an illustration of all aspects of the world coming together, representing one divine. The fact that all sides of the triangle are pointed can be thought of as an illustration of the victory of spirit over typical matter. Today, the pentacle used by Wiccans can be equated to the star of David in Judaism.

Witch's Knot

The witch's knot is also known as the witch's charm or the magick knot, and it is a representation of the aspect of protection. Wiccans use the knot by scratching it on their doors in order to protect themselves from evil spirits and all negative spells that may have been cast against them. The witch's knot has the ability to be drawn into a continuous motion, which increases its efficacy. The Wicca magicians also use this symbol to bind some things magically. Whenever the symbol is drawn, there is always a sense of peace, as any negativity is bound and cannot enter.

The Triple Moon

The triple moon is considered to be an illustration of feminine power, and it is used in the Wicca traditions to represent the goddess. The three moons are symbolic of the three phases of the moon: waxing, full, and waning. These are the three life cycles and progressions of a typical woman, as she starts out as a maiden, blooms into a mother, and eventually, she becomes a crone. The maiden stage is represented by purity, youth, and basically the magick of beginnings. As a mother, the aspect of fertility, fulfillment, and nurturing capabilities is achieved, since a mother typically cares for her little ones. The final stage is crone, where the female is a bit elderly and has acquired a considerable amount of wisdom and knowledge in the course of her life. Death and rebirth are part of this final phase, which makes it a rather bittersweet eventuality. In Wicca, the triple moon is largely an invitation for the women to begin celebrating each area of their lives.

The Horned God

The horned god is a Wicca symbol that represents the perfect union between the divine energy and the animal elements in nature, which are inclusive of human beings. Just like the triple moon, the horned god has three major phases which include the Father, Master, and Sage. However, unlike the triple moon, which is more inclined toward females, the horned god is considered to be more correlated to males and is actually thought of as encompassing the male aspect of divinity. Usually, the word "horned" leads one to think of the term horny, which is essentially where the males are known to get their virility.

This symbol is another major source of controversy in current times due to its association with the element of devil worship, although the truth is that there is no correlation.

The Ankh

The Ankh is considered to be one of the most powerful Wicca symbols, and it is mainly associated with healing. The symbol is drawn on entrances of either the houses of Wicca members or in their places of meeting, and it particularly comes in handy whenever there is the invocation of spells pertaining to healing. The Wiccans refer to the symbol as the key of life, since it is associated with the union between the god and goddesses, which therefore prompts the creation of infinite power in the universe. The top and circular loop usually represent the feminine energy, while the vertical bar facing down is a representation of the male energy.

The Elven Star

The elven star is a sacred symbol in most Wicca practices that was made particularly popular in the 1990s. The Wicca associate the symbol with the seven directions, with the original four being east, west, north, and south, and an additional three directions, including above, below, and within. In addition to the direction, some of the priests and priestesses view the symbol as an illustration of the faery path, which includes reputations such as connection, trust, magick, joy, honor, inspiration, and knowledge.

The Wheel of the Year

The wheel of the year denotes the eight seasons of the year, also known as the Sabbats. With the wheel, the Wicca are able to navigate through the ever-changing seasons with ease, just like a wheel moves and rotates easily from one point to the other. The wheel is divided into the eight Sabbats, and it is considered to serve as a reminder to the people that they should get moving, as nothing is constant.

Incorporating the Wiccan Symbols

Since you now have full knowledge about some of the most common Wicca symbols, it is worth knowing how it can be incorporated into the personal space of a member, as well as what exactly the Wiccans are supposed to use them for. There is no limitation as to where the Wiccan can incorporate the symbols, and they can paint them and place them all around the house, carve them into jewelry, or hand paint them on the walls. Every Wiccan member is free to display the symbols however they wish; at the end of the day, the ability to follow all of the regulations is what matters.

Principles

We exercise rituals to familiarize ourselves with the usual beat of forces of life manifested by moon stages, cross quarters and seasonal quarters.

We recognize that our understanding gives us extraordinary responsibility to the environment and trail living in harmony with the nature in ecological balance bringing satisfaction to life and mindfulness in an evolutionary observation.

We identify complexity of power greater than it seems to the usual person. It is called supernatural because it is far better than the ordinally one and we see it as dishonest in that, that is surely possible to all people.

We understand the inventive power in this world revealed through masculine and feminine divisions and this similar power of innovativeness is in the hands of all people and works via partnership of the masculine and feminine. We got value beyond the other knowledge each being helpful of the others. Sex is treasured as a manifestation and illustration of life and like one of the energy springs that is used in magical practice and religious worship.

We recognize internal and outside worlds or intellectual worlds rarely known as the heavenly world and seeing in the interaction of these two degrees, the basis for magical workouts and supernatural marvels. We contemplate neither measurement for the other one and for our contentment, all are looked at as essential.

We don't recognize harsh order but instead we do honesty forks that teach, honor people who share their better knowledge and acquaintance and even identify other persons who have courageously decide of themselves in managing.

We view wisdom, magick and religion in existence as joined in the system one sees and exists in the world. The opinion of the world and life thinking that we categorize as witchcraft- The wiccan technique.

Harm No One

This is a theme that is common in all Wiccan beliefs. Most followers keep to the belief that anything done in the practice of Wicca should not cause harm to anyone or anything.

Respect the Beliefs of Other People

In the practice of Wicca, people hold the belief that every person must find their own path in life and must be allowed to follow that path. Beliefs can be shared with other people but must never be forced upon other people.

Be Responsible for Yourself

Every individual is responsible for their own personal actions in life. Whether you are doing magick or just going about your daily activities you must be prepared to take responsibility for whatever you do.

Remember the Holidays

Wiccan Holidays are based on the cycles of the seasons and the rotation of the earth. Wicca celebrates eight major days of power, called Sabbats, and the Esbats which are celebrated monthly.

Honor Your Ancestry

No matter what our ancestors should be spoken of reverently and with honor. Many Wiccans feel that their ancestors guide them and watch over them because many Wiccans commune with those in the spirit world.

Life After Death and Karma

Many Wiccans believe in karma and life after death. There is a belief that whatever we do in this life will be visited on us in our next life. This is similar to the Eastern belief that however you live this life will determine what you return as in your next life and how your next life will be. In addition, usually, Wiccans do not believe in hell, heaven, or the concept of sin.

The Divine is Present in Nature

Wiccans believe that nature should be respected and honored because the Divine is present in and lives in elements of nature. Rocks, trees, plants, and animals contain elements of the sacred. This is similar to the Native American belief that life flows through all things, from the tree to the rock to the person to the animal, and if one part of the chain is broken or damaged, then the life cannot flow as well as it should. This is why many people who practice Wiccan are quite passionate about taking care of the environment. Also, the Divine is both male and female and is present in all people. Interacting with the gods is not a function of a select group of people because all people are sacred beings.

There are also the Principles of Belief that were set down by the Council of American Witches in the mid-1970s. They were a loosely organized group that did not stay together for very long, but they were able to give us a list of thirteen beliefs that many Wiccans follow to one degree or another. These are not meant to be hard and fast rules. They include practicing rites to mark the Holidays, being responsible to the environment, the natural potential of all people to have superpowers, the lack of animosity toward other religions and their beliefs, and the belief that people should improve their overall health by seeking what they need in nature.

There are certain laws often referred to the Rules of the Craft that present guidelines for the behavior of the follower. Most Wiccan will follow one or more of these and it is up to the individual follower to choose the one set of laws that are most in line with their personal beliefs and follow it. This would also be an entry into the front of the Book of Shadows.

The Witches Rede

This rule contains one line that almost all Wiccans follow even if this is not their guiding rule, and that is to harm no one. This is also the reason why many followers will close a spell with words like 'to harm no one' or 'to benefit the good of all.

The Charge of the Goddess

In Wicca, this is an inspirational text designed to honor the Goddess in ceremonies held in the Sacred Circle. It asks for the help of the Goddess to guide and teach the followers.

Seven Hermetic Principles

These are considered to be the seven ancient rules for one to learn to master oneself. This is done by pursuing knowledge that pertains to mysteries of a spiritual nature.

The Delphic Maxims

These are thought to have been delivered to man by Apollo himself and give guidelines for living a pious life, such as obeying the law, learning self-control, seek wisdom, and practice discipline in all things.

The Rule of Three

This rule states that the things you do will come back to you not once but three times.

Law of Power

This rule states that the power of a witch must only be used for their own good and for the protection of themselves and others if necessary. The power is a gift from God and the Goddess and must be treated as sacred.

Choose whichever lawsuits you the best and be prepared to follow it. This practice is a practice of individual choice. Just remember to place a copy of the laws you choose to follow in the front of your Book of Shadow so that you can refer to it often.

Present day

Wicca has truly blossomed across the world. In the year 1990, there were about 8000 Wiccans in the United States. As of 2008, there were 340,000. As the decades have rolled on, the numbers of people adhering to the Wiccan faith has grown exponentially. In just two decades, the number of people practicing faith increased over 42-fold. And they haven't stopped growing.

As of 2018, a grand total of 1.5 million people listed their religion as either "Wiccan" or more generally as "Pagan" in a research survey. "Pagan" is the umbrella term under which Wicca falls. This umbrella shelters other paths, such as Druidry, Reconstructionism (such as those worshiping Egyptian or Greek pantheons), and Alchemical traditions. The number of people practicing nature-centric faiths has exploded in since their revival in the early part of the 20th century.

There are many reasons that more and more people are flocking to Wicca and these other Pagan traditions. There is increasing dissatisfaction with the mainstream Abrahamic faiths of

Judaism, Islam, and Christianity. However, by and large, most converts to Wicca and Paganism come from a Christian background.

There is also an increasing awareness of our intimate links with the natural world, and the way we affect, and are affected by it. A growing awareness of pollution, climate change, and the ozone layer has led many people to a more empathetic ecological consciousness. This eco-focused consciousness not only informs their activism but can be viewed as causing them to seek a mystical connection with nature.

Though the original incarnation was Gardnerian Wicca, there have been many schools and lineages that have come into existence over the past century. As the number of adherents has grown and diversified, so too have the kinds of Wicca. These other lineages include the Alexandrian, Celtic, Dianic, and Eclectic.

Alexandrian Wicca is a slightly more liberal sister to Gardnerian Wicca. It heavily emphasizes the male-female duality. In terms of ceremonial structure, they are very similar, with some slight differences in the elemental association. The cycle of their rituals is heavily focused on the Holly King, who rules the winter, and his cycle with the Oak King, who rules the summer.

Dianic Wicca gives primacy to the Goddess in their worship. There are two branches; the first, called Old Dianic, has covens that are made up of both men and women. The second, called

Feminist Dianic Witchcraft, are women-only groups. Men are banned, and this second group has often been accused of transphobia for not allowing Trans women to participate in their rituals.

Celtic Wicca is also known as the Church of Wicca. By and large, they have been the most active publicly visible of the Wiccan groups, especially in the early days of the 1990s. Their ritual structure contains elements of Celtic traditions, based on a framework of ceremonial and high magick.

Finally, Eclectic Wicca rounds out the list. This variety of Wicca was founded in the 1960s. The hallmark of this tradition is the flexibility that it allows its adherents. Followers of Eclectic Wicca are able to take aspects from many traditions and faiths to meet their needs. They can incorporate ancient Celtic deities, a Catholic invocation of a saint, and a Gardnerian structure all within the same ritual.

There are many notable modern Wiccan and Pagan groups. These include Circle Sanctuary; The Pagan Federation; and the Order of Bards, Ovates, and Druids. These organizations have worked tirelessly to ensure that not only the spiritual tradition continues, but also that its practitioners can practice safely and openly without fear of retribution.

Up until fairly recent history, it was extremely common for practitioners of Wicca to be fired from their jobs, denied opportunities, and harassed by local communities on the basis of their faith. To this day, some fundamentalist groups still attempt to encroach on the religious freedom of Wiccans and Pagans.

In recent history, many great leaps and bounds have been made. Pagan Advocacy Groups such as the Lady Liberty League have formed a branch of legal defense for Wiccans and Pagans who find themselves discriminated against. Wiccans and Pagans today enjoy a far greater level of safety and freedom in the workplace and in their communities.

Wicca and Paganism have grown to be one of the largest minority religions in the United States. While they do not come anywhere near the number of adherents as Christianity, Wicca and Paganism have numbers of adherents similar to Sikhism and Hinduism in the USA. They are a significant chunk of the American demographic.

With grown numbers have come growing public acknowledgment, and greater rights. In 2006 an army chaplain named Captain Don Larsen was dismissed after requesting to become the first Wiccan military chaplain. Despite an exemplary record of service, he was dismissed. However, in 2007, things began to change in relation to the military. Spearheaded by Selena Fox of Circle Sanctuary, a lawsuit was settled; this settlement finally allowed the pentacle to be a symbol engraved on military headstones. Since 2007 many other Pagan symbols have been added, including Thor's hammer and the Druidic Awen, among others.

Wiccan and Pagan chaplains are now readily available in the military, as well as in places such as prisons. The freedom to have access to the ministers, rituals and symbols of one's faith has finally come around to include these ancestral religions.

The tradition of Wicca was based on the spirit of indigenous European religions tens of thousands of years old. This spirit was recaptured and reimagined by Gerald Gardner, who helped to reignite the light of witchcraft for the modern age. Today, Wicca and Paganism are one of the largest minority faiths in the USA, and it will surely only keep growing from here on out.

Chapter 2: Introduction to Crystals

Crystal

Crystals have been admired and preferred since the early days. Having been formed deep inside the earth over many years, and being some of the solidest materials we know, crystals can last beyond our life expectancy, so no wonder our attraction of them has been there over the years.

What are crystals?

Crystals are minerals, solid in nature with a natural symmetrical recapping design of atoms. They are able to take many thousands of years to form deeply in the earth's coating. They are in a diversity of various colors, shapes and sizes and each is unique in its own way.

Some of the crystals are very rare for example emeralds, rubies, diamonds and sapphires. They have been prized highly throughout history and are known as valuable gemstones.

Other usually crystals that always occur for example amethyst and rose quartz are recognized as semi-valuable stones. Historically, they were alleged to be gifts from gods and were used for medicine.

How crystals are used today

Today, crystals are useful for manifestation, meditation, in technology, for physical and emotional healing.

In technology

We stay in a technological world today, but in actual sense it should be referred to as the world of crystals. From silicon dioxide, we get quartz crystals. They preserve an accurate frequency standard which means that they can be useful in microprocessors i.e. the small computer processors which joins the computer processing unit functions. We wouldn't have smartphones, computers, watches without the quartz.

Crystal healing

This is an ancient technique of holistic medicine that many people in different cultures all over the world have used.

Naturally, crystals have some energies they release that you can use to heal others and yourself. During crystal healing, various crystals have exceptional vibrations and properties which work with certain mind and body parts. The texture and cut of the crystal all also impact its energy attention. Crystals are usually put on in jewelry to link the wearer to their energies that heal, but one can also benefit by putting them at various body points while laying down.

You can use them to alternate pain by putting the crystals in these parts as well as transfer the healing energies in your body.

Before using in crystal healing, various crystals are purified because each time the crystal are in touch with the person, they can transfer their energies to them. Through the process of cleansing those crystals, you remove all other energies they might have picked up prior to use. And to ensure that they are also kept at their most effective state, some of the crystals require to be charged frequently.

Meditation

Crystals enable you to feel more linked to nature since they originate from the earth. They can aid you in the meditation practice to make you feel more linked to the universe and earth or to lead you to some kind of thoughts if you hold them in your hand, wear them as jewelry or put them around you. For example, if you desire to lead your meditation to addiction thoughts, you can use amethyst because it is linked to helping in overcoming addictions and had strengthening and soothing properties.

Manifestation

One can manifest their desires via crystals through using them as lovely reminders of your dreams and goals and help you take one more step getting closer to them. This can be done by putting crystals that release energies which are in position with your manifestations in areas where you will regularly see them. For example, if you would like to manifest more confidence, you can put on citrine that is a sunny and a crystal that brings confidence as a necklace. You will be able to embrace it whenever nervousness comes to feel the confidence energies it brings and you will see it when you view yourself in the mirror and this will aid in reminding you to manifest the desires you have and be more confident. When it's used together with the attraction law, the trust that by being attentive on thoughts that are positive, you will bring about positive experience into one's life, use crystals that aid to restore your mindset and aid in taking you wherever you would want to be.

Mineral stones

If a solid piece of the Earth is made of more than one mineral, then they are referred to as a stone or rock. In other words, you can use these two terms interchangeably. However, the use of the term "rock" often brings the thought of drab to mind. In other words, they are less interesting!

When you are talking about a rock, you are simply referring to an organic substance that is composed of more than two minerals. They also do not have a consistent chemical structure. You may find chunks of minerals in rocks. However, what is even common is finding microscopic mineral grains in them instead.

Some of the substances that you will find used in magick and healing are stone-like lazuli and lapis. These are just but a mixture of diopside and lazurite. This explains the reason why the stones and crystals are used interchangeably among Wiccans and other magical practitioners.

The other thing to note is that amber is resin that has been fossilized from an ancient tree. Jet, on the other hand, is just derived from a decaying fossilized wood. On the other hand, is geode, which refers to a cavity that is spherical and is lined with crystals and other minerals.

Finally, there are sources that you might find using the term 'gemstones' when referring to minerals and crystals. Well, the truth is that this term is not rooted in magick or science. Instead, it is a category of attractive and rare minerals that are often used in making jewelry. Examples of these include fluorite and garnet, among others. The higher the cost of diamond and emerald, the lesser the chances of it being used in magick.

That said, the most important thing when it comes to choosing a crystal to use in performing magick is the intuition and the intention that you have. This is because they serve as the driving forces for transforming reality by way of using crystals.

The most important thing that you have to note is what magical association, spiritual healing properties, and emotional properties the crystal has. It is also vital that you know whether the crystal you are using is receptive or projective; which are the key features that determine their effectiveness in healing magick.

Projective Stones

One thing that you need to note is that projective energies can be linked to the Chinese system of yang energy. They simply refer to masculine energies that are said to be strong, active, hot, bright, electric, and physical.

The good thing with the projective stones is that you can use them when casting healing and protection spells. This is mainly because they are linked to masculine elements of Air and Fire, which makes them perfect when working to bring courage, vitality, and intellectual powers.

Receptive Stones

Did you know that if you held a receptive stone in your hands you are guaranteed having feelings of calmness? Well, it is true! It is believed that the receptive stone has the ability to absorb feelings of anxiety from your body. Just like the projective stone, the effect one experiences when holding a receptive stone varies from one person to another.

Additionally, this stone is thought to have Feminine elements of both Water and Earth. This is what makes them a perfect choice when you are meditating and would like to be grounded both physically and emotionally. It also has the ability to promote psychic abilities hence, great when working with the power of the subconscious mind such as casting love, compassion, peace, and spiritual development spells.

Exceptions

There are a few exceptions to the clear distinction between projective and receptive energies. Quartz crystal can exhibit both, depending on what it's being used for, and because it's a highly "programmable" stone, the user can choose which kind of energy to draw on before charging it for spell work. Some Witches attribute this dual quality to amethyst, opal, and crossstone, as well.

Furthermore, black stones may be projective or receptive, depending on their type. As you practice holding and attuning to crystals and stones, you will become more adept at noting which kind of energy you're interacting with.

Rose Quartz

Spell Description

A pink variety of quartz crystal, Rose quartz is universally associated with love and relationships, including friendship.

Rose quartz can vary slightly in appearance, from translucent to opaque pink, and the brightness of the color can depend on the amount of sun exposure the crystal has experienced. However, even the palest of these stones have great power.

Rose quartz has nurturing the energy and is good for recovering from emotional upset. It strengthens compassion and the ability to forgive others for past wrongs. This is required to attract relationships that are healthy and also creating inner peace. It encourages one to accept oneself like you are and to accept others just as they are.

Rose quartz is good for spell work devoted to all things love-related, including the love of friendship, whether you're working to bring new love into your life or heal from old relationship issues. It's also helpful for grounding yourself after spell work or divination.

Placed by the bed, it promotes the restoration of trust and harmony and is great for both children and adults as a sleep crystal. Place one under a child's pillow to relieve nightmares and fear of the dark. Rose quartz is also a good crystal to have near your computer, as it helps prevent eye fatigue and resulting headaches.

Occurrence

Zodiac Sign: Leo

Planet: Sun

Element: Fire

Ingredients

- A part of Rose Quartz (heart stone, love, happiness)
- A piece of Sodalite (cooperation, communication, wisdom)
- A portion of blue cloth (sized to wear as an amulet or medicine bag)
- Cord (long enough to be a necklace)

- Small piece of paper and a pen
- One head of dried lavender
- Blue candle
- White candle

Instructions

1. Start by casting your circle. On the small piece of paper, write the following words: I am committed to clear and open communication. I am open to all sides of the conversation and can listen as well as I can speak. My loved ones have something to say as much as I do, and we can share as we talk to each other.

2. Light the white candle on your altar and state the following words: With this candle, I do light; bringing the spirit, I do invite to help me open my voice of knowing, to speak with open heart and mind ongoing.

3. Light the blue candle and state the following: with this candle, I do swear to use my voice with love and care, for those, I am within sacred bond so that we may speak our true voice songs.

4. Set the blue square of cloth out between the candles. Place the paper on the cloth between the candles on the altar, and lay your stones on top of the paper. Place your

hands over the stones and visualize yourself having clear, honest conversations with those you love. See the calmness and creativity between you. See yourself speaking your mind freely and lovingly. Charge the stones with the energy of clear communication.

5. Spend as long as you need to in this visualization. Place the piece of lavender on top of the stones, and gather the corners of the cloth together to make a bag or pouch. Tie it with a long cord and then tie it around your neck so that it hangs over your heart. Blow out the candles and close your circle. You can wear this medicine bag whenever you need a clear voice and communication within your partnerships.

Citrine

Spell Description

Citrine is a yellow variety of quartz, usually transparent and ranging in color from pale yellow to gold, but is sometimes found as an almost-brown honey color. It is also referred to as the as "the Sun Stone" due to its bright color and often sparkling appearance, but the name "citrine" comes from the French word for "lemon."

Citrine is also good for helping to overcome negativity associated with having been ill-used by another person, either through direct manipulation or more subtle means. It can be hard sometimes to know whether some acquaintances are positive influences in our lives. Citrine can help illuminate which of your associations are worth keeping, and which to let go. It can do this for your thoughts as well, by clearing out negative or unnecessary mental "chatter" to help you realign with your inner wisdom.

Citrine is excellent in spell work for manifesting and maintaining wealth. It is sometimes known as the "Merchant's Stone" and kept near the cash register of many businesses. It's also good for issues of communication in interpersonal relationships and clearing and blocking negative energies from people around you. Wear or carry citrine as general protection against negativity, as a way to attract money or guard against excessive spending, and in any situation where you need to feel secure and confident.

Occurrence

Zodiac Sign: Gemini

Planet: Mercury

Element: Air

Ingredients

- A part citrine crystal
- A bowl of Water

Instructions

1. As you place the citrine and pour the water, visualize how you will feel when your particular challenge has been overcome, and welcome in a feeling of excitement about the future.

2. Because citrine is such a "sunstone," this elixir truly is best when charged outdoors, but if this isn't possible, you can place it under bright light (not too near the lightbulb) or near a lit candle next for a few hours. As you prepare to drink the elixir, take a deep breath, calm your mind, and state the outcome you wish to manifest.

Start chanting these words:

"I now activate my power to triumph over this challenge and stand in confidence about the future."

3. Then take a drink, and thank the citrine for its empowering energies. You may wish to continue sipping the full elixir over the next few hours, sprinkle some on your skin, or add it to bathwater. However, you choose to use it, be present and remember your goal each time you interact with the charged water.

Amethyst

Spell Description

Another form of quartz crystal, amethyst is considered by many to be the most beautiful of magical stones. It ranges in color from pale lavender to deep, very dark purple, and may be transparent or opaque. The color is created by the presence of manganese in clear quartz, and the variation in hue is caused by additional amounts of iron.

Amethyst frequently occurs in geodes, where it's not uncommon to see amethyst and clear quartz points clustered together. It is a stone of contentment, aiding in meditation and attaining higher states of consciousness and transforming negative energy into positive energy. It also helps enhance perception, on both intellectual and intuitive levels, and increases psychic ability.

In magick, amethyst is wonderful for clearing sacred space and maintaining a positive atmosphere anywhere it is placed. It is useful for healing rituals related to the addiction of all kinds, both physical and emotional. It increases luck and prosperity by curbing the tendency to overspend, as well as promoting motivation. It's a good stone for creativity and any projects requiring imaginative thinking and focus. Amethyst has been used traditionally in Wiccan magick for dispelling illusion and to bring about psychic healing.

Occurrence

Zodiac Sign: Aquarius

Planet: Jupiter

Element: Air

Ingredients

- Amethyst
- Pieces of moonstones
- Water

Instructions

1. When the hectic details of everyday life are causing you to feel disconnected from the spiritual and psychic realms, this elixir helps raise your vibration above the mundane level and get back on track with your higher self.

2. For best results, try charging this elixir with moonlight, and place pieces of moonstone around the water while charging when you're ready to drink the elixir, center, and ground yourself, holding the glass with both hands.

3. Take a few deep breaths, and speak your intention to the Universe. You might say:

4. "Thank you, the spirit of amethyst, for opening my path to communication with Divine Self. I am ready to receive any guidance waiting for me on the higher plane."

5. Take a sip, and then spend several minutes in meditation, continuing to hold the elixir in both hands. You will eventually feel at peace, released from mental clutter, and able to tap into your authentic inner wisdom.

Chapter 3:
List of specific Crystal that have a direct relationship with Wicca

List of all crystals and stones in detail

Agate

Is used in the process of healing and restoration. It brings about health, long life, wealth, happiness and grows the capability to remove inner bitterness and anger.

Amber

These changes and absorbs all the negative energy into the positive one and its also used for protection purposes.

Amethyst

It increases spiritual awareness, provides soothing and calmness, controls all types of destructive behavior and is also used for protection.

Aquamarine

This is good for protection against physical illnesses.

Bloodstone

This encourages selflessness, improves creativity, promotes renewal and courage, heals blood circulation problems and stimulates energy flow in the body.

Carnelian

It relieves sexual tension, feelings of hatred and anger, and stimulates precision and analytical capabilities.

Citrine

It transforms and disperses negative energy and also arouses endurance and mental attention or focus.

Diamond

It encourages Endurance, faith, inspiration, inventiveness, ingenuity, creativity and also removes the vacuums from one's atmosphere.

Emerald

It improves memory and brings about harmony and also increases domestic happiness, loyalty, sensitivity, fertility, love, prosperity and creative imagination.

Garnet

This is good for diseases related with blood, iron deficiencies, eliminates things that are out of order, creates energies, helps in love, cleansing and purification.

Hematite

This assists in balancing the mind, body, spirit and great mental attunement and is an outstanding grounding stone, reflects negative energy away and is protective.

Jade

It increases self-sufficiency and confidence, and is great for understanding and remembering dreams, it also brings riches and prolongs life.

Jasper

It is used for cultivating, and stabilizing the atmosphere and helps in safe astronomical travel. Yellow jasper helps in mind clearing, brown jasper helps in concentration and can also be used for centering and grounding and red jasper is used for protection purposes.

Lapis Lazuli

This helps in overcoming depression, assists in entering other realms, protects and improves a state of calmness, is used in expanding awareness, attunes creativity and fine tunes the feelings and instincts.

Malachite

This is great for gardening purposes, good for luck and money, simplifies emotions, captivates negativity, is good for healing purposes and a great source of warmth and maternal love.

Moonstone

This brings about calmness and awareness, improves all feminine aspects of one's nature, is trance-inducing and a great stimulator of composure and confidence.

Obsidian

This is great in healing, and provides clarity, excellent grounding and protective stone. Each obsidian type has its own qualities that are specific.

Onyx

This improves wise decision making, inspires great fortune and happiness, improves self-control, helps in banishing grief, concentration and absorbing negativity.

Opal

This has mystical and imagination qualities and also provides balance and helps in inspiration and creativity.

Pearl

This improves personal integrity, is soothing and absorbs attention, innocence, charity, negative energy induced faith and helps in obstacle overcoming.

Quartz (Clear)

This heals inner negativity, strengthens healing energy, unlocks mind abilities, also creates altered consciousness states and is used for logic, as a scrying crystal and for a mind that is clear.

Quartz (Rose)

It releases the imagination that is good for children, produces a calming and gentle energy, promotes happiness and love feelings and brings harmony.

Quartz (Smoky)

This dissolves all negative emotions, promotes the joy of life, is a great grounding stone, is good for mutable people or someone who is working with numerous behavior disorder and is a protective stone.

Ruby

This helps in improving psychological abilities.

Rock Crystal

This improves the powers of instincts.

Sapphire

This helps enhance the powers of the imagination and also brings about friendship and love into one's life.

Tiger's Eye

This promotes clearness in thinking.

Tourmaline

This promotes friendship and helps in goodwill.

Turquoise

This enhances good relationships between people.

Obtaining Stones

You can easily purchase all the stones you desire online for very cheap. This is risky as you typically do not know the exact stone you are getting as far as the shape and feel. It is recommended that you visit a local store or make a trip to a locally owned rock shop to find your stones. This is better than the Internet in many ways; you can 'feel' which stone is yours, you can hold the stone, you can be sure the size is fitting and you're also supporting small business, which is always best. If you need a certain stone and cannot find it, the Internet is useful, but overall the journey to finding your stones is half the fun.

When choosing stones you need to consider what you need them for. Do you want to use them for jewelry? Maybe you need a stone to hold planetary magick to balance your natal chart or detrimental transit. BE meticulous in your reasoning for obtaining certain stones for the best results.

Clear quartz is the go-to stone for beginners. Since it is clear it can be used for any number of magical uses. Quartz can house any type of energy and is very common all around the world. In fact, the Earth's crust is mostly comprised of quartz. This stone is a great clear alternative to diamonds and works as a great blank slate for you to scribe your magical workings into, literally or energetically. Be sure to cleanse your quartz once you obtain it to make sure you're not bringing any unwanted energy into your home. The following cleansing method can be used for any stone,

- Hold your stone in your hands and really feel its presence.
- Call upon any god or spirit you prefer to work with for assistance.
- Visualize pure white light from the heavens beaming down into the stone.
- Focus on this light and energy as it moves through the stone.
- Any energy that is already in the stone will be removed.
- The stone is now cleared.

With this technique in mind, we need to be aware stones may house very negative energy so it may come out and cause you discomfort or trouble. Protective precaution may need to be taken, as well as a clearing of the space you are cleansing your stones in. For general upkeep of stones and crystals place them in the light of a full moon, or even in sunlight during fitting times of the day.

Chapter 4: List of several spells and magical workings

Crystals

Quartz Crystals

Often thought of as the "quintessential" crystal, quartz is the second most abundant mineral on Earth, and one of the most common stones you will find in magical supply shops.

Comprised of just two elements—silicon and oxygen—it runs in color from completely "crystal clear" to milky white. Clear quartz is found as a six-sided prism and is often used in schools to demonstrate the ability of a mineral to hold the entire spectrum of light—held in sunlight, the prism will transmit rainbow patterns onto floors and walls.

The Aztecs, Egyptians, Romans, and many other ancient cultures used quartz in a multitude of ways that ranged from meditations to funerary rites. Among ancient lunar-aligned stone circles in Scotland, for example, lumps of white quartz were ritually broken and scattered, which may have mimicked the moonlight shining down on the participants. And according to some interpretations, quartz is among the "seven precious substances" of Buddhism. Today, it is widely used in alternative healing modalities as well as magick of various kinds.

Known to some as "the Witch's mirror" quartz is associated with both the Moon and the Sun and the Elements of Water and Fire. This stone is a potent tool for storing energy in the form of thoughts, memories and emotions, and can be easily "programmed" to activate previously stored energy when called upon. Quartz is often used to charge magical tools and spell ingredients, and can even be used to energetically cleanse other crystals and stones.

Quartz is also considered the "sage" of all minerals as it most easily facilitates the merging of the physical and spiritual realms. This is, after all, the original substance that crystal balls are made from!

Quartz absorbs and transmits energy from the Sun as well as from the life force of trees, plants and flowers, and like several other crystals it can be used to revitalize struggling plants around the home. Quartz is a great all-around rebalancing stone, replacing negative energies with positive ones and keeping harmonious vibrations going strong in any area where it resides.

In this chapter, you'll learn how to use quartz for storing and retrieving memories, energizing divination tools, improving your health, and boosting your energy toward achieving a specific goal.

Crystal Divination Recalibration

Quartz is often used to charge ritual and magical tools. As a stone of spiritual communication and psychic ability, it's ideal for sprucing up your divination tools—such as Tarot cards, runes, a pendulum, etc.—whenever you can sense their energy has become "fuzzy" or imbalanced in some way. In fact, many Tarot practitioners like to keep a quartz crystal with their Tarot cards at all times, to keep the energy of the deck in tip-top shape.

Technically, you can use any size crystal with any type of divination tools, but it's best to "match" the two as closely as possible. For example, a small crystal point may work well when rebalancing a pendulum, but when it comes to a Tarot deck or bag of runes, a more sizable crystal is ideal.

Ingredients:

- 1 medium to large quartz crystal
- White candle
- Divination tool(s)

Instructions:

1. Light the candle and spend a few moments quieting your mind.

2. When you're ready, place the divination tool in your left hand and the quartz in your right hand.

3. Gently bring them together until they touch.

4. Holding them together for at least one minute, visualize the divination tool being cleared of any unwanted energy, and then revitalized with the pure energy of the quartz.

5. When you feel that the recalibration is complete, thank the quartz and place your divination tool on the altar.

6. Repeat the procedure with any other divination tools you want to rebalance.

7. When you have finished, gently extinguish the white candle.

Crystal Quartz Memento Charm

As computer researchers have been discovering, quartz has the ability to store information, or "data," in the form of energy. But it also stores emotional information, which makes this crystal an excellent touchstone for positive memories that you want to hold onto.

This spell is a great one for experimenting with the energetic properties of quartz. Simply select a happy memory—whether recent or from the distant past—and charge the stone with the feelings it brings out in you.

Note: this works best with pure clear quartz, so try to find as clear a stone as possible.

Ingredients:

- 1 clear quartz crystal
- White, pink or yellow candle
- Journal or writing paper

Instructions:

1. Light the candle and spend some time quieting your mind.

2. Begin to recall the memory in as much detail as you can. If it's a memory from the past, you may want to spend 10 to 15 minutes writing about it, as this is guaranteed to bring up details you may not be able to access otherwise.

3. When you have a good grasp on the memory, take the quartz and hold it between your palms.

4. With your eyes closed, visualize every possible sensory detail about the memory—sights, sounds, tastes, noises, voices, your thoughts and feelings at the time, etc. Focus on the feelings that accompanied this memory and feel them again in the present moment.

5. Continue the visualization until you feel suffused with warm, positive energy. Then place the quartz in front of the candle, leaving it for at least one hour.

6. Now you can hold the quartz whenever you want to call up this memory and feel the positive emotions you've infused the stone with. You can place it on your altar or somewhere else where you'll see it often, or carry it with you in your pocket or purse.

Energy Amplifier for Reaching a Goal

When your heart is set on a significant goal, quartz is a powerful magical ally to help you literally crystallize your will and intent. Whether it's related to love, career, health or spiritual development, quartz can accelerate the fulfillment of your desires by amplifying the energy that is programmed into it.

As you perform this spell, it is important to not only consider the end result of your goal but to direct the energies of feeling successful and satisfied with your manifestation into the stone.

Ingredients:

- 1 pure clear quartz crystal
- Small slip of paper
- Small drawstring bag

Instructions:

1. Spend some time quieting your mind.

2. Focus on the goal you have made for yourself.

3. Write your goal on the small slip of paper. Remember to be very specific about what you would like to attain, as this will help concentrate the energy on the outcome you desire. For example, if the goal is a new job, don't simply write "new job." Focus on the type of job you want, and write a brief but specific description.

4. Wrap the quartz in the slip of paper.

5. Hold the paper and the quartz in your hands.

6. Concentrate on your goal by visualizing it being completed. How will you feel? What consequences or effects will the outcome have on your life?

7. When you have conjured the most detailed and positive visualization that you can, place the paper-wrapped quartz in the drawstring bag and tie it shut, while saying the following (or similar) words:

    "With stone of Earth and power of Fire

    I manifest my heart's desire"

8. Place the quartz where it can be close to you in your activities for completing the goal. This could be on your

desk, in your purse, in your car, on top of your computer, or in a room in your house.

9. Repeat this spell with a new goal and a new quartz whenever you need.

Rose Quartz

Widely beloved for its cheerful yet calming pink hues, rose quartz gets its color from trace amounts of iron, manganese or titanium found within what would otherwise be clear or white quartz. This is another widely abundant mineral that can be found in any magical supply shop, and is often made into pendants, rings, necklaces and other jewelry.

Archeological records dating back to 800 BC show that rose quartz was used in jewelry and cosmetics by the Assyrians, Greeks, and Romans. The ancient Egyptians said that the goddess Isis rubbed rose quartz on her cheeks and around her eyes to preserve her beauty. This skin-care method was a long-held tradition in Egypt, and now that crystals have seen a resurgence in interest over the past several years, it has recently come back into fashion in the West!

The delicate pink color of this crystal makes it a perfect symbol for love and compassion, and it can be used for all magical workings relating to these qualities. Known to many as the Love Stone, rose quartz opens the heart chakra to allow love to penetrate our lives. It aids in healing emotional trauma, resentments, guilt, and anger.

Associated with Venus and the Elements of Earth and Water, rose quartz helps to raise self-esteem and self-worth by reminding us to treat ourselves with gentle forgiveness and kindness, and is a very effective crystal to use during meditation. Indeed, rose quartz enhances one's inner awareness, teaching us that unconditional love is ever present and that we only need to be open to receiving the healing energies of the Universe.

Other magical uses for rose quartz include protection against nightmares and against anger projected by others around you. This is also a popular stone for fertility magick, as well as restoring peace to places disrupted by conflict. In this chapter, you will find rose quartz spells for raising the vibrational frequency of your home, healing and releasing painful emotions, cultivating self-esteem and attracting positive relationships.

Home Energy Transformation Spell

All homes need fairly regular energetic maintenance in order for the atmosphere to remain ideal. However, when there's been a traumatic or otherwise difficult event—whether involving the home itself or just the inhabitant(s)—it's especially important to address any resulting energetic imbalances. Rose quartz is uniquely suited for this work, as it has the ability to replace negative energy with positive energy.

This spell will help you to clear out and replace any pockets of negative or otherwise unwanted energy in your home. You will be replacing these undesirable energies with the warm, earthy glow of groundedness, peace, and well-being.

Note: This spell is powerful on its own, but for even greater effect, try sweeping and smudging your home with sage before you begin.

Ingredients:

- 1 medium to large rose quartz crystal per room or area
- White candle (optional)

Instructions:

1. If using, place the candle at the center of your home and light it.
2. Spend a few moments quieting your mind.
3. In each room of your house, find a place to sit in a comfortable position.
4. Hold the rose quartz between your palms for a few moments, concentrating on the peaceful, positive feeling it emits.

5. Now place it on the floor in front of you and visualize pink light radiating outward from the crystal, spreading throughout the room.

6. Feel any negative energy being replaced by a calming, loving vibration from the rose quartz.

7. When you feel the energy is sufficiently transformed, say the following (or similar) words:

8. "Love and light are ever present in this space. All is well."

9. Now pick up the rose quartz and place it in a safe space in the room so that it may continue to balance the energy.

10. Repeat this ritual in each room or in any area that contains unwanted vibrations.

Spell to Release Pain and Unexpressed Emotions

Sometimes we are unable to express emotions in certain situations or don't have the words to express our feelings. Stifling our emotions in this way can be a good short-term defense mechanism, but ultimately it will fester and become a source of unattended negativity.

Releasing these painful emotions will enable you to process grief or trauma, heal from emotional wounds, and clear your heart space so that you are open to receive love and compassion from the Universe and from others in your life. This ritual can be used for healing from specific past emotional wounds, or for simply clearing more general emotional clutter from your personal energy field.

Ingredients:

- 1 rose quartz crystal
- Pink spell candle
- Lavender essential oil

Instructions:

1. Light the candle and spend a few moments quieting your mind.

2. Hold the rose quartz in your left hand. (The left hand allows energy to flow directly to your heart center.) To increase the intensity of the spell, you can hold the rose quartz over your heart.

3. For three minutes, allow your thoughts to flow naturally, asking for anything that needs to be released to come into your awareness.

4. Don't hold on to any specific thought—instead, feel it, accept it, and let it move through you. Give the crystal

your permission to heal and soothe you by radiating love and understanding throughout your body.

5. As you breathe, inhale the calming essence of the rose quartz, and on the exhale allow any stuck energy from past pain and trauma to be released.

6. Anoint the rose quartz with 1 or 2 drops of lavender oil, if using.

7. Then bury it in the Earth to cleanse it from the energies of the old emotions.

8. Leave it there for one full night.

9. You can reuse the stone as often as needed.

Shining Light Self-Love and Confidence Spell

In a society focused on materialism and surface appearances, the concepts of "self-love" and "self-confidence" can be confusing. Often people look to their skills and accomplishments for sources of self-acceptance, but this approach is missing the point entirely.

True self-love comes from within, when we recognize that we are divine beings of light no matter how we appear or what we do (or don't do) in the exterior world. This spell is useful for anyone dealing with insecurities or issues of self-acceptance (which is basically everyone, at one point or another!).

If you like, work this spell with a rose quartz necklace or bracelet, for an easily-wearable charm.

Ingredients:

- 1 rose quartz crystal (or rose quartz necklace / bracelet)
- 1 pink candle
- 1 orange candle

Instructions:

1. Place the rose quartz between the two candles.
2. Take a moment to quiet your mind and then light the pink candle, saying the following (or similar) words:

    "This light shines as my love for myself shines."

3. Now light the orange candle, saying the following (or similar) words:

    "This light shines as my self-expression shines."

4. Pick up the rose quartz and hold it between your palms.
5. Take a moment to focus on the light that shines from the candles, and feel the love emanating from the stone in your hands.

6. Take a few deep breaths, close your eyes, and repeat the following (or similar) words seven times:

   "I accept myself. I trust myself. I love myself. From within, I shine for all the world to see."

7. Gently extinguish the candles.

8. Carry (or wear) the rose quartz every day until you feel more rooted in your own confident sense of self.

9. If you feel the need, you can repeat the spell periodically to recharge the stone (or jewelry).

Spell for Attracting Healthy Relationships

The Law of Attraction teaches us that "like attracts like," and that what we think about determines what we bring into our experience. This is true in all areas of life, but is often most clearly seen when it comes to relationships. If you always seem to date the wrong people, or find yourself surrounded by friendships that aren't fulfilling, you need to shift your energetic vibration in order to turn this trend around.

This is easier said than done, however, if you don't have a lot of experience with positive, healthy relationships. Whether you're seeking a romantic partner or a new friend, or both, this spell helps you open yourself up to guidance from the Universe so you can learn to recognize the difference between people who truly value your presence and people who are incapable of treating you well.

Ingredients:

- 2 small rose quartz crystals
- 1 white or pink candle
- 2 pieces of writing paper
- Fireproof dish

Instructions:

1. Light the candle and place one rose quartz on either side of it. Take a few moments to quiet your mind.

2. On the first piece of paper, write down the qualities of friendships and/or romantic relationships that have been unhealthy for you in your life. Don't use names or focus on specific people, but rather strive to articulate the actions that have hurt you and/or the resulting feelings from these encounters. Don't dwell too heavily on any one incident or person, and don't go into more detail than necessary—the point is not to reinforce the negative experiences, but simply to recognize and acknowledge what it is that you wish to be free of in your life.

3. When you're finished, tear the paper up into a few pieces, and ignite them one at a time on the candle flame, being careful not to burn your fingers.

4. Drop them into the fireproof dish and let them burn out.

5. Now use the second piece of paper to write about what you wish to manifest in your future relationship(s). Identify how you want to feel, how you want to be treated, etc. If you're unclear about what healthy relationships are actually like, feel free to write down questions. Let the Universe know what you need in terms of help in shifting these patterns in your life.

6. When you're finished, fold the paper four times and place it in front of the candle.

7. Place both crystals on top of the paper and say the following (or similar) words:

"As I value myself, I attract others who do the same

So, let it be."

8. Leave the candle to burn out on its own.

9. Bury the ashes of the burned paper or scatter them over the Earth.

10. Keep the folded paper in your journal, Book of Shadows, or somewhere else where you can refer back to it as a

"checklist" over the coming weeks and months, as new people make their way into your life.

11. If you like, carry the crystals with you in a purse or pocket when you go out.

Moonstone

Moonstone is probably one of the most captivating magical stones in any Witch's collection. This iridescent beauty is often white or cream colored, but can also contain blues, greens, yellows and browns, depending on the specimen. Comprised of two separate minerals, orthoclase and albite, moonstone is a type of feldspar, which is the most abundant mineral group on Earth. The largest deposits of moonstone are found mainly in Sri Lanka and India, but there are many deposits all over the world, ranging from Australia to Brazil to Norway.

Moonstone was highly valued in ancient Rome, where people wore the stone in various forms of jewelry. The Romans believed that moonstone was magically created from solidified moonbeams. Because of this it is strongly linked with the deities of the Moon throughout ancient Rome and Greece. The ancient Egyptians also revered moonstone, associating it with the goddess Isis, and in India it is still considered a sacred stone.

As a member of the feldspar family, moonstone is quite abundant, but the most beautiful specimens are becoming more and more rare due to high demand. Moonstone became hugely popular during the Art Nouveau period, where it was featured in a multitude of jewelry pieces, and men even wore moonstone in their cufflinks and watch chains.

Recently, the mineral has seen a resurgence of popularity in the jewelry world, which may put the most shimmering pieces out of reach for many of the magically inclined. But you don't need to have the most beautiful moonstone in order to work with its potent magical energies!

Not surprisingly, this stone's planetary association is the Moon, with Water as its Element. This makes it a great stone to work with in any spell related to serenity, tranquility, or feminine intuition, as well as any ritual honoring the Goddess. Fertility magick is a natural avenue for using moonstone, as is any working related to women's reproductive health, revitalizing romantic passion, and increasing psychic receptivity.

Traditionally, moonstone was also used for protection while traveling at sea. In this spirit, you'll find a spell below for ensuring safe travel on or over water, as well as spells to support efforts to conceive a child, energize a long-term relationship, and encourage prophetic dreaming.

Water Travel Protection Charm

Travel by sea isn't as common as it was centuries ago, when the tradition of calling on moonstone for safe passage over water would have been widely practiced. Nonetheless, moonstone's watery energy is perfect for a modern-day version of invoking travel protection, whether you're headed to the beach, going on a cruise, flying overseas, or taking a hike along a river.

Mugwort's association with the Moon makes it an ideal protection herb to accompany the moonstone. If you can't find mugwort, however, you can substitute another protection herb, such as valerian or bay leaf.

Ingredients:

- 3 small moonstones
- 1 teaspoon fresh or dried mugwort
- Small drawstring bag
- Work candle for atmosphere (optional)

Instructions:

1. Light the candle, if using.
2. Hold the moonstones between your palms and visualize the beams of the Moon entering each stone. See the white rays of light meeting the stones and charging them with

protective energy that will create a magical shield around you on your journey over (or near) water.

3. Place the charged stones in the drawstring bag, and sprinkle the mugwort over them while saying the following (or similar) words:

"As the Moon casts a glowing path across the sea,

the energies of protection will now surround me."

4. Close the drawstring bag and leave it under moonlight overnight, either outdoors (ideally) or in a windowsill.

5. Take it with you on your travels for extra safety.

Spell to Enhance Fertility

Deciding to bring a new soul into the physical plane can be exciting and somewhat stressful on a couple. Many times, conceiving a child does not happen instantly and each passing month may bring about a new level of disappointment. The resulting anxiety can adversely affect fertility.

Moonstone is a powerful magical ally when you are ready to become a parent. This simple but effective spell can soothe any fear about the ability to conceive and therefore enhance fertility. As an added bonus, moonstone is associated with protection of women during pregnancy as well.

Ingredients:

- 1 small piece moonstone
- Needle and thread
- Tee shirt or other often-worn item of clothing
- Small square of green fabric

Instructions:

1. Center yourself in the moment by placing the moonstone in your hands and breathing deeply.

2. Visualize your intent flowing into the stone. See yourself as a parent, welcoming a new life into the world.

3. When you're ready, turn the shirt or other item of clothing inside out and place the moonstone in a spot that won't get in your way when you wear it.

4. Place the green square of fabric over it and sew it onto the clothing. As you stitch around the edges, think of the moonstone pouch as a womb for your intentions to conceive a child.

5. When you have completely encased the stone in the garment, spend a moment holding it in your hands and say the following (or similar) words:

   "I welcome you, new child of mine, into this life."

6. Put on the clothing and wear it for the remaining part of the day.

7. Leave the stone in your special pouch and wear the clothing often.

8. Once you've conceived, you can remove the pouch and sew the fabric closed over the stone to make it into a keepsake for your new baby.

Moonstone Charm for Rekindling Passion

Every relationship needs a boost of renewed zest at one point or another. If you find yourself entering into a less-than-passionate phase with your partner, try working with enchanted jewelry to breathe new life into your current love routine. This working is best performed under the light of a full or waxing moon.

Prices for moonstone necklaces run from affordable to very expensive, but some online research will help you find one that fits within your budget.

Ingredients:

- 1 moonstone necklace
- Red candle

Instructions:

1. Light the candle.

2. Hold the moonstone necklace in your hands and take a moment to remember times when you felt passionate about your partner, and times when your partner demonstrated the same feelings toward you.

3. Visualize a new encounter with your partner that rekindles these energies.

4. If there is a single stone in the necklace, concentrate on holding that single stone as you visualize the past and future passion in your relationship. If the necklace has more than one moonstone, repeat the process with each one.

5. When you have fully charged your necklace with passionate energies, put it on, close your eyes, breathe deeply, and allow yourself to enjoy the anticipation of manifesting your desires on the physical plane.

6. Gently extinguish the candle.

7. Wear the necklace on your next date or other quality time with your partner.

Moonstone Dreaming Spell

When we're living fast-paced, hectic lives, our dreams can often seem like just a string of nonsensical "brain garbage" that don't lead to much in the way of insight. But traditionally, dreaming is meant to be a vehicle for important messages from the Universe and our higher selves.

There are many crystals that can help clear out the clutter of our subconscious and smooth out the path for clearer, more profound, and even prophetic dreams to come our way. Moonstone is one of the most powerful dreaming stones, as its energies are linked with the psychic, shifting tides of the Moon.

This spell calls for surrounding yourself with moonstone, creating an energy grid that will help you connect to the ethereal plane in your sleep. You can take it a step further if you like, asking for specific guidance to come to you in your dreams on the night you work the spell.

Ingredients:

- 4 small moonstones
- Silver candle
- Journal or writing paper

Instructions:

1. Light the candle and spend a few moments quieting your mind. If you have a specific question or issue that you

would like to have addressed in your dreams, write it at the top of a sheet of paper.

2. Hold the moonstones in your hands and visualize your personal energy infusing them until they glow. Silently ask the stones to harness the energy you need to receive dreams that contain useful information.

3. Now place one piece of moonstone on the floor at each corner of your bed. As you place each stone, say the following (or similar) words:

   "By the light of the Moon, my dreams will flow

   and tell me all I need to know.

   So, let it be."

4. Gently extinguish the candle before going to sleep.

5. Keep the journal or writing paper (and pen) near your bed so that you can record your dreams first thing after waking.

Hematite

One of the most common minerals on Earth, hematite is found in countries as far apart as Brazil, Norway, Italy, and Canada. This stone's outer appearance is a silvery-grey color that polishes to an immaculate shine, giving it the appearance of steel. Its inner core, however, is a blood red color derived from the iron oxide in its mineral composition. In its pure form, hematite can often develop into structures that appear to have petals like a flower. These forms are called iron roses.

The name hematite comes from the Greek word *haimatites* which roughly translates to "blood," due to its ochre interior. In fact, for many centuries, hematite was called "bloodstone," though we now use that name for the green jasper featured earlier in this book. At least one myth about the stone's origins was related to battle—as soldiers lay injured in the aftermath of a fight, large pools of blood would accumulate and sink into the earth, forming the mineral.

Hematite's smooth, glasslike surface made it a perfect crystal for using as a rudimentary mirror in ancient times. The powdered interior was used as a pigment in some cave paintings, and by the ancient Egyptians who painted their pharaoh's tombs and sarcophaguses to depict images of the afterlife. Native Americans also used hematite to paint their faces before going into battle.

Despite its many associations with blood and battle, hematite is also known as a stone linked to the higher mind. It helps to center and organize energy by grounding and calming the user. The ability to focus while experiencing multiple stimuli simultaneously can help to reduce stress and anxiety in social situations. Associated with Mars and Saturn, and the Elements of Fire, Earth, and Water, hematite is used in magical workings related to grounding, psychic awareness, healing, past life recall, logical and critical thinking, self-esteem and confidence, and dissipating negative energy in one's surroundings.

The spells in this paragraph utilize hematite to help you release worry and anger, transform pessimism into optimism, and ground yourself during social interactions that may cause heightened anxiety.

Spell to Boost Optimism

Anyone who understands the Law of Attraction knows that our thoughts create our reality. Therefore, keeping an upbeat and optimistic attitude is crucial to our ability to manifest what we desire. This is easier said than done, however, and even the most positive people occasionally find themselves slipping into pessimistic thinking. Hematite's grounding and healing properties can be harnessed to help you turn your attitude around, and go back to attracting positive thoughts and experiences.

The hematite in this spell works on two levels. First, it assists you in reprogramming your negative thoughts into positive statements. It also wards off any other general negative energy that you may have been unwittingly attracting during your bout with pessimistic thinking.

Although you may be able to identify a multitude of negative thoughts, it's best to just work with a small handful, in order to focus your intention on the act of transmuting the negative into positive. Otherwise, you may get overwhelmed or your focus may dissipate through the effort of rewriting too many separate thoughts. So just focus on the main issues that have been coming up for you repeatedly.

Ingredients:

- 3 to 5 hematite stones
- 3 to 5 small slips of paper
- White candle

Instructions:

1. Light the candle and spend some time quieting your mind.

2. When you're ready to begin, recall a particular negative thought that you have been having recently.

3. On one of the slips of paper, rewrite the negative thought into a positive statement. For example, if you keep thinking "I never have any money," you can write "I believe money can flow to me without having to know its source."

4. Wrap the slip of paper around the hematite stone so that the words are facing outward.

5. Secure the paper with a drop of wax.

6. Repeat this process with the remaining hematite and paper.

7. Leave the paper-wrapped stones on your altar or place them in an area where you spend a lot of time, to help you remember to transform your negative thoughts into positive statements.

8. When your pessimistic "funk" has lifted, thank the stones and recycle the slips of paper.

Spell to Ease Social Anxiety

Those who suffer from social anxiety know that it doesn't only occur in large group situations. Depending on your level of sensitivity to other peoples' energy, anxiety can crop up during all kinds of encounters with other people.

In this spell, you will create a helpful talisman to carry in your pocket, helping you to remember to ground and center yourself during social interactions.

Ingredients:

- 1 medium hematite stone

- White or black spell candle

Instructions:

1. Light the candle and spend some time breathing deeply to quiet your mind.

2. When you feel ready, spend a few moments visualizing the kind of social situation that makes you uneasy.

3. Ask yourself what triggers an anxiety producing response in your body during these situations.

4. When you identify a trigger, pick up the hematite and hold it between your palms.

5. Take a deep breath and exhale slowly, counting to seven.

6. Envision yourself in this imagined social setting, surrounded by white light.

7. Repeat this breathing process three times, focusing on filling the stone with tranquil, relaxed energy.

8. Now, place the hematite in front of the candle.

9. Allow it to charge there until the candle has burned all the way down.

10. Carry the charmed stone with you in your purse or pocket the next time you are entering into a social situation that may produce an anxious reaction. You can

hold on to the stone during any difficult moments without anyone even knowing!

Anger Release Spell

Anger is a normal human emotion that has its place, temporarily, in certain situations. However, it's best for your health—mental, physical and spiritual—to release anger once it has served its purpose. This spell will help you remove the energy of lingering resentments and move on so that you can experience positive emotions, like joy, love and hope, more fully and clearly.

Hematite's healing properties and its ability to dissipate negativity makes it a great stone for this kind of work. The Earth's power to transmute negative energy into neutral or positive energy is also utilized in this spell. Raw hematite is best for burying, but a polished stone will also work in a pinch.

Ingredients:

- Small to medium raw hematite stone
- Black or white candle
- Journal or writing paper (optional)

Instructions:

1. Light the candle, and spend some time quieting your mind.

2. Allow yourself to focus on the anger and/or resentment you're still carrying with you from an old situation.

3. If it helps, do some freewriting about the issue—try to identify the reasons for the anger you're still feeling.

4. When you're ready, hold the hematite between your palms.

5. Visualize the feelings you're looking to release flowing into the stone, making it grow warm and heavier in your hands.

6. Go outside and bury the stone in the Earth.

7. As you dig the small hole and cover the stone, say the following (or similar) words:

> "Let this pent-up anger cease.
>
> These old feelings I now release.
>
> Blessed Be."

Spell to Release the Habit of Worry

Planning ahead is a valuable skill to have in life, but constantly worrying about what may or may not happen is actually counterproductive to manifesting the reality you desire. If you're a chronic worrier, you're certainly not alone.

However, you can empower yourself to ditch this habit with the help of the powers of Nature. The soothing effect of running water in this spell combines with the transmuting power of hematite to help you release your habit of worrying and clear up your energy field for a smoother, more carefree life.

If you don't live near a stream or creek, you can place the stones in a bowl and run water from the sink or bathtub over them for several minutes and then scatter the stones over the Earth. However, it's highly recommended that you make the effort to bring them to a natural body of water, even if you have to go out of your way to get there.

Ingredients:

- Several raw hematite stones
- Small cloth bag

Instructions:

1. Spend some time quieting your mind.
2. When you feel ready, take one stone and hold it between your palms.
3. Think of a specific worry that you are currently experiencing and let the hematite absorb the worry.

4. Place it in the small bag.

5. Continue this process with as many stones as you need.

6. Bring the bag of hematite to a nearby stream, river, or creek.

7. Sit quietly for a few moments at the edge and allow the sound and sight of the moving water to soothe your spirit.

8. When you feel ready, gently empty the bag of stones into the running water.

9. Thank the Elemental spirits of the water for cleansing your energy of worry and fear.

10. The next time you find yourself starting to anticipate something negative happening in the future, return in your mind to the water running over the hematite stones.

11. If you can, get into the habit of listening to recordings of a bubbling brook, a waterfall, or even the ocean in order to help you maintain a calmer state of mind.

Elixirs

Crystal Elixir for Physical Health

Crystal elixirs—the infusing of water with the vibrations of crystals and other mineral stones—have been used for healing purposes since at least 3000 B.C.E. in various cultures.

The rebalancing powers of quartz crystal can be used to bring about physical regeneration and revitalization in the body by working at the subtle energy level. This elixir is great for those who have been feeling low on energy, are recovering from a minor illness, or would simply like an all-around rebalancing "lift" of healing energy.

Note: Some of the stones and crystals are very toxic, and they shouldn't be used internally in any way. So, if you're wanting to explore this particular magical technique further, be sure to do thorough research on any stone you're considering for use in an elixir!

Ingredients:

- 1 small piece of clear quartz
- Cup of filtered water

Instructions:

1. Place the quartz in a small glass of water and leave it in the sunshine for one day. The following day, perform the healing ritual.

2. Remove the quartz from the water carefully and place it on your altar or table. Keep the water in the center of your altar or table.

3. Take three deep breaths to relax and focus.

4. Take a moment to meditate on your body. Allow your mind to scan your body from the top of your head down to your feet. Notice any areas that may need attention.

5. Return to the first place you noticed an imbalance in your body. Focus on healing that area as you take a sip of the water.

6. Visualize the power and ancient wisdom of the quartz healing that area, releasing any tension, discomfort, or other unwanted sensations.

7. Repeat this with each area of your body that needs attention and healing.

8. When you are finished, allow yourself a moment to feel the vibration of the quartz throughout your body, healing and reviving your being.

9. You can repeat this ritual whenever your body needs a boost of healing energy.

Candle spells

Below are several spells that help in matters of money, health, employment, and other things that contribute to having a life full of enjoyment. Each of these has one or more candles as its attention and some including few more ingredients many of which should be available. Please remember that you can modify any of these spells to the needs you want and you can pay attention to your goals through your influence that makes the difference.

You will realize that every spell, the perfect moon stage and week day are listed for working this magick type. Mostly the waxing stage of the moon is for the type of magick that appeals things in your life and the waning stage is usually for discharging unwanted or old things from your life.

Similarly, week days have old magical relations. For example, Friday is suggested for spells that involve beauty, reconciliation, friendship and love. However, its fine if you can't target your spell work accurately to these suggestions, but doing so is very probable to boost spell power.

Lastly, be sure that you have some time to get prepared for the magick, instead of unconsciously going through the waves as if you are preparing lunch you will take to work tomorrow. Whether you desire to meditate, and exploit other approaches for adapting to the unseen reams, by doing something to spot a difference between the magick time and the rest of the day to realize that you are in a right mind frame to have an effect.

Love Spells

Heart matters are perhaps the most joint reason that people pursue magick. Its reasonable to want to do all it takes to bring love into one's life. Nevertheless, there are lots of irresponsible spells that are out there appealing to have the ability to bring to you the kind of person you desire.

Spells whose intention is to manipulate another person, no matter how eventually well-meant, are not accountable for magick and its very possible for them to fail. So, one must concentrate on the condition you crave rather than the person, when working on these spells. You can never tell what is around the corner, because the one you may have a crush on today can pale in contrast to the person you will meet tomorrow or next week.

Passionate Relationship Spell

When you are prepared for a new lover, you don't just cast a universal spell before taking time to reflect on what you need out of the relationship. Or else your strong magick can bring you more of the same categories of the people that you have already moved away from.

So, take some time to plainly outline what exactly you are looking for. You may need to organize a list of abilities that you want in a lover before time since you will be speaking and writing about them during the spell casting process.

A healthy, true and passionate relationship should include self-confidence and appreciation in both partners so, you will also pay attention to yourself in this particular spell. Devote some time confirming to yourself the qualities that are positive you have to bring to a new relationship so that you have then in mind undoubtably as you start the work.

Ingredients

- Cinnamon, jasmine
- Crystal point, athame
- Scissors
- Wax paper
- White paper
- Red pencil or marker
- One red spell candle

Instructions

1. Cut a heart shape or any other love symbol into the candle and smear it with oil. Light the candle and let the wax to start the melting process
2. In the meantime, cut two heart figures like the size of your palms from the paper. Take one of the hearts, and

on it, write the very crucial qualities that you need in a romantic partner, using a red marker or pencil. Also write down the list of all qualities that you have to offer to the other partner.

3. For a moment, hold the hearts in your hands as you pay attention to bringing the new love to your life. Now,

Hold the hearts in your hands for a moment as you focus on bringing new love into your life. Now, place the hearts so that they overlap each other on a sheet of wax paper. Speaking out loud, take turns listing the qualities written on each heart.

4. As you list each one, drip a few drops of wax onto the hearts to seal them together. When you have finished speaking, and the hearts are sealed, say the following words:

    > "Passionate hearts, passionate minds,
    > Passionate souls, we now entwine.
    > So let it be."

5. Place the hearts on your altar or in a special space in your home. Allow the candle to burn out on its own.

Moonlight Love Attraction Spell

For singles wanting to enjoy the dating scene, here's a simple spell to heighten your ability to attract potential suitors. This is particularly good for those who have been single for a long time and may struggle to remain optimistic about their prospects.

Moon phase: Waxing

Ideal day: Friday

Ingredients

- 1 Pink candle (spell candle sized)
- A small vial of wearable essential oil blend (or cologne/perfume if preferred)
- Cinnamon, jasmine, or lavender incense
- Crystal point, athame, or other ritual carving tool

Instructions

1. Light the incense. Using the crystal point or another carving tool, carve a heart in the center of the candle. Place the candle in a window, ideally one with a direct view of the Moon. (If this isn't possible, visualize the moon as you set the candle down.) Place the vial in front of candle so that it stands between the candle and the window.

2. Take a few moments to call up the feelings of well-being, excitement, and companionship. Hold this feeling as you get ready to light the candle. As you light it, say these (or your own) words:

    "By this moon's light, let love shine bright."

3. Allow it to burn down. Wear the oil (or perfume) when you go out to help you stay confident in your ability to

attract new love. But be careful not to overdo the scent—that never helps!

Rekindling the spark in your relationship Spell

Those of us already in long-term relationships may sometimes long wistfully for the rush of feelings that accompany the beginning of a romance. While you can't turn back the clock to your relationship's early days, you can rejuvenate the atmosphere between you and your partner with this simple spell.

This can be done during any point in the Moon's cycle—if you're working during the waning phase, focus on ridding the relationship of any "humdrum" feelings or stagnant-seeming energy.

Moon phase: Any

Ideal day: Tuesday or Friday

Ingredients

- Two red votive candles
- Plate to melt them on
- Jasmine oil (or homemade blend)
- Pinch of rosemary (fresh or dried)

Instructions

1. Anoint the candles with the oil and stand them next to each other on the plate. Sprinkle the rosemary on top of the candles and in a circle around them.

2. Chant these words; *"As these flames dance side by side, so we two renew our stride, in love and desire."*
3. It's ideal for letting the candles burn out in one sitting, but it's also fine to snuff them out and repeat the spell the next night, if necessary. Once they're all the way gone, take some time to look at the melted wax and see if any impressions or messages about your relationship emerge.

Finding an ideal lifetime partner Spell

For those who are ready to move beyond casual dating and want assistance in manifesting a solid, healthy relationship. This spell asks you to identify what you're truly looking for in a partner, so spend some time considering this beforehand.

As an added "boost," you can consult color meanings and choose a candle color that aligns with the qualities you feel are most important in a partner. For example, if you know that sharp intelligence and ability with language are key, you might choose a yellow candle. If no colors or qualities jump out at you as being at the top of the list, then feel free to use a white candle.

Moon phase: Waxing

Ideal day: Friday

Ingredients:
- A pen and a piece of white paper
- One small candle (white, or color of your choice)

- One gold or silver ribbon, long enough to wrap around your palm at least twice

Instructions:

1. Light the candle, and wrap the ribbon around your non-writing hand. On the paper, write down the specific things you desire in a partner for a long-term relationship. Spend a good while on this part. Be sure to include how you want to feel around and be treated by this person, as all the desirable characteristics in the world won't matter if you're being ignored or abused in any way.

2. Fold the paper into a small square, then unwrap the ribbon from your hand and tie it around the folded paper. Hold the bundle together in your palms as you meditate on how you will feel in this relationship once it is underway. Place the bundle under your mattress for one week, then bury in a potted plant or the yard.

Prosperity Spells

Many skeptics of magick will ask, "If it works so well, why don't people just cast spells to win the lottery?"

Well, one thing that you have to remember is that magick works in cooperation with physical reality. This means that the mathematical odds are still in play. You're also competing with the wishes and dreams of many, many people and whether they're working spells or not, their intentions matter.

Wiccans and other Witches know that we have to do our part in manifesting wealth by working, making smart decisions about our money, etc. As you develop your magical abilities, be sure to acknowledge and express gratitude for all gifts from the Universe—even for the penny you find on the sidewalk. Let no luck be too small—otherwise, the spirit realm may interpret your attitude to mean you're not interested in experiencing good luck!

Magick Cash Spell

There are many spells out there that involve charging actual cash—either coins or paper bills—to attract more cash. This version draws very directly from the power of the green spell candle, with a little help from prosperous patchouli oil.

Ingredients:

- One green spell candle
- Patchouli essential oil
- One five-dollar bill
- Green rubber band

Instructions:

1. Anoint the candle with the patchouli oil. Fold the five-dollar bill in half lengthwise and wrap it around the candle. Secure the bill with the rubber band, leaving at

least an inch of space between the bill and the candlewick so that the flame will not ignite the bill.

2. Now hold the wrapped candle between your palms and summon up the feeling of being flush with cash, with all of your basic needs met and the ability to spend some money on yourself! When you have a solid hold on this feeling, say the following (or similar) words three times:

"As above, so below.
So money in my life does flow. Land to the sky,
shore to shore, this money brings me money more."

3. Light the candle and allow it to burn down to the top of the five-dollar bill. Gently extinguish the candle, and when the wax has cooled, unwrap the bill. Carry it with you in your wallet, but don't spend it—instead, whenever you see it, remind yourself that you are attracting more cash into your life each day.

Getting rid of money blocks Spell

Unlike most money-related spells, this one is done during a waning Moon, as it focuses on releasing these unhelpful, and often unconscious, attitudes and fears. If you've been unsuccessful at other spell work to attract money, you might want to give this one a try—it could be that you've been unknowingly getting in your way!

Moon phase: Waning

Ideal day: Thursday, Sunday, or Monday

Ingredients:

- One black candle
- One piece of white paper
- Scissors
- Cauldron, sink. or another safe place to burn paper

Instructions:

1. Light the candle and sit quietly for a few moments. On the paper, write down your fears about money. Go with the first few things that pop into your mind—these are usually the thoughts that block our progress toward prosperity.

2. Name each fear in a simple, single sentence. Leave space in between each sentence so that you can cut them into strips. Cut the first "money fears" sentence from the top of the paper. Read it silently, and then speak its opposite out loud. For example, if you've written, *"I will always have scarcity,"* then say, *"I always have more than enough."*

3. Then light the paper on the candle and allow it to burn out in your cauldron, sink, or another fireproof container. Gently snuff or wave out the candle. Repeat this spell each night, burning one fear sentence per night, until you've burned them all. The ideal length for this spell is 3 to 5 consecutive nights.

Quick Money Spell

This is one of the greatest spells you can start practicing as a beginner. This is mainly because it is often immediate and the outcome is impressively surprising. All you need to do is relax and stay open to possibility of money coming your way quite unexpectedly.

Moon phase: Waxing

Suitable day: Thursday

Ingredients:

- One green spell candle
- Crystal point or any other carving tool
- One coin

Instructions:

1. Start by carving the dollar sign or any other currency that you use onto your candle. Now, take the candle and hold it in your hands for a couple of minutes and start saying these words:

   "As like attracts like, this money brings more."

2. After chanting these words, light the candle and let it to burn down to the coin. Take the coin and it with you in your wallet or pocket every day.

Rent and Bills Stability—7 Day Spell

If you often end up scraping to get the bills paid, or are in a transition period and unsure of how your finances are going to work out shortly, this is a good spell to aid you in establishing some peace of mind about staying afloat.

Once you've sent this spell energy out into the spirit world, you can focus on manifesting more long-term improvements to your financial life.

Moon phase: Waxing

Ideal day: Thursday or Sunday

Ingredients:

- One check from your checkbook (or piece of paper)
- One 7-day candle, preferably gold, grey, brown, or orange
- A pinch of basil
- Almond, patchouli, or bergamot oil

Instructions:

1. Anoint the top of the candle with one or two drops of the oil. Sprinkle the basil over the oil. Focus on the feeling of ease that comes with having everything in order financially. Light the candle as you say:

"All is provided to me exactly as I need it, with harm to none. So, let it be."

2. Sit with the candlelight for a few moments and write some positive affirmations about money and stability on

the check or piece of paper. Be sure to write as if the magick has already worked—for example; you might write, "All bills are paid, and I can move forward with confidence."

3. Make sure you use words that resonate with you and help you strengthen your belief in your ability to manifest positive change. Fold the check (or paper) into thirds, then keep folding until it's as small as you can make it. Place it in your purse or wallet and carry it with you until your bills are paid.

4. Leave the candle to burn out on its own. This typically takes seven days, though if things are manifesting at a more rapid rate, the candle may burn out more quickly.

Healing Spells

We know that, like anything else, the body is essentially made of energy. Many popular alternative healing modalities make use of this understanding, such as reiki and therapeutic touch. With this in mind, it makes perfect sense that magick can positively affect our health.

However, you should never substitute magick for actual medical care! As with any other "alternative" practice, magick should be used in addition to, not instead of, any necessary medical interventions. Just as in money or employment matters, you're expected to do your part to manifest the change you seek.

These spells can work well during any phase of the moon since any healing involves both sending away disease (imbalance) and attracting health (balance).

Harmony Spell for Domestic Conflicts

The Blue Perimeter Home Protection spell above is excellent for maintaining healthy and positive energy within your home. However, interpersonal conflicts among roommates or family members can still flare up and even persist over time. After all, we learn through our relationships, all of which are bound to have their thornier aspects at times.

This spell can facilitate that learning, and the resolution of the conflict, by providing sacred space and time for honest and healing dialogue. This spell is particularly effective because blue is the color of peace, and also because it requires that both parties be willing to work through and resolve a disagreement.

Ingredients:

- One blue pillar candle
- Two pieces of blue or white yarn, long enough to wrap around the candle

Instructions:

1. You should sit facing one another with the candle placed between you, either at a table or on a raised platform, so that the candle is safe to handle once it's lit.

2. Take a moment to breathe and center yourself by visualizing a white light surrounding you both. Ask the other person to do the same, so that you both come to the ritual with healing intentions.
3. Light the candle and open an honest discussion about how to restore harmony in the home. Be frank but respectful to one another. Practice using "I statements" throughout the spell.
4. It is important to avoid an attitude of blame or right and wrong; rather, invite the person to work *with* you to solve the argument. This may take some time, so allow space and time needed to truly clear the air and find a resolution.
5. When you are each satisfied that you have been heard by the other and peace is restored, each person should carefully tie their piece of yarn around the candle to signify their commitment to keeping harmony in the home. You can gently extinguish the candle at any point after this and relight it on each successive evening until the candle is spent.

Simple Healing Spell

For everyday ailments such as the common cold, or more chronic issues such as arthritis flare-ups, this spell gently supports the body's natural healing abilities.

It can be worked all at once or over a series of days, depending on the nature of the imbalance you're seeking to heal and your general preferences. If you choose to work it over more than one night, be sure to use a new pinch of yarrow each time.

Moon phase: Any

Ideal day: Sunday or Monday

Ingredients:

- One blue candle
- A pinch of dried yarrow

Instructions:

1. Light the candle. Close your eyes and visualize white light filling and surrounding the part of you that needs healing (for example, if you're dealing with a bronchial infection, focus on the lungs).
2. Once you have this image firmly in your mind, then visualize the white light growing and expending until it surrounds your entire being. Hold this image for a few moments and notice the shift in your body as you mentally flood it with light.
3. When you're ready, open your eyes and sprinkle a small bit of yarrow into the flame. Thank the Universe for its healing powers and close the ritual with words of confirmation, such as:

    "For the good of all and harm to none, this magical healing work is done."

4. If you aren't leaving the candle to burn out completely, wait at least 15 minutes before snuffing it out.

Casting out depression Spell

Depression is often described by those who suffer from it as an unwanted presence in the mind that turns every thought into a sour, mucky experience. It can be very challenging to make use of positive imagery when under the "spell" of depression, so it's helpful to first do some work toward banishing the negative influences underlying this harmful condition.

Because the focus here is on banishing, the spell is most powerful during a waning moon, but don't let that prevent you from using magick to take care of yourself—it can still be done at any time!

Moon phase: Any (waning is ideal)

Ideal day: Saturday, Sunday, Monday, or Wednesday

Ingredients:

- One black candle (preferably with a shorter burning time)
- Three white candles
- One small black crystal or stone (such as obsidian, black tourmaline, or jet)
- A piece of quartz crystal (or other white stone)
- Small black cloth

Instructions:

1. Arrange the white candles in a triangle, and place the black candle in the center. Hold the black stone between your palms and spend a few moments directing all negative energy from your body and mind into the stone. When you feel ready, place the stone next to the black candle and light it.

Say the following words, or use your own:

"I release and banish all negativity from my being."

2. Next, hold the quartz crystal (or other white stone) between your palms and focus on pulling in healing, loving energy from the Universe. Visualize your entire body flooded with, and surrounded by, white light. When you feel ready, light the white candles, repeating this mantra as you light each one:

"I welcome and trust all positivity and Universal love into my being."

3. Once the black candle has burned down, discard any remaining wax, and clean the candleholder before putting it away. Use the black cloth to pick up the black stone so that you avoid touching it with your skin. If possible, toss the stone in a moving body of water, such as a stream, river, or ocean. If this isn't possible, bury it somewhere away from your home.

4. Keep the quartz crystal (or white stone) in your pocket or in a pouch that you keep near you at all times. You may

also want to keep it near your bed while you sleep. You can snuff out and relight the white candles as much as you wish—they can be very comforting as you continue to heal from the depression. Just be sure to use all three of them until they are completely gone.

Healing Spell for Loved Ones

It can be a wonderful experience to work healing magick for others, rather than for yourself. However, if you're going to do spell work for someone else, it's strongly recommended that you get permission first. (If you're not able to be fully open about your magical life, you could just ask the person if they'd be comfortable with you praying for them. Magick is, after all, a powerful kind of prayer.)

Also, if you're troubled by worries about this person, do some work to release those feelings before working the spell, so that you don't cloud up the message you're sending to the spirit realm!

Moon phase: Any

Ideal day: Sunday or Monday

Ingredients:

- One white candle
- Crystal point
- Eucalyptus oil

Instructions:

1. Carve the name of the person you're working the spell for into the candle, beginning at the base and working toward the top.
2. Anoint the candle with a few drops of the oil, starting at the bottom and working up to the middle, then starting from the top and working back down towards the middle. As you prepare the candle, focus your mind on a vision of your friend or loved one glowing radiantly in good health. When you feel ready, light the candle and say the following words, or use words of your own:

"Bright light, this healing white surrounds and makes [name of person] new."

3. If at all possible, leave the candle to burn all the way down on its own.

Charms

Anti-Nightmare Protection Charm

Jet is a great stone to use in sleep magick, especially for those who suffer from nightmares or other sleep disturbances.

Jet beads can be found through crystal and mineral retailers and at craft stores (though be sure to double check at craft stores that you're not getting imitation glass beads). If nothing else, you can buy a jet necklace or bracelet and unstring it in order to create this sleeping charm from scratch.

Ingredients:

- 10 to 15 jet beads
- Several inches of thick silver thread
- Scissors
- Thumb-tack or hook
- Work candle for atmosphere (optional)

Instructions:

1. Light the candle, if using.
2. Spend some time taking deep breaths and quieting your mind.
3. When you're ready, begin by cutting a long piece of silver thread.
4. Tie a knot at the end of the thread, making it large enough that the jet bead will not slip off.
5. Place one bead on the thread and say the following (or similar) words:

> *"Peaceful sleep I shall find,*
>
> *all my nightmares I now bind."*

6. Tie a knot and then repeat the chant as you place the next bead on the thread.

7. Repeat this process until all the beads have been strung.

8. Use the scissors to cut the thread, leaving enough to tie a small loop.

9. Use the loop to hang the pendant on a tack or hook above your bed.

Lapis Communication Charm

Effective communication is essential to healthy relationships. Even when a conversation or discussion will be difficult and potentially painful, it is ultimately necessary to the longevity of a relationship. Lapis lazuli is associated with the throat chakra, the place from which our words flow. Here, you will charge a lapis necklace or pendant with the energies of honest and respectful communication.

If you don't have a necklace or pendant featuring lapis lazuli, you can make one by wrapping wire around the stone and attaching it to any type of necklace cord (see the instructions for "Charm for Intellectual Confidence and Motivation," above). You can also find simple cords with small wire "baskets" that allow you to place crystals of your choice inside them, effectively serving as an all-purpose crystal pendant.

Ingredients:

- Lapis lazuli necklace or pendant

Instructions:

1. Place the necklace the table or altar in front of you.

2. Hold your hands above the lapis lazuli stone(s) with palms facing downward.

3. Take a moment to focus your intention on the qualities of honesty, wisdom and courage.

4. When you are ready, send your positive, loving energy into the stone, visualizing the stone and your hands connected by a bright blue light.

5. After you have charged the stone with your energy for a positive conversation, place the necklace or pendant on your altar until you need to use it.

6. Wear it during the next difficult and/or deep conversation you have to have in any relationship, to support honest and wise communication between both parties.

Anti-Bullying Protection Charm

Warriors of the past were known to wear a bloodstone amulet close to their hearts in order to give them courage when facing their opponent. The red flecks of fiery Mars energy combined with the deep Earthy green hues imbue a feeling of well-fortified security.

If you're in the unfortunate situation of dealing with someone who behaves in a bullying manner toward you, this protective amulet can shield you from their negativity. Because bullies only target people they think they can have an effect on, you'll soon be well out of their radar and left alone. This is defensive magick at its best!

If you don't have a necklace or pendant featuring bloodstone, you can make one by wrapping wire around the stone and attaching it to any type of necklace cord (see the instructions for "Charm for Intellectual Confidence and Motivation" in the lapis lazuli chapter). You can also find simple cords with small wire "baskets" that allow you to place crystals of your choice inside them, effectively serving as an all-purpose crystal pendant.

Ingredients:

- 1 bloodstone necklace or pendant
- Black spell candle

Instructions:

1. Light the candle.

2. In a sitting position, place the necklace or pendant in your lap.

3. Begin by visualizing a beautiful green orb at the center of your lap. See the orb gradually grow as it envelops you within it. This is your magical force-field, protecting you against your opponent.

4. On the outer edge of this shielding energy, visualize vibrant patches of red flaring up to warn away anyone who would do you harm.

5. When you've summoned a peaceful, protected feeling, hold the bloodstone between your palms and say the following (or similar) words:

   "With the Heart of Earth and the Fire of Mars,

   I am protected from all who mean me harm

   This amulet shields me from their gaze

   and sends them on their way.

   So, let it be."

6. Place the amulet in front of the candle and allow the candle to burn out on its own.

7. Then wear it around your neck whenever you may come into contact with those who would bully you.

Citrine Charm for Maintaining Wealth

The ancients of every culture saw the Sun as the source of abundance and prosperity, which could be depended upon to return at the start of each new day. Citrine's association with the Sun makes it an excellent representative of security and long-term abundance.

When you work this simple spell, you reaffirm your appreciation for what you already have, as well as your receptivity to more wealth to come.

Ingredients:

- 1 small piece citrine
- 1-dollar bill
- Green or black ribbon or thick thread
- Small drawstring bag
- Work candle for atmosphere (optional)

Instructions:

1. Light the candle, if using.

2. Hold the citrine in your dominant hand and the dollar bill in your other hand.

3. Take a deep breath and concentrate your energy on merging the yellow light and energy of the citrine with the dollar bill, which symbolizes your current wealth.

4. Wrap the dollar bill around the citrine.

5. Now secure the dollar bill with the ribbon or thread, while chanting the following (or similar) words until you have secured it tightly in place:

    "I open the path to wealth without end."

6. Place the wrapped citrine in the drawstring bag and keep it near your safe, checkbook, fireplace, or somewhere else in your home that symbolizes wealth.

Confidence Speaking Charm for Introverts

Many people who are quite articulate in a one-on-one setting find themselves reluctant to speak in group situations, whether it's a college classroom, a meeting at work, or even a social night out. It's not that they don't have anything to say—often they have great insights to share, but just don't quite feel comfortable enough to be the center of the group's attention, no matter how briefly.

If this describes you, try bringing this simple charm with you the next time you're interacting with others. You just might be surprised by the difference it makes!

Ingredients:

- 1 small piece carnelian
- Yellow, orange or white candle

Instructions:

1. Light the candle and spend some time quieting your mind.

2. Think of a recent time when you had something to contribute to a conversation, but kept it to yourself rather than sharing.

3. Now pick up the carnelian and visualize the scene again, but this time see yourself saying what you wanted to say. See the energy of your statement spreading light like a beacon throughout the atmosphere of the scene. See the other people in the room acknowledging your contribution.

4. While still holding the stone, repeat the following (or similar) words nine times:

"My voice has value and I am heard by others."

5. If you like, think of another scene to "rewrite" in this manner, and then repeat the words nine more times. Continue this process until you feel a shift of confidence in your energy.

6. Carry the carnelian with you next time you are in a group setting and watch as you begin to communicate your thoughts and ideas with confidence.

Chapter 5: How to apply spells in everyday life

There will be times when you will want to write your own personal spell. While it is perfectly acceptable to use the spells that other people have put out there for us to use sometimes you need a spell that is personalized just to you. And it is easy to write a personal spell in just five steps.

First, you must decide what the purpose of your spell is. What is it that you are hoping to accomplish by casting this spell? It can be anything from a new house to a new love, or a new car. Whatever the desire is just make sure you are very clear on what you want to receive. Next, decide what materials you will need in order to complete the spell. Will you need stones, candles, or herbs? Gather everything together before you begin. And keep in mind that magick will rely heavily on the use of symbols, so using a toy car to represent that new car or a toy house to represent that new house is not only acceptable but is very desirable.

You will then need to decide if the timing is particularly important to you and your spell. Some spells are best cast at certain times of the moon but do not get too caught up in the details of timing. If Sunday night seems like a good time to cast a spell to assist with the Monday job hunt then do it on Sunday night. In addition, the words that you choose to use must be considered very carefully because words have power and need to be used with caution. Your spell might be something as simple as using silent meditation. Then one you have the spell planned just do it, make it happen. And if a particular working is not helping in a reasonable amount of time such as two weeks to one month then it may be necessary to revisit the spell and try something new. And if it is a spell that works and you want to use it again do not forget to write it down in your Book of Shadows.

How to Create Your Own Spells

Why create your own spells? It can be daunting to do so. Perhaps you lack confidence or are unsure that you are skilled enough to create spells. Don't worry. Below is a simple process that will help shape your spells so that you can embrace your spiritual creativity. Taking ownership of your practice is the key to becoming the greatest Wiccan you can be.

The first step in creating your spells is to define what they are and what you want to happen. It is very difficult for the divine and the elements to grant you what you want if they are unclear about that is. Spells should have a clear intent. If the spell involves other people, it is important to take them into consideration, especially if you know who those people are. After all, their energy and auras will surely affect the spell. Once you have a clear idea of what you want to happen, the next step is to gather the materials or resources you need.

It is important to have the correct materials when creating new spells. This can include known spell correspondences such as which day of the week corresponds to which type of spell as well as the magical tools one might use (see Chapter 5). One can choose a tool or tools based on the elements associated with the spell.

The next step is to find the words or incantations involved in the ceremony. What words will invoke power from the spirits or lend their selves to the healing ritual? While words in spells are not required, using them can help focus your magical energy. You can use a basic chant; many are available online, or you can create your own. The words of the spell might be a poem, with rhyming lines and other poetic devices. You can even use song lyrics that you have a deep and personal connection to; though those should be used sparingly as they are not as potent as words the practitioner comes up with.

Finally, it comes time to cast the spell. It is possible to go through all the motions of a spell, from reciting the words or making gestures, and still not be actually casting the spell. Casting the spell involves not only the process of the spell, but also the energy the practitioner can summon, visualize, and control. That energy has as much to do with the outcome as the magical tools, words, and gestures. It is also a good idea to meditate on the spell's outcome before attempting to spell.

Once a spell is created, it can be used or modified later. It is a good idea for the witch to record his or her spells in a book.

Different Types of Spells

There are several types of spells. The major types of magick are divination, high, low, elemental, sympathetic, talismanic, folk, and petition magick. Each form of magick has its own pros and cons.

Divination

Divination is the art of seeing the future, be it an outcome or an event. There are several methods for divination. These methods are discussed in Chapter 5.

High Magick

Despite its name, high magick is not better or worse than low magick. It simply indicates the amount of ritual and ceremony involved in the spell. High magick covens use a lot of specific words, gestures, movements, and tools in a very precise way in order to cast their spells. High magick is the most ritualized version of Wiccan magick, and it is especially prevalent in Gardnerian covens.

Low Magick

Low magick is common earth and nature magick. Low magick is the magick that is minimally ritualized in contrast to high magick, where everything is ritualized. Low magick relies less on ceremony and more on inspiration, intuition, spontaneity, and creativity.

Elemental Magick

Elemental magick deals with energy tied to the five elements of air, earth, fire, water, and aether. Elemental magick is raw and powerful, and its practice involves the precise association of the element with magical tools, chants, timing, and gestures. In elemental magick, it is important to include a strong symbol of the element such as a stone or crystal for the earth, a feather for air, a match for fire, or a cup or goblet of water or other magical concoction.

Sympathetic Magick

Sympathetic magick is magick that uses an association between a person and an object. Through magick, the two become linked so that what happens to one happens to the other. While this process is often used in voodoo dolls and black magick, it is also useful to give the linked person healing, love, and positive energy.

Talismanic Magick

Talismanic magick centers on the creation and wearing of a talisman or an amulet that is generally worn but can also be carried. Talismans are used to gather or repel certain types of energy, ward off an evil spirit and entities, or to act as a magical focus for other spells. Many magical tools are consecrated as talismans before they are used in ceremonies.

Folk Magick

Folk magick is the common magick that is typically passed down from one generation to another. It is done around the home such as cleansing with a smoke stick. While folk magick is common, that does not mean it is less advanced or potent than other magics.

Petition Magick

Petition Magick is where the witch makes a deal with an entity, spirit, or divinity. This spell is much like a contract, with the witch promising or giving something in return for the spirit's help. It is important to be clear about your intentions; spirits contacted through petition magick may have their own goals that might not coincide with the Wiccan practitioner.

Conclusion

Thank you for making it through to the end of Wicca Crystal Spells. Let's hope it was informative and able to provide you with all of the tools you need to achieve your goals whatever they may be. Next, take the information from this book and explore Wicca for yourself.

The next step is to put this book down and begin practicing the craft. No matter if you are already a Wiccan or just interested in the subject, you can take the information from this book and take it to the next step. For many, it means beginning to practice witchcraft and the Wiccan religion.

If you feel overwhelmed, don't worry. Wicca is a broad subject with many fascinating aspects, but learning about it can be a daunting and it may require patience and perhaps a touch of creativity as you delve deeper into the mysteries of Wicca. To help keep from getting overwhelmed, it is important to purchase a blank book or use a word processor to create your own Book of Shadows.

It will be easier to understand Wicca if it is absorbed over time. The craft is a complex religion, but taking it in small parts and setting deadlines will help you learn it at your own speed. This is vitally important as many new Wiccans are too eager to skip to the magick and not ingest the rest of the book as they need to. Setting realistic goals will help the reader to fully comprehend the subject.

Once you have finished your initial preparations, note that they are just that, preparation. The next step is to take it to the next level and to begin worshiping the Goddess and God, practicing magick and performing rituals and ceremonies.

Made in United States
Orlando, FL
04 November 2024